ULTIMATE

Motorcycle Tours

ULTIMATE

Motorcycle Tours

GRANT ROFF

Hardie Grant

EXPLORE

INTRODUCTION

You'll know extreme, hardcore adventure riders immediately when you meet them: their bikes will be covered in stickers and they'll be happy to endlessly entertain you with stories about the Road of Bones in Siberia and how they had to eat 'plov' at every meal for three months.

They deserve great respect, of course, but this book isn't for them.

The rest of us may be happier talking about the coastal scenery in Northern Ireland or the seafood chowder we ate in the restaurant in Monterey that John Steinbeck wrote about in *Cannery Row*.

When you're cornered in a saloon or pub by your riding friends, you'll invariably be asked, 'What's the best ride you've ever had?' It can be a hard question to answer – one ride rarely covers it. Many factors go into the mix to determine a result. Rarely is it 'just one ride'. An easier contemplation is perhaps the 10 or 20 best rides.

The components of a great ride can include the company you're in, the road conditions, the weather, the time of year, the quality of your bike, how relaxed you are, if you have everything you need in your luggage, if the pace suits you, if the schedule allows for plenty of socialising, if you can afford it, if the balance of 'knowns' and 'unknowns' is right, if the people you meet make you feel welcome, if the scenery is varied and interesting, if you have the time to alter the schedule to take advantage of new discoveries and if the level of adventure suits your temperament.

Yes, many of these issues are entirely subjective: you can be miserable on an iconic ride and delighted by a gallop down the little-regarded by-ways of England's Yorkshire Dales. Lists are fragile: they can change according to mood and inclination.

Most riders, though, harbour a short list of aspirational rides – places they'd visit (or revisit) in a heartbeat if the circumstances were right. These are the legendary rides talked about in their friendship circles and mythologised in motorcycle media.

In this book, we're going to visit some of these legendary rides. We'll reveal how to go about the planning and give you some practical details. We'll deconstruct both the journey and the destination and, if we do it well enough, it will inspire you to plan your own trip or, at the very least, have a virtual sense that you've already been there simply by reading about it.

Our list includes some rides you'd expect to feature and some you probably haven't even thought about. We've focused on rides for those of us who ride regularly on conventional road or dual-purpose bikes. You'll require a skill level that keeps you safe and the maturity to ride within your limits – but there are no other expectations.

You may also be surprised that some of the iconic rides of the world don't feature in our list. Sometimes that's because they're now inaccessible – motorcycle travel today can be difficult, particularly if you want to take your own bike. More pressing is the issue of personal safety. In this post-pandemic, fractured world, there are great riding destinations that will have to wait some years, if ever, before reopening.

Geopolitics is now important in your planning. The great motorcycle adventures of riders like Elspeth Beard (first English woman to ride around the world) and Ted Simon (author of *Jupiter's Travels*) are now impossible to replicate due to wars, border closures and international tensions that could spill into conflict when you least expect them to.

The great rides described in this book weave through the international clutter and can be achieved with minimum risk to health and safety. You don't have to be jealous of those who rode before you in more liberal times, as our rides can fully engage the senses and leave you with just as much awe as Elspeth and Ted experienced in their grand adventures.

Here's a secret that motorcycle riders usually keep to themselves about why they love riding: you get that rarest of things – uninterrupted, quality time in your own head.

These aren't journeys you can do the same way in a car. Riding gives you maximum physical and mental exposure to the environment you're in at the time. You can't escape it by winding the windows up and retreating to an electronic entertainment system. Your memories of these rides will be intense in a way car drivers simply can't understand. Riding sears the journey into your soul and educates the person you are constantly in the process of becoming.

So. Enjoy what follows. Some of these rides might remain dreams, but others may be possible and forever rewarding if you can devise the ways and means of engaging with them.

Do it, and may the road gods smile on you.

Grant Roff

Above The author powers through South Island, Aotearoa/New Zealand

Map of the World

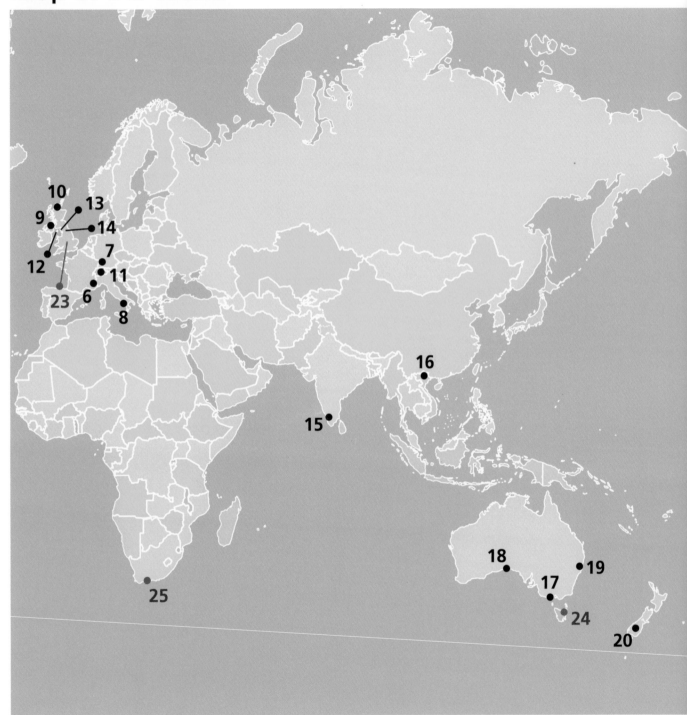

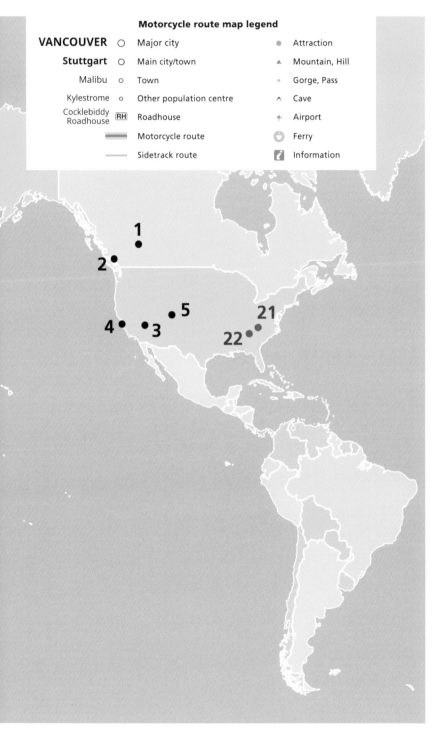

Motorcycle route map legend

VANCOUVER ○	Major city	●	Attraction
Stuttgart ○	Main city/town	▲	Mountain, Hill
Malibu ○	Town	·	Gorge, Pass
Kylestrome ○	Other population centre	∧	Cave
Cocklebiddy Roadhouse [RH]	Roadhouse	✈	Airport
▬▬	Motorcycle route	⛴	Ferry
──	Sidetrack route	ℹ	Information

NORTH AMERICA

1. Icefields Parkway: Canada
2. Vancouver Island, Sea To Sky & Highway 99: Canada
3. Death Valley: USA
4. California's Highway One: USA
5. San Juan Skyway: USA

EUROPE AND THE UK

6. Route Napoleon & Cime de la Bonette: France
7. Black Forest High Road: Germany
8. The Amalfi Coast: Italy
9. Causeway Coastal Route: Northern Ireland
10. North Coast 500: Scotland
11. Five Passes: Switzerland
12. The Mountain Course: Isle Of Man
13. Lake District: England
14. Yorkshire Dales: England

ASIA

15. Kerala: India
16. Ha Giang Loop: Vietnam

OCEANIA

17. The Great Ocean Road: Australia
18. Nullarbor Plain: Australia
19. Oxley Highway & Thunderbolt's Way: Australia
20. South Island: Aotearoa/New Zealand

More Rides

21. Blue Ridge Parkway: USA
22. Cherohala Skyway & Tail of the Dragon: USA
23. London to Anglesey: Wales
24. Tasmania East Coast Loop: Australia
25. Garden Route: South Africa

HINTS AND TIPS

WHICH BIKE?

For long rides in developed countries (USA, Europe, Australia and the like), size matters. Larger capacity bikes are more relaxing to ride and generally more comfortable than their smaller brethren. While Indian is making inroads into the American market, Harley-Davidson has the culture sewn up and has a dealer network so well-sorted that help is never far away if it's needed. Touring H-Ds have provision for luggage and a riding position that allows for long, comfortable miles.

Bike hire companies in the US usually have a range of H-Ds available but the roads suit touring rather than glamour models.

The UK isn't big compared with countries like the US and Australia so mid-size and smaller bikes can make more sense with their versatility and economy. Triumph, the iconic British brand, was rescued in 1983 by John Bloor and offers a range of bikes eminently suited to the local conditions. The prince among them is probably the Bonneville, which is a great all-rounder, but Triumph's adventure bike range also lends itself to touring with the Tiger 900 and 1200, both offering touring luggage options.

Despite the best efforts of other manufacturers, motorcycle touring in Europe is owned by BMW which offers kitted touring bikes including its adventure GS range that covers bikes from the G 310 GS to the R 1300 GS. BMW also offers plenty of midrange, vertical twins in both road and adventure form easily set up for long-distance riding. If you score a Triumph in the UK, though, it's easy to bring it to Europe for a holiday.

Using the bike you actually own makes the most sense if your destination is achievable without fraught border crossings. But if you live in Germany and you want a three-week holiday in New Zealand, hiring a bike makes a lot more economic sense. There's a hire-bike option for every ride in this book.

LEFT OR RIGHT?

Moving between countries and continents can mean changing the side of the road you'll be riding on. While most of the world (about 66 per cent) drives on the right, locations influenced by British colonialism largely drive on the left, including: Australia, New Zealand, India, South Africa, the Isle of Man, and, of course, the UK itself.

Here are some tips on how to make the change successfully:

- Follow the traffic in front of you. They'll be doing it properly.

- Concentrate. You need to be 'in the moment' while you're riding so old habits don't interfere with your decision-making process.

- You'll most likely make mistakes when you do something routine like stop for fuel. When you pull out of the garage, you need to reset your thinking to the new environment.

- If you lose your direction and take a wrong road, you'll be thinking about that rather than which side of the road you should be on. Always keep it in mind.

- Turning at crossroads is often a challenge. Sit behind a car going where you want to go and follow it when the lights change.

- It's easier on divided road freeways but if you're from a country that rides on the left, the far right lane becomes the slow lane, not the fast lane. The reverse is true if you normally ride on the right-hand side of the road.

How long does changing sides of the road take to get used to? Old habits die hard so it's something you'll have to focus on continually. Mistakes can be fatal. From personal experience, it will be two months before you can relax.

Opposite top Triumph Bonneville T100
Opposite bottom **Traffic jam in Vietnam**

LUGGAGE

A dear, departed touring companion and legendary motorcycle writer, Peter Smith, used to take a red pen with him whenever he went for a long ride. Anything he used in his luggage he'd mark with the pen – anything not marked would be excluded from the next ride. In the end, while our bikes looked like elephants, his luggage consisted of the barest essentials: a bed roll, a tooth brush, a few changes of underwear (not many) and a few t-shirts. Most of us overpack and, if we adopted the Smith method, we'd take a lot less with us.

If you're travelling on your own bike, chances are you've already got luggage sorted. It might consist of hard or soft panniers, luggage perhaps including a bed roll on a rear rack or the pillion seat, and maybe a tank bag.

Lockable hard panniers may be useful in environments where you want to protect their contents as well as possible but soft panniers tend to be more flexible in use. They're also easier to carry and easier to fit if you're going international and you'll be using hire bikes.

The images you see in this book – including the Triumph Tiger 1200, the Harley-Davidson Street Glide and a Suzuki 800 Boulevard – are fitted with genius Australian Andy Strapz AA bags (www.andystrapz.com), which swallow an enormous amount of gear and will tie onto any make or model of bike with a rear rack or rear seat. It's great for international riding in that airline baggage handlers can't hurt it and, once it's attached, it can't shift or fall off..

Flying to your riding destination? Wear all your riding gear (boots, pants, jacket) onto the plane because its heavy and you don't get weighed. Annoy your fellow passengers by getting almost completely undressed on the plane and taking up most of the overhead locker space. Your checked-in luggage should then be below the maximum limit. Most airlines will allow you to carry your helmet onto the plane, which is another bonus.

If it turns out that you're hot or cold at your destination and you haven't prepared for it, just relax: that's why the road gods invented thrift shops.

Right Following the Rocky Mountain trail in Colorado towards Durango (*see* p. 39)

RIDING GEAR

If you knew exactly what kind of crash you were going to have, you could design a perfect helmet for it. Because we can't do that, the safest helmet is the one that fits your head best and meets international standards. It doesn't have to be an expensive brand. Fit is the most important safety feature. The helmet should be snug but not tight. Put it on, hold the sides of the helmet and try to turn your head to the left and right. You should be able to move your head a little but not excessively.

Mesh jackets are the most versatile. Most come with a padded liner for cold weather and a waterproof liner as well to keep the rain out. In hot weather, with these removed, the mesh allows cool air to flow but you always have the protection of the jacket's armour. DriRider is a reputable, inexpensive brand.

Depending on where you're going, take a set of warm and summer gloves so you can match the conditions and still have good hand protection.

Riding jeans are more versatile than leather pants. You want Kevlar lining but not too much weight.

Again, depending on where you're riding, the best boots are the ones you can walk in as well as ride in. There's nothing worse than a sign that says, 'Waterfall – 400m', and you feel it's too onerous because walking is uncomfortable. Ankle boots are a good option – protection and versatility.

In tropical climates such as India and Vietnam, the heat will tempt you to ride with less protection. It's true that crashes will be at a slower pace and you're less likely to be injured, but knee pads, elbow pads and a back protector can be fitted over your long-sleeve shirt and jeans to give you comfort as well as protection. Abrasions from crashes in Asian countries have to be treated seriously as infections can be hard to treat and can lead to loss of limbs.

Here's the thing not many will tell you about riding gear: if you hit a fixed object such as the back of a stationary bus or a tree on the side of the road at a speed of over 80km/h, you'll probably die irrespective of what you're wearing. Your internal organs can't stay in place if you come to a dead stop from that speed. Safe riding gear is designed to protect you from abrasions and possible minor internal damage as long as you don't hit anything while you're sliding along the road. Keep this in mind when you're deciding how fast to ride in riding environments with plenty of fixed objects on the roadside.

TEN TACTICS FOR SURVIVAL

1. Watch the big picture. When you're riding, things happen around you all the time that influence your level of safety. Examples include cars, trucks and buses leaving an oily strip in the middle of traffic lanes; native animals appearing on roads, especially at dawn and dusk; and the likelihood of erratic behavior from drivers stuck behind slow-moving vehicles.

2. Keep your distance. Keeping a safe distance from other road users, parked cars and fixed objects on the side of the road will give you more time to react if something unexpected happens.

3. Be seen. Wear bright riding gear and ride with your headlight on during the day. Ride in a road position so you can be seen in both the rear and outside mirrors of the vehicle travelling in front of you.

4. Be predictable. If other road users can see you, be sure to signal your intentions well in advance and ride at the same pace as other road users, and you'll be less likely to get caught up in surprise incidents.

5. Think like them. If you understand how car and truck drivers think and you understand the limitations of their vehicles, you can anticipate their possible behavior and ride to suit it.

6. Read the road. All roads are different. Even the same road can change overnight because of rain, different patterns of road use, roadworks or unexpected oncoming traffic. Experienced riders 'read' the road and adapt their riding to suit.

7. Pace yourself. The safest speed for a motorcycle in traffic is generally the speed at which all the other vehicles are travelling. Riding slower or faster than this increases risk. On open roads, adjust your speed to accommodate your skill level and the road conditions.

8. Ride straight. Alcohol and other drugs, including cold and flu tablets, affect your ability to ride. They may make you clumsy and less careful than you might otherwise be. Excessive alcohol will affect your balance.

9. Trust your bike. A bike in good condition allows you to trust its performance and concentrate on the other issues of riding. Do regular checks of suspension, steering-head bearings, fluid leaks (from forks, brakes, suspension and engine), lights and instruments, and the tread depth and condition of the tyres.

10. Trust yourself. The experience that builds knowledge and confidence usually has to be gained in the complex environment of the road. Tactics to allow this knowledge to grow include allowing yourself plenty of time to complete rides, choosing routes that minimise hazards, listening and learning from experienced riders you respect, and not riding with others who pressure you to ride outside your comfort zone and beyond your capabilities.

Opposite Riding through Kerala, India (*see* p. 124)

Q & A
Lavi and Ollie

Lavi and Ollie are attempting a Guinness World Record to be the youngest pair to circumnavigate the world by motorcycle riding two-up. They've made a start, but the trip is going to take them two years. Their average age at the finish will be 33. You can follow their adventures on www.youtube.com/@LaviandOllie

What got you into riding?

We weren't bikers to begin with. We just wanted to see the world. We tried walking (3000km) but it was too slow, we tried cycling (2000km) but it was too exhausting, so we decided motorcycling would be the best option to get us around.

Where did the idea of the world record come from and will you be able to keep it once you've set it?

We had a friend who attempted (and failed) to become the youngest male to circumnavigate the globe by motorcycle so after we had decided we wanted to ride around the world, we looked online to see if a record had been made circumnavigating the globe by motorcycle two-up. Turned out it hadn't, so we went for it.

Once we have completed the journey we will be the youngest pair to circumnavigate the globe by motorcycle. This record can be broken by a younger pair if they are brave enough!

Do you think motorcycle adventures have changed you?

Definitely! We have seen so much of the world in a single trip. Ridden roads that connect countries and continents together. Overlanding gives you a level of detail not possible by any other form of travel and really allows you a rare insight into the lives of the communities living along the way. Seeing the real life lived away from the tourist areas, it shows you other ways of living which change your perspective.

How did you end up selecting the Suzuki as the best bike for the trip and how's it going?

Actually the bike was selected for us. A local dealership in Ollie's home town offered it to us as a sponsorship for the trip, so of course we couldn't say no!

It has been a blessing though because this bike is incredibly reliable and strong, so we believe it was meant to be as it has turned out to be the perfect bike to take us around the world and we are sure it will make it to the end!

Given your experiences so far, what have you learned and would you do anything differently if you could start again?

We have learned that if you set yourself a goal, no matter how crazy it seems, and work hard at it, you can achieve almost anything.

However, shipping a bike from Senegal to Brazil is an incredibly hard and expensive goal so perhaps in this case we should have set ourselves an easier shipping route! (Spain to Argentina would have sufficed for the purposes of the record).

Opposite Lavi and Ollie out and about in the desert landscape of Morocco

North America

Icefields Parkway: Canada

Some judge this the best motorcycle ride in the world. It's a big call, but if the conditions are right and scenery is your thing, it's hard to argue with.

SNAPSHOT

The Icefields Parkway was built to show off the incredible scenery of the Rocky Mountains in this part of Canada.

It's an easy ride on a good surface with plenty to look at, and a speed limit of 90km/h allows you to focus as much on your surroundings as you do on the riding itself.

There are plenty of attractions very close to the road that suit riders who will be bulked up for occassionally unpredictable weather, but take some walking shoes just in case.

Geologically, the Rocky Mountains are brand, spanking new. Yes, there was stuff happening before but what you see now may only be somewhere between 50 and 75 million years old.

Compare that with 3.6 billion years for the Barbertown Greenstone Belt in South Africa and the Hamersley Range in Australia, which is 3.4 billion years old.

The Rocky Mountains are bigger and more dramatic than their competitors, though, which is a product of their youth and formation. They're much longer as well: they stretch from New Mexico in the south through British Columbia and Alberta in Canada to Alaska. It's a distance of around 4800km (3000 miles).

The Aseniwuche Winewak Nation (Rocky Mountain People) are descendants of the early First Nations People who have lived and used the area for thousands of years. European interest in the area was largely from explorers and mountaineers, many of whom were trying to find two mythical mountains either side of the Athabasca Pass. In 1827, a botanist had incorrectly recorded the height of the mountains which triggered numerous unsuccessful expeditions to try to locate and climb them. All expeditions failed, of course, but one of the explorers, Arthur Coleman, took a route in 1884 from the Sunwapta River to Jasper that laid the foundations for the Icefields Parkway route.

How long?
We're riding from Jasper to Lake Louise on Hwy 93. It's 230km on a great road so it's easy to do it in a day. There are, however, plenty of distractions.

When to go
Mid June to the end of September. July and August are crowded. From November to April, most accommodation, restaurants and the only fuel stop along the route are closed.

Need to know
- This ride combines parts of the Jasper National Park and the Banff National Park so you'll need a park pass to ride it; available online, at park entrances, or at tourist information centres.
- Ride on the right-hand side of the road.
- The speed limit is 90km/h so just relax and enjoy the views.
- There's not much in the way of roadside dining, accommodation or fuel on the 227km route so fill up with picnic supplies and fuel in Jasper.
- Most businesses close in winter so plan accordingly.
- Don't feed the bears.

Ride rating
Easy. The Icefields Parkway route is fully paved with wide shoulders. Vehicles exceeding 4550kg are not allowed to use the road so there's almost no commercial traffic. Buses and RVs, however, are common.

Distances
- Jasper to Lake Louise is 230km (143 miles).

This route was so beautiful that Arthur Wheeler, a chiefland surveyor responsible for establishing the border between Alberta and British Columbia, had a premonition that he expressed in a 1920 journal entry:

'Through dense, primeval forests, muskeg, burnt and fallen timber and along rough and steeply sloping hillsides, a constant flow of travel will demand a broad, well-ballasted motor road'.

Jasper National Park was established in 1907 and the Grand Trunk Pacific Railway reached Jasper in 1911, bringing tourists into the area in greater numbers.

Guides would take visitors down the 'Wonder Trail' but it would take three weeks and the pressure was on to build a more useable road.

The opportunity arose during the Great Depression when the Canadian government signed up 600 unemployed men to build a road along the Wonder Trail. It was done by hand to employ as many workers as possible. They were paid CA$5 a month with a little extra for clothing and tobacco and the job took 10 years, but, finally, the Icefields Parkway road could accommodate the flood of cars arriving.

The road was re-aligned and paved in 1961 and that's the Icefields Parkway road motorcyclists have come to know and love. It gets more than 1.3 million visitors each year so you can expect it to be a little crowded in summer but, if you pick the shoulder seasons, you'll have plenty of 'me time' on your journey.

 Temperatures
- July to September: minimum 3°C to 8°C (37°F to 46°F); maximum 15°C to 22°C (59°F to 72°F)
- The weather can be unpredictable in the Rocky Mountains and temperatures can vary considerably during the days and nights even in the summer months

 More information
www.hikebiketravel.com/everything-you-need-to-know-about-camping-on-the-icefields-parkway

Below The Rocky Mountains on Canada's Icefields Parkway route

Lake Louise at the end of the Icefields Parkway

North and South

We're riding the Icefields Parkway from Jasper downwards because it makes a nice loop from Vancouver (*see* p. 11, the Sea to Sky route) and our plan afterwards is to ride into Montana in the US to visit the Glacier National Park.

A fly-in, fly-out option for those wanting to experience the Icefields Parkway is to touch down in Calgary and hire a bike from **Calgary Harley-Davidson** (www.calgaryharley davidson.ca). You could then make a return trip to Jasper via Banff and see the route in both directions – win-win. Calgary to Jasper via the Icefields Parkway route is 490km.

Calgary Harley-Davidson hires out a variety of current models but a good option would be a Road King Special for three to six days for CA$235 per day. Add an extra CA$10 a day if you want a Road Glide or a Street Glide.

Jasper is a nice little town to start your adventure. It houses about 5000 people but the facilities suggest a much bigger population because it allows for a massive influx of visitors during the summer months.

A good place to start is the visitor centre where you can pick up the latest information on weather conditions and buy a compulsory national park pass so you can ride the Icefields Parkway. The pass is CA$10.50 per day. Cars need to display it on their dashboards but the rangers ask motorcyclists to carry the pass with them and be able to show it on request. It's one of the few roads in Canada where a pass is required even if you have no intention of stopping. You're paying for the view.

While you're in Jasper, stroll its main streets, admire the steam engine in the middle of the town and consider a trip on the Jasper Sky Tram to the summit for a serious view of the town and its surrounds.

Not just Jasper but the entire area is set up for adventure tourism, with skiing, walking trails, ice climbing, mountain climbing, mountain-bike riding and everything else you can imagine to wear yourself out. We're primarily interested in the ride, but bring walking shoes with you so you can take advantage of some of the incredible spectacles close to the road.

Rollin' down the road

This is a relatively wide, well-made road with mostly sweeping corners rather than hairpin turns and hence will suit touring bikes rather than knife-edge sports bikes. The speed limit is 90km/h with a couple of slower areas around the Saskatchewan River crossing and the Columbia Icefields area.

In some ways it seems a waste of a terrific road surface and wide, open spaces but this ride is really all about the scenery. You'll enjoy it more if you chill. Buy a lunch pack (and a bottle of wine) from Jasper so you don't have to rely on the scant supply and high prices of food on the route.

Around 33km from Jasper is **Athabasca Falls** which is known for its volume and force rather than its height. It's a very short walk from the car park so you don't have to take your boots off and you'll enjoy the noise.

Not far past there (56km from Jasper) is **Sunwapta Falls**. The upper falls are close to the road as well, but the lower falls require a short hike. Both of these falls are genuine experiences of Canadian wilderness and remind you that life isn't always about big cities.

Located 108km from Jasper is the **Columbia Icefields Centre** where you can organise yourself a glacier experience. The **Athabasca Glacier** is the largest south of the Arctic Circle, but, thanks to global warming, is retreating. The Icefields Centre has a few options for you to explore. If you like to watch, pay CA\$37 and take the regular bus (included in the ticket) from the centre's car park up to the **Glacier Skywalk** which is 6km away. The Skywalk is a 1km walk around a man-made,

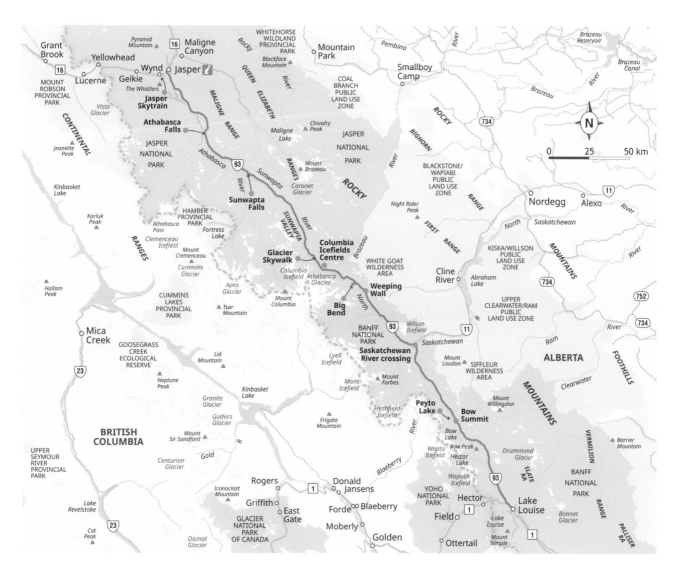

glass-bottomed bridge that is 280m over the Sunwapta Valley. You already know if you don't like heights so I won't bother you with the warnings.

Option two is the CA$92 Skywalk and Ice Explorer tour. You walk the Skywalk but a purpose-built bus also takes you onto a parking area on the actual glacier where you can alight and spend some time on the moving ice.

There are also a few licensed businesses that will take you for a walk on the glacier without the bus trip, which would be interesting if you're fit enough. There's a short, free hike onto the toe of the glacier from the end of the car park but there's always some danger – a 12-year-old died there in 1990 from slipping into a tapered crack in the ice.

The centre is full of information on the glacier and the Icefields Parkway experience. It's free to enter, but if you're watching your budget you can just enjoy views of the glacier from the parking lot. Job done.

Turns and tears

To snap you out of your 90km/h fug, the **Big Bend** is 180km from Jasper. It's a hairpin turn on a descending road that wraps in a circle and reminds you that, sometimes, 90km/h is pretty fast.

The **Weeping Wall** is also worth a look. It's 8km past the Big Bend and a short walk from the road. Conditions need to be right, but it can look like a crying mountain – water seeping out of the rock face.

Your next stop will probably be at the **Saskatchewan River crossing**. Turn right at the signs and you'll enjoy public bathrooms, a fuel stop and a restaurant. The truth is, if you need fuel and food, it doesn't really matter what it costs but spare a thought for the transport and storage costs the providers have to live with. Besides, if you took my earlier advice, you will already have had a nice picnic by a brook or lake with a couple of glasses of wine to steady your nerves. This is the only fuel stop on the route and it's 153km from Jasper, so take advantage of it.

The **Bow Summit** just ahead of you is the highest point on the Jasper to Banff run and the highest elevation (2840m) crossed by a public road in Canada. Enjoy the view. The turquoise colour of **Peyto Lake** (and Lake Louise) is created by suspended

Right Columbian ground squirrel *Opposite* Highway 93 from Jasper to Lake Louise runs mostly in a valley overshadowed by the wild Rocky Mountains

Wildlife

The Jasper and Banff National Parks have 53 species of mammals so it's unlikely you'll finish your Icefields Parkway ride without encountering quite a few of them.

The cutest is probably the Columbian ground squirrel which is in plentiful supply, much to the delight of the bigger carnivores in the park that eat them. If you're camping, you'll probably see porcupines in the campsites.

Keep your eye out for beavers as well. They were trapped to near-extinction in the past because of the value of their pelts, but thanks to protections afforded by the national park system, they're recovering. Even if you don't spot one, you'll see the dams they're constantly in the process of building.

Elk are relatively common. They have been reintroduced after being decimated by hunting and are happy to walk around campgrounds and townships to the point where they occasionally have to be relocated. Coyotes are similarly unafraid of humans and you'll often see them in built-up areas looking for garbage or stray cats.

Not so with wolves. They don't like human contact and tend to stay in the wilderness areas of the parks where they pack-hunt deer, moose, sheep, beavers and mice. Mountain lions (cougars) also live in the parks and can end up weighing as much as 70kg.

The glamour animals are the bears. There are two types: black bears and grizzlies. They're both scavengers and are omnivorous. You're most likely to see black bears in spring and autumn. They hang around the roadside and frequently visit campgrounds.

The grizzlies can grow up to 250kg. They eat mostly plant material but don't bet your life on that if you see one.

rock particles reflecting light, but climate scientists (what would they know) predict that the water will eventually become blue as it fades due to receding glaciers and reduced impact on water flows. Enjoy the turquoise while you can.

Lake Louise

The Icefields Parkway eventually finishes at **Lake Louise**, which, if it didn't continuously have a million tourists around it, would indeed be one of the world's prettiest sights.

The only good news is parking is free for motorcycles and you can amble around the foreshore and marvel at the lake's popularity.

I'll tease Chateau Lake Louise further in the 'Best Sleeps' section, but be forewarned: find somewhere else to stay.

By the time you get to Lake Louise you'll already have been blinded by the magnificence of this ride. You slide, twist and turn mostly in a valley between giant mountain peaks and the 90km/h limit gives you time to look at them and be bedazzled by their magnificence.

Canada is the wild end of the Rockies and the Icefields Parkway run lets you enjoy it (apart from the speed limit) to the fullest.

Being there

Canadians run a tight riding collective, which is probably because there really is a 'riding season'. In many places in Canada the bike gets to hibernate for the winter, so in the summer months riders are generally very pleased to see each other out on the road.

Canadian bikers acknowledge one another with the traditional low, left-hand wave and they probably do it more than any other country in the world, although Americans would come a close second.

If you stop where there are other bikes, there will always be a conversation, and if bikes pass by you while you're stopped, there will almost always be an acknowledgement.

The rider of a Harley-Davidson Sportster cruised by on the Icefields Parkway route on one occasion and gave an enthusiastic wave. The camping gear and luggage on the back was piled high enough to make me initially think it was a pillion passenger so we stopped to say hello about 20km farther on when we saw the bike at a scenic stop.

The rider's name was Nicky and it turned out she was Australian. It's a small world. She'd been living in the US for some years and had made the recent decision that she wanted to take up riding. I wouldn't have thought a H-D Sportster would be an ideal first bike but there she was and she was loving every minute of it.

She'd camped the night before at Jasper, and when we'd turned up there at around 10am that morning it was still only 5°C. It must have been a bloody site colder during the night.

Riding constantly teaches you things about yourself. You think you're tough and then you meet someone like Nicky. Ride on, sister.

Left Harley-Davidson's Street Glide - perfect for the Icefields Parkway *Opposite* Fairmont Chateau Lake Louise - proud and pricey

BEST EATS

Whistle Stop Pub, Jasper
You'll recognise most of the items on the menu at this pub within the Whistler's Inn. Pricing is good for a resort town like Jasper and the pub has a cosy vibe. The nachos are recommended. It's near the Jasper Parks info centre. www.whistlersinn.com

Patricia Street Deli, Jasper
This deli sells a small range of boxed lunches that you can take with you for the Icefields Parkway ride and it's better (and cheaper) than anything you'll find along the way. It means you can find a spot with a fabulous view (a million to choose from) and eat well.

The 'Hungry Hiker' box has a sandwich of your choice, chips, a cookie, some fruit and either a juice or water for around CA$20. Oh, take a bottle of wine, too, and some paper cups. www.facebook.com/patriciastreetdeli/

Bill Peyto's Cafe, Lake Louise Village
Named after a Banff guide who was a local legend, this cosy cafe offers a variety of traditional Canadian fare. It's licensed as well. You can't book and, in season, it gets very busy so you may occasionally have to queue. Once seated, though, you'll enjoy the experience. It's a good time to try that most traditional of Canadian dishes: poutine. It's fresh, hand-cut potatoes double fried and then topped with cheese curds and gravy. The locals swear by it. www.hihostels.ca/en/about/hostels/bill-peytos-cafe

BEST SLEEPS

HI Jasper
Recently refurbished, this hostel has the normal bunk rooms but also family and private rooms. Among its amenities are a shared kitchen, media room, a coworking bar, sauna and on-site café; however, it's only a short walk to the restaurants in the middle of town. Your bike will be safe here. www.hihostels.ca/en/destinations/alberta/hi-jasper

Fairmont Chateau Lake Louise
Okay, I confess I didn't actually stay at the five-star Lake Louise resort. It's possible no motorcyclist ever has, but at least you can catch a glimpse of how the other half live from the outside. Rooms start from CA$1059 a night for the Mountain View king room and go to CA$3979 for the Marquis De Lorne suite. Oh, that doesn't include taxes and fees, and it doesn't include the CA$40 resort fee. Geez Louise … www.fairmont.com/lake-louise/

Rampart Creek Campground, Banff National Park
Got your tent? This basic campground is 40km south of the Columbia Icefields on Icefields Parkway. There's a fire pit at each campsite and wood is provided. There are kitchen shelters with cooking stoves and pit toilets. You need to keep any food you bring secure as the site has frequent wildlife visitors. Cost is CA$18.75 per person per night. You need to book online in advance. www.reservation.pc.gc.ca/

Overlooking Qualicum Beach on Vancouver Island *Overleaf* Trees aplenty along the Sea to Sky Highway near Squamish

Vancouver Island, Sea to Sky & Highway 99: Canada

Forests, mountains, valleys, rivers, gondolas, craft beer and great roads with a couple of ocean voyages thrown in as well. What more could you possibly want?

SNAPSHOT

This ride starts with the best of ferry rides: 90 minutes from the US mainland to Vancouver Island. There's another ferry ride to get back but this time you're dropped off in Canada at the start of the legendary Sea to Sky route.

Stay on Hwy 99 when the tourist road stops and enjoy isolated mountains and valleys on a glorious road until you intersect with Hwy 97.

Then it's decision time – but adventure waits both to your left and right.

'Well, that's not going to go anywhere'. So say millions of people who've tied their bike down in the back of a pick-up/ute/truck/trailer to move it from one place to another. They're usually right, too, as amateurs regularly practice overkill on the various ropes and straps they use.

Imagine my surprise, then, when I saw how my bike was secured on a ferry the first time I went to the Isle of Man. I was asked to leave it in first gear and rest it on its sidestand. The deck hand then used just one bit of rope around the handlebar to secure it to a tie-down point on the floor.

The theory is that the rope will prevent the bike from falling to the right, the sidestand will prevent it from falling to the left and the gearbox will prevent it rocking backwards or forwards. It's simple and effective but if you're in one of the ship's upper deck bars enjoying an ale, particularly if the crossing is rough, it's hard not to think about your bike pitching about down in the hold.

The MV *Coho* ferry that took our bikes from Port Angeles at the top of Washington State in the US across the Juan de Fuca Strait to Victoria on Vancouver Island was even more minimalist in its approach. Leave the bike in gear with the sidestand down and kick a stepped block of wood underneath it from the other side. Tie-down points and straps were available if the bike's owner couldn't be convinced that this was enough. Keep in mind that the ferry has been transporting motorcycles since 1959 and its advice is based on over 60 years of history.

 How long?
It depends on the route you eventually decide to take, but three days will get you there.

 When to go
June to September will give you the most sunshine and the least rain but the Sea to Sky route gets very busy during July and August.

 Need to know
- It's wise to book yourself and your bike on the MV *Coho* in advance. It's also cheaper.
- You don't need a visa if you enter Canada by land or by ferry from the United States. Your passport will be checked, though.
- You can't book a motorcycle ferry ride in advance on BC Ferries from Nanaimo to Horseshoe Bay: turn up one hour before the scheduled departure time, buy your ticket and wait in the motorcycle queue. You won't be left behind.
- Ride on the right-hand side of the road.

 Ride rating
Mostly easy with a few challenges in the upper reaches of Hwy 99.

 Distances
- 500km (311 miles) to the end of Hwy 99.
- 977km (607 miles) loop ride back to Vancouver via Hwy 1.

 Temperatures
- Victoria (June): 12°C to 18°C (54°F to 64°F)
- Whistler (June): 8°C to 20°C (46°F to 68°F)

(i) More information
- Getting to Vancouver Island from USA: www.cohoferry.com
- Getting from Vancouver Island back to the Canadian mainland: www.bcferries.com
- Tourism information on Vancouver Island: www.hellobc.com
- Tourism information on the Sea to Sky route: www.hellobc.com/places-to-go/sea-to-sky/

Life on the high seas

At least we didn't have to leave the bikes alone for long. It's a 42km crossing and takes about 90 minutes – in my mind the perfect length for an ocean voyage.

Captain James Cook's voyage was a lot longer (and far less comfortable) when he 'discovered' Vancouver Island in 1778. He stayed there for a month while claiming it for Britain. The Spanish had arrived just before him and there was a dispute over ownership between the two countries that came close to a war.

The Kwakwaka'wakw, Coast Salish, Nuu-chah-nulth and other First Nations People had, of course, been living there for thousands of years before Cook arrived and had the usual experience of mass deaths due to the introduction of smallpox by the Europeans.

Victoria (population: 91,867), the capital of Vancouver Island, is a beautiful harbour town. It was, until the train line arrived in Vancouver on the mainland in 1886, the premier town of British Columbia.

Arguably the best ride on the island is up to Qualicum Beach; turn left across the Vancouver Island Ranges and then ride a short distance up the west coast to the holiday town of Tofino. That was plan A in our itinerary, but Canada was on fire when we arrived and the Tofino road was closed due to landslides created by water-bombing. Next time, maybe. There was no indication of when it was going to open again so plan B was enacted, which involved a ride along the coast to Port Renfrew, a pub, then an engaging gallop through forests on the way to the port of Nanaimo. Second prize wasn't bad.

The forests are full of Canada's tallest and largest Douglas firs, cedars and spruce trees. To see is to believe.

Nanaimo is the port to use to get back onto the Canadian mainland and BC Ferries are surprisingly inexpensive for the 3.5 hour trip to Horseshoe Bay in North Vancouver that positions you perfectly for the ride up the Sea to Sky route. A motorcycle passage was about CA$35. You can't book in advance, but they can always fit motorcycles onto the ferry so just arrive an hour early for your proposed trip, buy a ticket and wait in the queue. Securing your bike involved the same procedure used by the MV *Coho*.

As the entry to Canada is largely done in the trip from Port Angeles, getting out of the terminal at Horseshoe Bay is relatively simple.

Now it's time for you to engage with the Sea to Sky route.

Up, up and away

It's hard to get lost here. The Sea to Sky route is so well sign-posted that all you need to do is what the signs tell you.

If you accidentally turn left, you'll be in the ocean and if you accidentally turn right, you'll crash into the cliffs.

It's undoubtedly a great road but it's very heavily biased towards conventional tourism. We're dressed for the road, right? There's a limit to how much walking we can do to look at waterfalls and views. The road itself has a splendid seal and the initial ride along the coast before you start to climb is visually sensational.

At Britannia Beach you'll find the **Britannia Mine Museum National Historic Site** where you can get a comprehensive understanding of copper mining. Even if you're underwhelmed by that prospect, you'll like **BOOM!**, a part of the museum that is a live-action, multi-sensory experience that works well. You can also join a mining train for an underground adventure – as long as claustrophobia isn't one of your hang-ups.

The stop at **Shannon Falls** is worth it because it's a short walk and you get your first taste of Douglas fir, Western red cedar and Western hemlock. You'll never be able to ignore trees in the future. These are magnificent.

Close by Shannon Falls is the **Sea to Sky Gondola**. This takes you to three viewing platforms at the top of the ride, a 100m suspension bridge and a restaurant. It's a good experience but you'd want it to be at CA$70 a ticket. The trip lasts 10 minutes each way.

Camping

Canadians love the great outdoors and camping is part of that experience. The best campgrounds usually involve a long walk beforehand, which doesn't always suit riders who, understandably, don't want to leave their bikes unattended.

The **Klahanie Campground** (www.klahaniecampground.com) is popular as it's opposite Shannon Falls and within walking distance of the Sea to Sky Gondola.

Its tent sites are great. They include a fire pit and a picnic table. To make sure you get a spot in busy periods you need to book in advance; although if you just turn up and there's something available, you'll get it.

Another worthwhile camping site is **Riverside Camping and RV Resort** (www.campingrvbc.com) near Whistler. It's a 10-minute walk to the tent sites from where you can securely leave your bike, but the advantage is you're away from the noise and fuss of the RVs. The tent site is very scenic and is usually available even if the RV park is full. Sometimes you might be the only one camped there.

Very cool yurts are also available with good views and picnic tables outside the front door.

A little farther on is the village of **Squamish**, which exists to satisfy outdoor adventurers. There are 600 or so mountain biking trails to follow through the forests. No, unfortunately, you can't ride your motorcycle on them. Enjoy one of the many craft beers available instead.

Just north of Squamish is **Brackendale**, famous as a viewing area for North America's highest concentration of bald eagles. They gather between November and March to feast on the salmon in the alpine rivers. The 'Eagle Run' viewing facility is your best bet to see them in action, with December and January being the best months. What a pity that it is in the middle of winter.

It's a 50km gallop from Brackendale to Whistler but you will have already seen the best of the road conditions on the climb to Squamish. It's not that the road surface to Whistler is in any way bad, but the trip to Squamish from Vancouver sets a very high standard.

The Sea to Sky highway was extensively refurbished before the 2010 Winter Olympics that were co-hosted by Vancouver and Whistler. Such a good job was done that *The Guardian* newspaper declared it the fifth best road trip worldwide.

Whistler and beyond

Whistler (population: 13,982), in case you hadn't already guessed, is a ski town but there are still some worthwhile adventures there in summer. It, too, has a gondola experience and you can learn about the First Nations People with a visit to the very impressive **Squamish Lil'wat Cultural Centre** (www.slcc.ca).

While the road conditions deteriorate past here on Hwy 99, the ride actually gets better. There's far less traffic and the highway winds and drops through Pemberton and on to Lillooet in Fountain Valley. Once again you have a sense of wilderness in a country where it's prolific but sometimes hidden by a veneer of civilisation.

The Lil'wat First Nations People lived in the Pemberton Valley for thousands of years before European explorers arrived in the first half of the 19th century and the cultural centre in Whistler provides some idea of how difficult they found it. Smallpox devastated many communities and a recent apology from Premier Christy Clark indicates that smallpox was

spread intentionally to make land theft easier. Storyboards in Pemberton confirm the betrayal of the trust of the Lil'wat People.

You'll be sorry to arrive at the Hwy 97 intersection as it's the end of the Hwy 99 road. If you turn left, you can weave your way up to Jasper where you can start the Icefields Parkway ride. If you turn right, you can join Hwy 1 at Cache Creek and head back to Vancouver on another largely wild road where wilderness becomes your friend.

Decisions, decisions ...

Opposite top The Sky Pilot Suspension Bridge is part of the Sea To Sky Gondola experience *Opposite bottom left* The main street of Squamish *Opposite bottom right* The Sea to Sky Gondola

Being there

Highway 99 is a road in two sections. From Vancouver or Horseshoe Bay, it's hard to understand how a road that climbs like this one does could be in such good condition, until you discover it was vastly improved for the 2010 Winter Olympics.

Once past Whistler, the road goes back to what it probably always was before the Olympics: a two-lane road through the wilderness with great physical beauty and lovely riding.

We caught it through huge bushfires and, ironically, driving rain past Whistler. We stopped at a bus shelter in Pemberton to thaw out and, while we were waiting, read the information boards on how the Lil'wat Nation was treated after the arrival of the colonisers.

To the credit of the locals who erected the boards, the content was direct speech from the Lil'wat chiefs who expressed their bitter disappointment over how they'd been lied to by various levels of government and how they'd lost trust in any attempt to progress the relationship. For them, an agreement coupled by an appropriate ceremony was an unbreakable truth. For various interest groups among the colonisers it was just a means of making it easier to claim land and look for gold.

Standing in the rain and reading this was a faint glimpse of the misery that was inflicted on the First Nations People of Canada. Every colonised land in the world has a similar story.

Below Shannon Falls *Opposite top* Squamish Lil'wat Cultural Centre *Opposite middle* Qualicum Beach *Opposite bottom* Bald eagles are known to gather in Brackendale

BEST EATS

Ile Sauvage Brewing Company, Victoria, Vancouver Island

It's probably true that you're most likely to go there for the incredible craft beer, but Ile Sauvage (French for 'Wild Island') knows you have to eat as well, so they have a food truck onsite; but not just any old food truck. The food on offer has been paired with the beer to provide complementary tastes and it's easy to spend an afternoon there without realising it. Craft beer is big on Vancouver Island and Ile Sauvage is among the best.
www.ilesauvage.com

Port Renfrew Hotel, Vancouver Island

This is a traditional pub on the edge of the world. It can't help but have great seafood and the seafood chowder is made from fresh, local salmon and cod. All the usual pub favourites are there, and, if the sun is out, the back deck offers lovely harbour views. Perfect.
www.wildrenfrew.com/renfrew-pub

Naked Sprout Café, Whistler

Here's one for breakfast (or lunch) and set up to please vegans and vegetarians, although carnivores will get pleasure from it as well. Locals eat here, which is always a good sign, and it gets great reviews. Smoothies are half-price if you order something from the breakfast or lunch menu.
www.facebook.com/nakedsprout

BEST SLEEPS

Pangea Pod Hotel, Whistler

Not all Whistler accommodation is expensive. This is a hotel rather than a hostel but well designed with modern, pod-like accommodation and extras like en-suites and balconies. It's right in the heart of Whistler and rooms start in summer from CA$80 up to CA$95. Very nice.
www.pangeapod.com

Pemberton Valley Lodge, Pemberton

This is a little upmarket for long-distance motorcycle tourers but if you treat yourself occasionally, this is a good place to do it. It's set up for skiers but you can take advantage of free underground bike parking and a very comfortable, well-equipped suite. Summer pricing starts at CA$240. Oh, it has a cool pool as well.
www.pembertonvalleylodge.com

Bear's Claw Lodge, Cache Creek

A good hotel in a natural environment with clean rooms and a restaurant onsite. It has safe bike parking and it's close to Cache Creek if you want to explore other dining options. Rates start well under CA$100 a night.
http://bears-claw-lodge.britishcolumbiahotels.net

Death Valley: USA

Death Valley is very hot, very low and very dry. The harshness of the environment led to place names in the valley including Hell's Gate, Coffin Peak, Funeral Mountains, Dante's View and the Devil's Cornfield. Hades can't be far away …

SNAPSHOT

A natural fit for the countless cowboy and sci-fi movies that have been shot in the area, there's nothing quite like Death Valley anywhere else in America. But to ride it, timing is everything. This is one you carefully need to pick your time to avoid the searing heat and bitter cold. The road surface of Hwy 190 is good, which is fortunate as there aren't many alternatives. There are a surprising number of corners going into and coming out of the valley. Take plenty of water.

It's official: California's Death Valley is the hottest place on earth. A temperature of 134°F (57°C) was allegedly recorded in 1913 but the temperature was certainly 130°F (54°C) in July 2021 and at least 128°F (53°C) in July 2023. Mountains ring the valley, trapping heat and cooking the floor of the valley to the point where the surface can deliver third-degree burns to bare skin and melt the bottom of your motorcycle boots if you try to walk on it!

 How long?
Using Las Vegas as a starting point, it's possible to ride through Death Valley National Park in one day. Four days would do it justice, however, particularly if you decide to camp for a night to catch one of the best night skies in the world.

 When to go
Death Valley is crazy hot in summer and very cold in winter. Spring and autumn are the best times to ride, but even then it can be hot enough to fry an egg on the roadway. March, April and May are the months when the limited rainfall brings the desert flowers into bloom.

 Need to know
- Ride on the right-hand side of the road.
- Entrance fees apply to all visitors.
- Some 93% of the park's 3,422,024 acres is wilderness with either restricted or no access. Hence riding off-road is prohibited and you need to stay on established roads. National park rangers are vigilant about enforcing this and protecting the integrity of Death Valley.
- It's illegal to feed birds or animals.
- Your mobile phone won't get a signal in most of the park and GPS devices can mislead you into taking 'shortcuts' that don't exist. Get a paper map from the visitors centre at Furnace Creek.
- The use of drones is prohibited.
- Take plenty of water with you. Rangers recommend you drink a gallon (four litres) each day.
- Don't disturb potential wildlife habitats - given local species include rattlesnakes, scorpions and black widows, we probably don't need to tell you that.

While I could go on with plenty of other disincentives to visit, the truth is it's an extraordinary ride. The trick is to pick the right season. It's hottest from early June to late September. Spring and autumn are probably the best times to cross it, with late March to early April usually coinciding with wildflower blooms. If you thought you might get to cool off in the rain, only 2.2 inches (43mm) falls each year. Oh, and it's also the lowest place in North America, with Badwater Basin being 86m below sea level.

 Ride rating

Easy. The roads you'll be riding on are all sealed and the surface is generally very good. Concentration is required through the mountain sections due to the lack of safety barriers. The most common cause of death in the park is a single vehicle crash. Enjoy the scenery but don't become too distracted by it.

 Distances

- Las Vegas to Lone Pine via Death Valley: 232 miles (373km)
- Las Vegas to Death Valley Junction: 112 miles (180km)
- Death Valley Junction to Furnace Creek: 30 miles (48km)
- Furnace Creek to Panamint Springs: 55 miles (89km)

 Temperatures

- January: 39°F to 66°F (4°C to 19°C)
- July: 88°F to 117°F (31°C to 47°C)

 More information

www.nps.gov/deva

Left Salt lakes are a feature of the road network in Death Valley *Opposite* The entrance to Death Valley National park

Top Weaving through the Panamint Range towards the exit from Death Valley *Bottom left and right* Death Valley entertainment options

Life's a gamble

If Death Valley is on your itinerary, **Las Vegas** (population: 646,700) in Nevada isn't a bad starting place. You probably already know enough about Sin City without the need for further explanation, but if you've never been there or have deliberately avoided it, here's a chance to widen your horizons.

Accommodation in the giant casinos mid-week is astoundingly cheap and you'll be able to find a range of options in the middle of town for well under US$80 a night. Obviously the casinos want you to stay there because you might gamble with them and, mid-week, they have plenty of spare rooms.

Las Vegas is well serviced by transport options from just about anywhere in America. So with limited time, it's possible to fly in, rent a motorcycle, explore Death Valley and be out of town again in two days. EagleRider (www.eaglerider.com) is a well-established operator renting bikes ranging from a Triumph Bonneville T100 for US$80 a day to a full-dress Harley-Davidson Road Glide Ultra at US$225 per day.

If you've got your own bike, most accommodation options provide secure parking.

We're not here to gamble, though – we're here to ride. Set your on-board satellite navigation system for Death Valley Junction and get ready to roll.

Highway to hell

Death Valley Junction (formerly Amargosa; population less than 20) is 112 miles from Las Vegas, accessed mostly along Route 95, with a left turn at Amargosa Valley onto Route 373 for the final 23 miles.

Rapidly falling into disrepair, Death Valley Junction started as a railway town in 1907 with a saloon, a store and a brothel. Borax (salt) turned out to be the biggest mining enterprise in the area, and between 1923 and 1925 the Pacific Coast Borax Company built a grand, Spanish-looking complex in the town with a theatre, offices and a hotel. It became derelict within 10 years and was rediscovered in 1967 by Mara Becket, a dancer and actress, who restored it and turned the theatre section into the Amargosa Opera House. It's falling apart again now but the hotel is both an inexpensive and interesting place to spend a night. Check beforehand if the cafe is open as it's the only game in town. Otherwise, you may have to bring along your own food.

The ride from Las Vegas to Death Valley Junction has moved you from Nevada into California. Head north from Death Valley Junction very briefly before turning left onto Route 190 on which you'll largely stay until you exit for the Death Valley

National Park on its west side. The distance from Death Valley Junction to Lone Pine on the other side of the park is 135 miles but you need to add around 60 miles to that to allow for detours.

You'll be welcomed into the national park by a giant sign and an unmanned booth where you'll be expected to pay the entry fee. It's US$30 for cars for seven days and US$25 for motorcycles. It seems unfair, doesn't it – five people in a car versus one person on a motorcycle! If you're visiting more than one national park, it's cheaper for riders to get an Interagency Annual Pass for US$80 – plus, if you're riding with a comrade on another bike, you can share the same pass, which evens things up considerably.

So you're finally in **Death Valley**. Well, not quite – you have to climb over the Amargosa Range and your first deviation will be to **Dante's View**, which is well signposted and 12 miles east from Route 190. Caravans and camper trailers can't do it, but bikes can make it to the major viewpoint 4920ft above the floor of Death Valley. It's unlike any other view you'll ever get in the US and it's an engaging ride on a twisty, narrow road.

Retracing your ride to Route 190 and turning left will take you to another lookout: **Zabriskie Point**. This is an easier ride in that it's only a quarter mile elevation. There's a car park at the base but, if it isn't busy, you can ride the paved road to the lookout point. It provides a view of the badlands and, in some spots, it looks like the surface of the moon. It's weird but wonderful. From here it's a short, downhill run to the administrative centre of Death Valley: **Furnace Creek**.

Camera, action!

Lone Pine and the Alabama Hills on the western edge of Death Valley National Park is a hotbed of cinematic history dating back to the silent film era. Over 400 films have been shot there. The landscape is perfect for cowboy movies and early stars included Tom Mix, John Wayne, Errol Flynn, Gene Autry, Gary Cooper and Roy Rogers. More 'recent' stars included Robert Mitchum, Gregory Peck, Randolph Scott, Steve McQueen, Clint Eastwood and Mel Gibson. More recently, *The Lone Ranger* with Johnny Depp was shot there in 2013.

The Death Valley area also attracts its share of sci-fi films. Along with *Star Wars, Star Trek V* was also filmed there. If 'sword and sandal' epics are more your thing, it's also where parts of Russell Crowe's *Gladiator* were located.

So Lone Pine might seem like just another innocuous small town, but keep your eyes open - you never know who you might be sitting next to in the pubs and cafes.

Into the furnace

Somewhat unbelievably, the Indigenous Timbisha Shoshone People have lived in Death Valley for over 1000 years. The environment is so fragile that it could only support a small community and it's estimated that only 200 of the Panamint Shoshone Nation spoke the Timbisha language.

Death Valley remained undisturbed by European colonisers until the gold rush in California in 1849 when miners passed by, seeking a shorter route to the goldfields from the east to west. For those who attempted it, the route was a disaster, but some noticed potential in the valley and moved there to run cattle, explore for minerals and exploit the small areas of fertile land.

The then-US President Herbert Hoover created the Death Valley National Monument in 1933, which subsumed all tribal homelands. Without access to the few waterholes, and with cattle trampling the subsistence vegetation, the Timbisha Shoshone were eventually reduced to living on a 40-acre block near Furnace Creek.

Timbisha Shoshone women – who made up the majority of inhabitants of the Furnace Creek camp while the men worked away – fought back and got recognition as a group in 1982,

eventually winning back 7500 acres of ancestral homelands and, unlike other Indigenous Americans, their reservation is still on their original homeland.

Golf? Seriously?

A reminder of civilisation in an otherwise alien environment, **Furnace Creek** (population: 136) is the go-to place in the middle of Death Valley. It has fuel, accommodation, a visitor centre, post office, general store, camping sites and a few places perhaps inappropriately named as 'restaurants'.

It also has two magnificent accommodation options: the Inn at Death Valley and the Ranch at Death Valley (www.oasisatdeathvalley.com), but be prepared to pay for the privilege. The Ranch actually has a golf course which, in its opulence, must astound locals. It might also astound golfers in that hitting a ball at below sea level is unique in its results. Abandon all hope ye who enter.

Just before you arrive at Furnace Creek, there's a turn-off to the left to **Badwater Basin**, which is the lowest point in North America. It's a 35 mile return-trip but worth the effort, particularly if you take the boardwalk onto the salt flats.

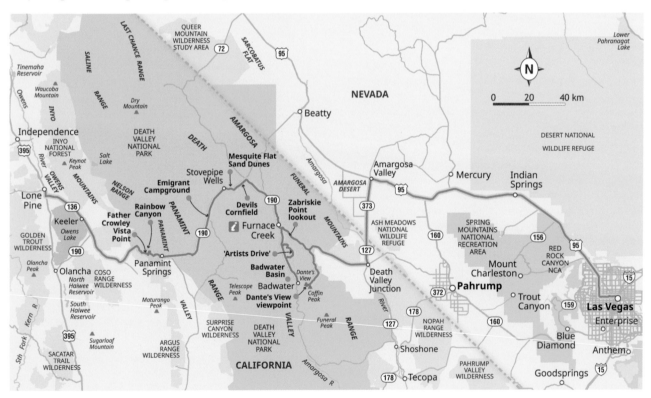

Above Death Valley is the location for many western and science fiction movies - it has atmosphere aplenty

On the way to Badwater Basin, take the one-way, scenic loop called 'Artists Drive', which is 8.5 miles left on the Badwater Rd. It's worth it for the hilly, rugged terrain and how the colours in the hills change depending on when you're doing it.

The Badwater Basin run is a fitting introduction to what lies ahead.

Westward ho

Route 190 from Furnace Creek initially runs north up the valley. It's a well-maintained road mostly at sea level and it's another chance to pick up the mysterious vibe emanating from the land. Within minutes of leaving Furnace Creek, you feel very much on your own. It's easy to understand why the decision was made to film parts of *Star Wars* and *Return of the Jedi* here as the setting for the planet of Tatooine.

Thirty miles up the road there's a left turn to stay on the 190. You'll pass (and probably stop at) the **Mesquite Flat Sand Dunes** on your right after passing the Devil's Cornfield on your left. **Stovepipe Wells Village** is only 9 miles from the turn-off where there's a store, fuel and a very welcoming bar with a limited but interesting menu. George Lucas wasn't the only filmmaker to see the potential in Death Valley. A film poster collection in the bar includes Roy Rogers in *Saga of Death Valley* (1939) and Ken Maynard in *Death Valley Rangers* (1943).

Heading west for 8 miles will take you to the **Emigrant Campground** where, if you have a tent, you might consider stopping for the night. Why? Death Valley National Park is part of the International Dark Sky Places program that certifies locations where the night sky is protected and preserved through public education and managed, artificial lighting. The free-of-charge Emigrant Campground (first-come, first-served) is tent-only with just 10 sites available. It has minimal facilities but it's one of the best sites after dark to observe the billions of stars that light up the sky. In total there are 15 authorised camp sites in Death Valley, some that close in either summer or winter, but all of which offer excellent night skies; the more remote ones provide the greatest rewards.

From Emigrant you'll start to climb the Panamint Range, leaving the straight road behind as you engage once again with its twists and turns. While the road surface is very good, there's not much in the way of protection if you happen to go off from being over enthusiastic with your cornering. Cliffs on one side and drops on the other are common. Make sure you look at your surroundings occasionally, however, as the colour changes in the hills are surreal.

Once off the range you'll cross a Panamint Valley salt lake before arriving at **Panamint Springs** (population: 2082), another small but welcome reminder of civilisation.

Before you leave the park proper, stop at the **Father Crowley Vista Point** for a look at **Rainbow Canyon,** named because of the layered landscape created by lava flows. It used to be a magnet for photographers when the military used the canyon for low-flying exercises and you could actually look down on fighter jets traveling at 600mph below the lip of the canyon. However, a crash in 2019 that killed a pilot and injured seven tourists has understandably paused the program.

Reality finally kicks in again on the 40-mile exit from Death Valley on the other side of the Inyo Mountains to **Lone Pine** (population: 1484) where most of the Western movies you've ever seen were probably shot.

Death Valley will be one of the strangest rides you'll ever do. Transitioning from the completely artificial lights and noise of Las Vegas to the absolutely silent night sky of Emigrant in one day will fray the edges of your understanding. Doing it on a motorcycle gives you maximum exposure to the experience and will remind you once again why you love riding.

Above The sound and light show that is Las Vegas *Opposite* The bar of the Badwater Saloon at Stovepipe Wells village

Being there

Aha, Las Vegas. My comrade on this trip, Stuart, determined that we'd only invest US$50 each on gambling for our two nights there. We'd get to know what it was all about without losing too much money.

Along the main strip near our hotel, I helped one of two bikini-clad women approaching me whose butterfly wings were being buffeted by the wind. They were grateful and suggested a photo of the three of us before telling me that they expected US$40 each for the images! That's what they do for a living. I gave them $20 to split but was unnerved by the experience. Human compassion can have a cost in Sin City and encourages the feeling that if anyone talks to you on the street, it's probably part of a scam.

You can, however, enjoy Vegas without spending much. The traffic in the main strip, human and mechanical, is a constant source of entertainment and there's no entry fee to the casinos where you can watch gamblers losing thousands without seeming to notice.

Stuart and I lost our US$50 playing blackjack but, to the dealer's annoyance, we dragged it out for as long as possible with small bets and conservative decisions.

BEST EATS

Margaritaville, Las Vegas
You might be asking, 'where is Margaritaville?' *It's in your mind.*

Vale Jimmy Buffett (1946-2023). The prolific and much-loved American recording artist created not just music but an entire ecosystem of presence; his Margaritaville restaurants being just one example. This one in Las Vegas is typical with its nautical themes, boat seating and Key West menu. Try Jimmy's Jamin' Jambalaya (shrimp, chicken and Andoville sausage simmered in a spicy broth). Have the Key Lime Pie for dessert and drink a toast to Jimmy.
www.margaritavillelasvegas.com

Last Kind Words Saloon, Furnace Creek
The historic ranch in Death Valley was refurbished in 2018 and the Last Kind Words Saloon was born. It looks like a big Western movie set and it's full of reminders of the Wild West. This extends to the menu, which is slightly meat-heavy but does make some provision for vegetarians. You're reminded of the 'wild' side of the Wild West with random antique firearms on display along with taxidermied game animals. Don't say you weren't warned …
www.oasisatdeathvalley.com

Stovepipe Wells Village Hotel, Stovepipe Wells
Located 40 miles past Furnace Creek is Stovepipe Wells, which has a general store, the Badwater Saloon, the Toll Road Restaurant, hotel accommodation, a caravan/camping site and a swimming pool.

You can get counter-type meals in the Badwater Saloon along with cold beer but it's a step up to the Toll Road Restaurant where the menu is more extensive and thoughtful with an emphasis on the history and traditions of food in the area. Try the Ancho Tortilla soup (anchos are chillis) or the flat pan steaks. The self-contained nature of the village makes it an attractive place to stop for a night and everything you might want is available.
www.deathvalleyhotels.com/our-hotel/

BEST SLEEPS

Ellis Island Hotel Casino & Brewery, Las Vegas
As mentioned earlier, you can find some amazing deals with the major casinos for mid-week stays and it's worth checking online booking sites. Otherwise, Ellis Island Hotel is a great alternative. It's a block east of the main strip and an easy walk. The rooms are clean and consistently cheap. The gambling in the casino is old-school - you can get involved with $5 chips. The hotel has guest parking out-of-the-way around the back for your bike.
www.ellisislandcasino.com

Stovepipe Wells Hotel and Caravan Park, Death Valley
The hotel has a variety of rooms available starting with the smaller patio rooms with space for one or two for US$144 a night, all the way up to deluxe rooms at US$226 a night. If you have a tent strapped to the back of your bike, you can pitch it in the caravan park for just US$14 a night. Use of the shower facilities has a slightly additional cost but access to the pool is free. And, of course, you can drink at the Badwater Saloon and dine at the Toll Road Restaurant if you so desire.
www.deathvalleyhotels.com

Panamint Springs Resort, Death Valley
Originally owned and operated by Buffalo Bill Cody's cousin, Agnes Cody, Panamint Springs Resort is about 10 miles inside the western border of Death Valley National Park. Though it's situated along Hwy 190 it doesn't have a physical address because it doesn't receive US mail. Despite that, it's not too hard to find.

It has hotel rooms, a restaurant, a general store, fuel and a bar. Cabin-style motel rooms start from US$140 and move up to US$290. If you have your own sleeping bag, a good option for riders is a two-person tent cabin for US$55 a night. The tent cabin has no facilities but you can access the caravan shower facilities for free and there's a fire ring outside the tent cabin if you want to prepare food yourself.
www.panamintsprings.com

Q & A
Michelle Lamphere

Michelle Lamphere threw a corporate life away to pursue motorcycle adventures. She's a major player in American motorcycle life, author of two books and you can hear her as a regular contributor to the world's top motorcycling podcast: www.adventureriderradio.com

What got you into riding?

Although I was born in Sturgis, South Dakota, home to a world famous motorcycle rally, no one in my family rode motorcycles. I was a ranch kid and used horses and four-wheelers as tools for getting work done. My high-school boyfriend used a dirt bike for ranch work and taught me to ride in a prairie dog town one summer but I didn't get my licence until more than a decade later.

What have been your three best rides?

The Karakoram Highway in Pakistan, Portachuelo Llanganuco Pass in Huascaran National Park in Peru and Iron Mountain Road in South Dakota are probably the roads that are the most memorable for me. I've loved riding gorgeous coastal roads, desert vistas and salt flats, but there is nothing more dramatic for me than traversing a mountain pass and riding sweeping curves through a valley surrounded by rugged peaks.

Do you think motorcycle adventures have changed you and how?

Although I have always been a traveller, motorcycles have allowed me to experience the world in a much deeper way than ever before. Exploring a part of the world on a bike allows you to choose your own path and take your time as you go. I've seen stunningly beautiful landscapes, met kind people and soaked up cultures in a way that I wouldn't have been able to do when travelling by any other means. And riding has taught me to slow down, be more present in the moment and go with the flow. Those are things that transfer to my life off the road as well.

You're president of the USA division of WIMA (Women's International Motorcycle Association) and an instigator of Rev Sisters. Are you a born organiser or were these roles forced on you?

Most of the roles I've taken on in my life have come about from the standpoint that they were things that I believed strongly needed to be done and I wanted to do my part to make them happen.

The Women's International Motorcycle Association was created by American Louise Scherbyn in 1950 and is the oldest international group of women riders in the world.

The USA division had become dormant in the last several years before I took on the role of national president. I wanted to see Louise's legacy honoured and for her mission to serve a new generation of women. I'm blessed to know some incredibly generous, hard working and passionate women motorcyclists and together we have worked hard to revive the American division. Thanks to them, it's becoming a thriving organisation again.

Rev Sisters was a passion project created by two friends and myself to provide online film festivals celebrating all things 'motorcycle' during the pandemic and for a short time after. It was a lot of fun and hopefully entertained the motorcycle community at a time when we all needed it.

You're the author of two books. What are they and where can we get them?

The Butterfly Route is a memoir of my motorcycle travels from home to Ushuaia and beyond. What started out as an extended vacation and break between careers turned into a two-year journey from South Dakota to South America including random experiences, new friendships, rugged mountain roads to Andean villages, desert camping, two broken bones, countless accidents (happy and otherwise) and a marriage proposal.

Tips for Traveling Overland in Latin America: Things I Wish I had Known Before I Rode my Motorcycle to Mexico, Central and South America is a small handbook I put together after returning from South America in 2015 to share tips with others who might be considering a similar trip.

Both books are available in print and e-book formats from Amazon.com

What advice would you now give to yourself as a 20 year old wanting to engage in a motorcycling life?

Go have fun! Be safe and smart, wear all the gear all the time, take classes and grow your skills. Learn how to maintain and work on your bike and change your tires and ask for help. People are more generous, kind and alike than you know, but always use your head and look out for yourself.

Opposite Michelle Lamphere - motorcycle wonderwoman

California's Highway One: USA

America's cultural imperialism has turned Highway 1 into myth and legend but, somehow, it's still worth the effort. Americans invented the 'road trip', right?

SNAPSHOT

Highway 1 is an absolutely iconic ride for motorcyclists due to its construction and association with the literary traditions of American writing on 'the road trip' being a metaphor for self-discovery. The popularity of the route affects the quality of the ride, but it's still worth the effort. You'll enjoy it most in the section of Hwy 1 north of San Francisco, where you might actually have an encounter with the 'real' America, or the version popular culture will have you believe, anyway. Do the ride soon, before the west coast of the US slides into the Pacific Ocean permanently.

The Great American Road Trip existed before Jack Kerouac wrote *On the Road* in 1957, but Jack sure-as-hell cemented it into popular culture. Prior to the late arrival of Europeans, multiple groups of Indigenous Peoples populated California from between 16,000 and 25,000 years ago and they developed an extensive network of trade routes, many of which the Europeans eventually turned into highways. The Rocky Mountains encouraged isolated groupings and there are around 135 identified dialects among the First Nations Peoples in the state, with plenty of evidence of sophisticated trading over long distances.

The wagon trains that headed west in the 1800s were on an early form of a European road trip, seeking freedom, wealth and discovery without really knowing what they'd find. Similarly, John Steinbeck's *Grapes of Wrath* (1939) had the Joad family on a road trip along Route 66 to what they believed would be both work and financial salvation in California.

For motorcyclists, Robert Pirsig's *Zen and the Art of Motorcycle Maintenance* (1974) philosophically covered a road trip from Minnesota to Northern California on a Honda C77 in 1968, and it became America's all-time best-selling book on philosophy. Pirsig later claimed it wasn't very accurate on Zen Buddhism and it was equally inaccurate on motorcycle maintenance, but it did successfully enunciate the ideas of 'road trip' and its relationship with 'quest'.

As a motorcycle road trip, *Zen* was arguably eclipsed by the film *Easy Rider*, which was released in 1969. Wyatt and Billy are permanently etched into road trip folklore.

Right Bixby Creek Bridge on Highway One between Point Lobos Marine Reserve and Little Sur River

 How long?
Two days will get you from Los Angeles to San Francisco and another day will get you to where Hwy 1 ends near Leggett. A more relaxed and enlightening schedule will be three days on the first leg and two days on the second.

 When to go
November to April will give you reduced traffic on this well-loved route and the coastal location means winter isn't too cold. Summer is fine as well, of course, but the traffic reduces the pleasure of the ride.

 Need to know
- Ride on the right-hand side of the road.
- Be aware that visitors will park in inconvenient locations while taking images of the coast so don't presume the road is clear around the next corner.
- The little-heralded second leg of Hwy 1 north from San Francisco is one of America's greatest rides.

As for Kerouac, he told a student in 1961 that he and Neal Cassady (Dean Moriarty in the book) had embarked on a journey through post–Walt Whitman America to *find* that America and *find* the inherent goodness in the American man.

'It was really a story about two Catholic buddies, roaming the country, in search of God. And we found him'.

That would be news for Allen Pietrobon, a history lecturer at Trinity Washington University who teaches a course on the meaning of the 'Great American Road Trip'.

'There's no "real America". If you set off on your journey to find some myth that doesn't exist, you'll always be disappointed'.

Regardless, Hwy 1 is part of the mythology of the American road trip. For many, it begins and ends at either San Francisco or LA, depending on which way you travel. In fact, it extends past San Francisco for another 182 miles near to Leggett where it joins with Hwy 101 heading north.

We're setting out from LA and heading north, singing Simon & Garfunkel's *America*, which we've 'all come to look for'.

 Ride rating

Mostly easy, but remember it's a two-lane road and the traffic can be unpredictable.

 Distances

- San Diego to near Leggett north of San Francisco: 656 miles (1056 km).
- Note taking Hwy 1 instead of Hwy 101 adds an additional 200 miles (322km) depending on the routes you select.

 Temperatures

- January: 46°F to 57°F (8°C to 14°C)
- September: 57°F to 72°F (14°C to 22°C)

 More information

www.visitcalifornia.com
www.visittheusa.com.au/trip/pacific-coast-highway-road-trip

Just about every town on Hwy 1 considers itself a tourist destination and has its own tourist web address. Google the towns you're interested in and you'll get the hard-sell.

North America

Above Blind corners are common on Highway One

Leaving Los Angeles

Any advice for riders in LA? Yes, leave it as soon as possible. It's the death of riding: too packed on the roads and nowhere to park. If you're starting your ride from LA, though, you'll probably be stuck there for a few days getting your bike sorted so you should make the most of it.

If you're flying in, there's a Motel 6 about 5 miles from the airport with a free shuttle bus service. Motel 6 is an American chain of cheap motels of very mixed quality but always relatively inexpensive. This particular one is well located. The nearest metro line is a 15-minute walk away and there's a 117 bus stop across the road that connects with LAX City Bus Centre and multiple metro stations to help you get around the city . There's free parking for motorcycles and if you park near the entry doors, your bike will be in sight of the 24/7 security guard.

It's also well located in that it's on the right side of LA to easily get to Hwy 1 via a freeway.

Got your own motorcycle? Great. No problems. Fly-ins will probably be renting a bike when they get there from myriad bike hire companies. Two mainstream options are **HertzRide** (www.hertzride.com), which offers a BMW R 1250 RT with luggage for US$150 a day (as an example) and **EagleRider** (www.eaglerider.com) where you can pick up a Yamaha FJR1300 with luggage from USD$143 per day. HertzRide is in the same suburb as Motel 6.

Out of left field, you should also consider **Riders Share** (www.riders-share.com), which is easily half the price of the mainstream hirers. How about a 2002 Harley-Davidson Ultra Limited for USD$65 a day?

If you find yourself with time to kill, popular LA attractions include tours of Universal Studios and Warner Brothers, a walk down Hollywood Blvd or a visit to Santa Monica boardwalk where Route 66 is claimed to end – or start – without it being strictly true. You're in Hollywood so who cares?

You can also easily spend a day at the Petersen Automotive Museum (www.petersen.org) where exhibitions can include movie cars (the Batmobile!) and motorcycles from the Barber collection in Birmingham, Alabama.

Northern lights

So we're finally on the road. The trip along Hwy 1 can initially feel a little disappointing as LA is spreading up the coast and what used to be discrete villages are now becoming part of the urban sprawl.

30

A particular annoyance is a failure of planning laws that have allowed houses and businesses to be built right on the beachfront. It's only one layer deep but in places it completely obscures views of the beaches from Hwy 1. Iconic Californian locations including Malibu and Ventura are probably still great for the people who live there but you hardly notice them as you ride past. There's a pier in Malibu adjacent to Surfrider Beach but it's hard to find a park, even on a motorcycle, and you could easily pass it without noticing.

It gets a little better as you get to Santa Barbara and better still the farther north you ride.

Santa Barbara's highlight is Sterns Wharf which, when you think about it, is incredible. It's the oldest working wood wharf in California, built in 1872, and it's still strong enough to allow around 140 cars (and bikes) to drive up it to enjoy its views, restaurants and other attractions. How much do 140 cars weigh? It's probably around 130,000kg – not bad for an old wharf.

Cars are free for 90 minutes and then it's USD$2.50 per hour afterwards. Nobody seems to care about bikes so just ride in and out of the barrier as you see fit.

If you have time, visit the Bait and Tackle shop on the wharf, buy some bait, hire a hand-line or rod and spend an hour or so wetting the line. The locals do it so there must be some fish out there.

Mercifully, Hwy 1 starts to lose its population after Santa Barbara and you can start focusing on the ride and the views as you head towards Santa Maria and on to Pismo Beach.

Pismo Beach

Pismo Beach (population: 8000) has a great pier as well where you can indulge in most of the popular water-related activities, but, if that's your want, you can ride your bike on the beach at **the Oceano Dunes State Vehicular Recreation Area**. There are camping areas near the beach if you've brought your tent. This is the only beach area in California you can legally ride and camp on.

Pismo Beach is famous for its clam chowder but, with overfishing, clams are getting harder to find. Enjoy it while you can.

The road north from here becomes less busy and more twisty as it weaves in and out of the coastal shore with your next destination being **Morro Bay** (population: 10,757). It's a quaint, old town dominated by the Morro Rock, a volcanic plug that sits in the middle of the harbour. It's a beautiful sight at sunset. Main St and Morro Bay Blvd provide the best walks and, at last, you feel like you're being dragged free of LA.

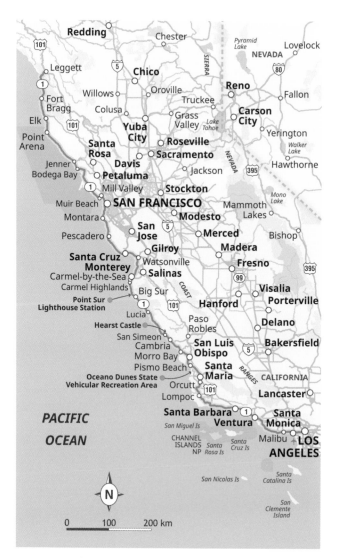

It can be a bit confusing following Hwy 1 due to the complicated signage. You'll see signs saying CA State Hwy 1, Pacific Coast Hwy, Cabrillo Hwy and other highways. For brief sections, you'll also join Hwy 101. The plan here is to keep left. The closer you are to the coast, the more likely it is you'll be on Hwy 1.

You're now about to ride the most impressive part of the whole trip. It's still Hwy 1 but it's also regularly called the Pacific Coast Hwy. It's a 71-mile section starting at San Carpoforo Creek near San Simeon and finishing at Malpaso Creek near Carmel Highlands. It's a winding, narrow road often cut into the face of cliffs. The incentive to build it was due to a shipwreck near Point Sur Lighthouse Station in 1894 and the difficulty involved in getting medical help to the scene. Building this section of road was started in 1921 and not finished until 1937.

Australian painter Francis McComas called it the 'greatest meeting of land and water in the world'. Riding it requires focus because of the narrow road and the consequences of you getting it wrong, but you need to leave enough in reserve so you can enjoy the interplay of the road and the view. Often, you can see the road in the distance weaving in and out of the cliffs. These days it's busy but this section tends to be less busy than the section between San Francisco and Big Sur.

You should be aware that the road is often closed due to mud- and rock-slides, usually as a result of heavy rain. Local gossip is the blasting that occurred while the road was being built made the cliff faces unstable. The road has been closed around 55 times by landslides. In 1917 the slide was so severe that the road was closed for 18 months. In early 2021 the land under the road at Rat Creek south of Big Sur collapsed into the sea,

Route 66

Okay, this isn't exactly on our route but it finishes where we start from on our examination of Hwy 1. It's not a ride in itself in that there are large parts of it that are relatively uninteresting, but it's still of tremendous cultural significance to America.

It was established in 1926 and ran for 2400 miles (3862km) crossing eight states, starting from Chicago and ending (more or less) at Santa Monica.

For John Steinbeck, it was the 'mother road' that gave access for destroyed farming families from Middle America to the promised land of California.

On the way, the road crossed Illinois, Missouri, Kansas, Oklahoma, Texas, New Mexico and Arizona.

The road was so well used that it developed its own culture of motels, gas stations, diners and tatty tourist attractions. The route was decommissioned in 1985 but around 80 per cent of it is still rideable with a few landmarks on the trip that celebrate its history.

One of these towns is **Williams** in Arizona. which has an entire street devoted to Route 66-themed accommodation, food and merchandise.

If you have time, you know where to get your kicks …

and the route was repeatedly closed during the heavy storms of 2022 and 2023 for periods of up to six months. You can check current highway conditions on 1-800-427-7623.

Here's the problem. Because the road is largely cut into cliff faces, there are no detour opportunities if a landslide occurs, even if you're on an adventure bike. To proceed north if the road is closed, you need to get onto Hwy 101 at San Luis Obispo and you can't rejoin Hwy 1 without difficulty and dirt roads until you get to Monterey via Salinas. It means you'll have missed 130 miles of riding glory.

Treat Hwy 1 being open when you want to ride it as a gift from the road gods.

The American Dream

Cambria (population: 5555) is around the mid-point of the LA to San Francisco ride and isn't a bad place to set up camp. It has an historic downtown area that's well worth a walk around, but most people are here to visit the extraordinary Hearst Castle in San Simeon, which is 10 miles away.

Hearst Castle was built by newspaper magnate William Randolph Hearst between 1919 and 1947 and is a monument to the confusion new wealth brought to Americans. Hearst clearly couldn't decide how money could be converted into culture, so not only did he build an inappropriate castle but he filled it with out-of-place objects. It's 'a museum of the best things I can secure,' he said.

The weekly guest list included Charlie Chaplin, Carey Grant, the Marx Brothers, Greta Garbo, Buster Keaton, Clark Gable and Winston Churchill, among everyone else in showbiz or politics who was important at the time.

An invitation to Hearst Castle was a two-edged sword. To 'manage' his alcoholic actress girlfriend, Marion Davies, there was a limit of one cocktail before dinner and no alcohol in any of the guest rooms. Hearst's wine cellar had 7000 bottles.

Hearst left the Castle due to ill health in 1947 and died in 1951. His family donated it to the state of California in 1958 and it's been open to the public since then.

Another regular guest, George Bernard Shaw, had this to say about the 82,000 acres surrounding the castle: 'It's what God would have built if he had had the money'.

San Simeon, the 500-resident-strong town nearest to Hearst Castle, is a little expensive but worth visiting to see the **elephant seal rookery** where, if the season is right, you can see hundreds of elephant seals relaxing on the beach.

Big Sur

Big Sur itself isn't actually a village. It's a vibe, man. There are small settlements, cafes, national park entrances and a beautiful road, but it's not a village you can actually visit.

The area is famous, though, for the people it attracted. You need to drop into the Nepenthe, a restaurant that was once owned as a holiday house by Orson Welles and Rita Hayworth. Welles' most famous film, *Citizen Kane* (1941), was based on the life of William Hearst and demonstrated the inherent uncertainty and conflict in the American Dream. Nepenthe (*see* Best Eats section) bloomed from 1958 when Hearst Castle was opened and was well used by stars including Kim Novac, Steve McQueen, Salvador Dalí and Clint Eastwood.

The road north from here is still a good ride but loses a little of its natural charm. **Monterey** (population: 29,874) is worth stopping at for its pier (great seafood chowder) and access to Cannery Row, made famous by the John Steinbeck novel.

Carmel-by-the-sea

Carmel is a long way from being a bike town but it's an example of what America could have been if the government had been run by artists rather than politicians.

Its council in 1929 declared that the town was 'primarily, essentially and predominantly, a residential community'. It was agreed that it was a village in a forest overlooking a white, sandy beach and that's what its residents wanted. Rather than let the town be overrun by rampant capitalist enterprises, planning regulations protected its original charm. New buildings had to be built around existing trees. The village has no streetlights or parking meters. There are no street numbers on the houses, so there are no postal deliveries to individual houses. The village occupies just one square mile and anything that threatens its cultural establishments are denied planning permits.

Clint Eastwood was its mayor for two years to ensure summary justice was handed out to anyone who disagreed with the council's decisions. He still owns a hotel complex in town.

Left Fish art on Monteray Pier *Right* The end of Route 66 - Santa Monica Pier

Are you going to San Francisco …

The 1967 song by Scott McKenzie wasn't news to Americans – they already knew that San Francisco was the place to be for the flower-power generation. Haight-Ashbury hosted the summer of love in the same year but, for a variety of reasons, the hippy movement fell apart afterwards. Important parts of its philosophy survived, though, and its influence changed a generation.

San Francisco (population: 815, 201) is a city and riding there, like in most cities, isn't much fun. Have a look at the remnants of Haight-Ashbury, go to Fisherman's Wharf for great, local seafood and, perhaps, book a tour to Alcatraz before you head north to discover what is probably the best bit of Hwy 1.

To get across the city on Hwy 1, you need to cross the **Golden Gate Bridge**, which, if you haven't done it already, will be another tick on your bucket list. Use GPS or a good map to take you farther along the coast road until you get to Mill Valley where you'll turn left where Hwy 1 breaks away from 101.

The road is Shoreline Hwy and will be signposted to Muir Beach. Shortly you'll quit Tamalpais Valley and find yourself largely free of traffic and enjoying a twisty, climbing and descending run towards the Pacific Ocean.

When I say, 'largely free of traffic', the secret is out with riders and on weekends you can join up to 200 of San Francisco's best at the fuel station in Mill Valley for a stop over the hill and up the coast.

Highway 1 north of San Francisco is now like what the LA to San Fran section must have been in the 1940s: a quiet road with great views passing periodically through small, quaint villages. It's two-lane all the way and full of corners as it tries to hug the coast. It lacks the spectacle of the Big Sur route but is naturally quite beautiful in its own way. Sections like the **Sonoma Coast State Park** offer grand views of the Pacific, which usually involve rocky outcrops randomly stretching into the ocean.

Below Coastal scenery along Highway One *Opposite top left* Flowers blossom along the route *Opposite right* Santa Monica Pier *Opposite bottom left* A stop at Point Arena

The road surface is generally good to excellent, although clearly, the population density isn't there to justify keeping the roads in perfect condition. It's certainly good enough to make riding a hoot.

Oysters are big business, especially around **Tomales Bay**. You can call in to the Tomales Bay Oyster Company along the highway and buy a fresh bag, but you can't eat them there. Choices include buying a shucking knife and riding a few miles farther on to the beach, or calling in to a number of close-by restaurants and ordering them off the menu. Not sure how to use a shucking knife? The people running the Tomales Bay Oyster Company stand will show you how. Of the restaurants, William Tell House is the pick. Share a dozen Tomales oysters and then tuck into the house seafood chowder. Yum.

Point Arena houses that most unexpected of thing in this part of the world: a motorcycle shop specialising in Italian exotica. It's called **The Zen House: The Art of Motorcycle Maintenance** (www.thezenhouse.net). Co-owner David Harris was service manager at GP Motorcycles in San Diego before deciding to head north. Call in and have a look at the bikes on display. Some are customer bikes but others will be Zen's award-winning builds.

Not far past Point Arena is the tiny settlement of **Elk** (population: 200) with the best general store on the entire road. They have food to go, but you can eat there if you like or take it across the road to the beach.

Farther on you'll ride alongside Fort Liberty where 52,000 military personnel are stationed. It was called Fort Bragg until 2021, when the department of defense decided to update all military installations named after Confederate Civil War figures. Confederate general, Braxton Bragg, was a slave owner and, according to his contemporaries, a short-tempered, merciless tyrant. Historians say he was the 'worst and most hated of the South's generals'. Despite the name change costing over six million dollars, presidential hopefuls including Ron De Santis have said that, once elected, they'll reverse the decision.

It might be an idea to top your bike's fuel up at Fort Liberty as supply will be unreliable until you get to the end of Hwy 1 near Leggett.

Alas, Hwy 1 is coming to an end but there's one little treat left in store: the final 25 miles before Hwy 1 intersects once again with Hwy 101. It will remind you of your earlier ride from Mill Valley to Muir Beach in that it's tight, undulating and remote. If there were tigers in America, this is where they'd live.

Your three choices at the intersection with 101 are to turn left and head up towards Canada, turn right and head back towards San Francisco, or do a U-turn and see how Hwy 1 unfolds in the opposite direction. The oysters and chowder you had at William Tell House might just be the thing that helps you decide ...

Being there

Here's a thing about travelling generally, and Hwy 1 in particular. The last time I was there in 2023, Hwy 1 was closed. As is the way with luck, it happened about a month before I wanted to ride it again and as I write this, it's still closed.

I complained already about when it's closed you can't just ride around the obstacle and complete your journey - you have to backtrack and take Hwy 101 and you miss the best bits of the coastal route, namely the Big Sur section.

You can ride up to the mud slide or mountain slide before having to turn back. You can use 101 to get back onto Hwy 1 somewhere near Monterey and ride down to the obstruction before being turned around again. Sometimes, the slide blocking the road is less than a mile long but it still means you can't actually say you've completed the trip.

Above Sterns Wharf at Santa Barbara

Such are the blessings of my life that I've done it before when Harley-Davidson launched its Project Rushmore bikes in 2014. I had a beautiful ride the full length of Hwy 1 but I was focused on the bikes and not paying much attention to the environment.

The Rushmore bikes have passed into history (only 103ci - really?) but Hwy 1 has increased in importance.

As far back as 1977, the US Forest Service said the highway had reached its design capacity during peak-use periods; which basically means spring, summer and fall. There's no joy in being in a traffic gridlock on a road like this, but if you ride it off-season (November to April) there's a chance you'll still get to enjoy it.

San Francisco tourists often don't make it past Big Sur and LA tourists often turn around at Morro Bay, so the best part of the ride can still have little traffic.

Ride it while you still can.

BEST EATS

Neptune's Net, Malibu
This is a seafood restaurant and a proud biker's bar in Malibu not far out of Los Angeles. It's been around since 1956 with not many owners and if it sounds familiar to you, it might be because of how often it's been the setting for scenes in Hollywood movies. It makes sense, being so close to LA.

Keanu Reeves (who is now a co-owner of a business building motorcycles - Arch) was there in *Point Break*, the *Fast & Furious* boys were there, and even the *Bachelorette* graced the restaurant. So iconic is Neptune's Net that the building was recreated in Florida for the filming of *Iron Man 3*.

Its sourdough bread bowl with a pint of clam chowder in it for USD$15 is worth the visit alone, but if you want a longer lunch, order the Peel 'n Eat large shrimps for US$24 per pound.
www.neptunesnet.com

Nepenthe Restaurant, Big Sur
Once owned by Orson Welles, this restaurant blossomed when Hearst Castle opened to the public, but has become an institution in itself because of its location 29 miles south of Carmel and 63 miles north of San Simeon. It also has one of the best views of the coast of any restaurant, so people go for the visual spectacle as well as the modest menu.

Its signature dish is the Ambrosia Burger for US$25, which is a ground steak sandwich served on a French roll with ambrosia sauce with either Swiss or cheddar cheese. Did I mention the view?
www.nepenthe.com

William Tell House, Tomales
It's been there since 1877 and only been burnt down once so it's obviously a stayer. It's a good place to sample Tomales Bay oysters and does a mean seafood chowder featuring smoked ham, rock cod, shrimp, mussels and clams. It's the oldest saloon in Marin County and has a good take on sustainability and seasonality in its menu.
www.williamtellhouse.com

BEST SLEEPS

Pigeon Point Lighthouse Hostel, Pescadero
Once again, a youth hostel has come to the rescue for impoverished motorcycle tourists. No commercial enterprise could hope to secure a location like this. As the name suggests, it's a lighthouse in Pescadero that has free, safe parking with bunk beds for US$40, and private twin rooms for US$150. Beat that.

The Highway 1 Brewery Company is only 2 miles away for dinner and there's a beach attached to the property.
www.pigeonpointlighthouse.com

HI Point Montara Lighthouse, Montara
What, another lighthouse? Yep. Not far up the road to San Francisco, this hostel has a variety of rooms available, on-site beach access and is only 4 miles from Mavericks Beach, where one of the most famous surf competitions in the world is held.

The catch here is there's a two-night minimum stay from September 15 to June 15 and a three-night minimum stay from June 15 to September 15. Go on - you deserve a break from the road.
www.hiusa.org/find-hostels/california/montara-8800-cabrillo-highway

Muir Woods Lodge, Mill Valley
This probably shouldn't be in the 'best sleeps' section as it's a fairly humble, ordinary motel but you'll be pleased to get there as it means you got through San Francisco and you're only a minute away from the turn-off that re-engages you with Hwy 1. On top of that, it's relatively cheap and the rooms are clean.

Walk across the road and there's a bar and restaurant, which, like the accommodation, aren't excellent but are adequate and convenient. Oh, and you can park your bike directly in front of your room.
www.muirwoodslodge.com

San Juan Skyway: USA

The San Juan Skyway is a microcosm of the making of America with its good and bad on rich display. Understand the Skyway and you'll understand the country.

SNAPSHOT

This ride has pretty much everything: scenery, history, adventure, corners, passes, near-death experiences, food and wine. It's 233 miles of the 'American Dream'. The good, the bad and the ugly are on full display with its towns and mountain scenery straight out from most of the Westerns you've seen. Go in autumn as the red and gold leaves on the route help hide the scars of past treatment of the Indigenous population and the environment.

Lies, damn lies and statistics. According to multiple sources, the most dangerous road in America is Route 1 in Florida. However Route 1 isn't in itself a dangerous road. Instead it's the behaviour of people using it that causes death and injury; and possibly there's a correlation with a lack legislation banning folk taking calls on hand-held mobiles while driving. The Million Dollar Hwy in Colorado, on the other hand – which often comes second – absolutely deserves the title. That's because the road itself is the challenge. It's averaged seven deaths a year but numbers are jumping with 400 deaths recorded between 1992 and today. Admittedly, some of these are from avalanches rather than rider and driver mistakes, but it's not a road to be taken lightly. Oh, and it's only 25 miles long.

It's part of the 233 mile San Juan Skyway route and, despite, or maybe because of, the Million Dollar Hwy, it's one of America's best rides.

How long?
You can ride it in a day but if you want to learn as well as lean, allow a minimum of three days. It will be worth every second.

When to go
June to October will give you the best riding weather, but the route gets busy in July and August. Around late September to early November, the autumn colours are legendary. While the road is open year-round, snow can be heavy from late November to late February.

Need to know
- Ride on the right-hand side of the road.
- The mostly two-lane road is narrow in places with cliffs on one side and steep drop-offs on the other.
- Towns are well placed along the route so fuel, food and accommodation is readily available.

Ride rating
Mostly easy but intermediate over the Million Dollar Hwy, and advanced for some of the forest trails if you decide to go exploring.

Distances
- The loop from Durango is 233 miles (375km).

Temperatures
- June: 33°F to 69°F (0°C to 20°C)
- October: 22°F to 54°F (-6°C to 12°C)
- January: -4°F to 34°F (-20°C to 1°C)

More information
www.durango.org
www.colorado.com

Opposite Approaching Red Mountain Pass on the Million Dollar Highway

Gold blindness

Less than 40 miles from Cortez, along the lower eastern end of the San Juan Skyway, is the **Four Corners Monument** where you can stand in one spot and be in four states: Colorado, Arizona, Utah and New Mexico. On the way there you'll pass through the **Ute Mountain Reservation**, which is one of the three major reservations established for the Nuche People and other Indigenous Peoples dispossessed of their land after Europeans arrived in the area around 1765.

The biggest changes occurred when the first gold rush into the Rocky Mountains began in 1859. The Ute Nation (Nuche Peoples) agreed to a treaty in 1868 that allowed them most of the western slopes of the Colorado Rockies (which included the San Juan Mountains) but the reservation was quickly overrun by gold and silver prospectors ignoring the treaty terms. A subsequent treaty that allowed for mining but protected Nuche farming land was also ignored. So it goes with imperialism and colonialism.

Gold fever drove the development of trails to link up the towns in the San Juan Mountains and were quickly replaced by rail lines connecting Durango, Silverton, Ouray, Telluride and Rico. The remote rail link still exists between Durango and Silverton and is serviced by arguably the most committed trainspotters in the world. It's a great adventure but nothing quite beats a circuit of the San Juan Skyway on two wheels.

Wild, wild west

Durango (population: 19,223) makes a good starting point for this ride as there's plenty of accommodation. As most of Durango's development took place around its rail line, the area around the train station holds the most interest for visitors. Yes, it now looks a little like a movie set, but rest assured a lot of the buildings in the area are genuine from the early period. The substantial build quality of the 1887 Strater Hotel just eight years after the township was established gives you some idea of how much money flooded the area when mining began. Here you can take a drink in the front bar which is a bit 'Hollywood' with its piano player and costumed barmaids, but it has the right vibe for the period.

There's no right or wrong direction for the San Juan Skyway loop, but if you're starting in Durango, the temptation to do it anti-clockwise is close to overwhelming. Head north on Route 550 up the **Animas River Valley**, which is scenic without being a challenging ride. The road surface is good and the riding improves once the road turns into two lanes.

Make a note of the signs to **Trimble Hot Springs**, 9 miles out of town. It's too early to stop now but if you're going to do the loop in one day, it's a great place to refresh afterwards. If the fates collide, you might see the Durango–Silverton train pass under the highway at Shalona Bridge where it deviates from the highway and follows the Animas River northwards.

Back on the 550 you'll pass **Purgatory Resort** on the left. It's an odd name for a resort in a country that invented marketing! From here, 550 twists and turns as it climbs and lowers from **Coal Bank Pass** (3243m) and **Molas Pass** (3325m), the latter claiming to have the purest air in the US.

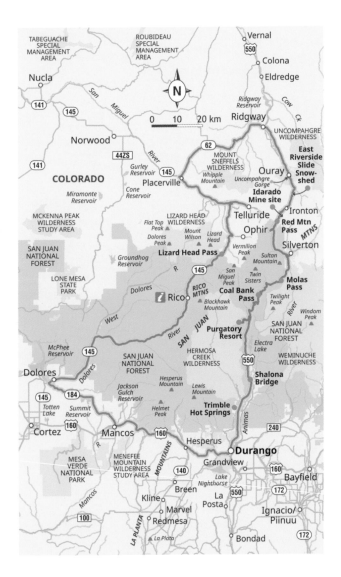

North America

Above Heading into Silverton on the Million Dollar Highway

Gunslinger Trail in Colorado

It's no secret that life in the Old West wasn't much like it's been depicted in countless Hollywood movies, but there's no doubt parts of it were genuinely wild.

Colorado boasts two prominent female gunslingers: Mountain Charley and Jane Kirkham. Charley was married at 12, had two children by age 15, had her husband shot by a man named Jamieson and then dressed as a man to make money before ending up owning the Mountain Boys Saloon in Denver. Charley wrote an autobiography, one copy of which survived into the 1960s before it was reprinted. Jane Kirkham, meanwhile, loved gold and robbed stagecoaches until she was gunned down by a sheriff who also happened to be her husband!

When it comes to Colorado gunslingers, Tom Horn was one of its more ruthless. The subject of the Steve McQueen film *Tom Horn* (1980), he worked variously as a gun-for-hire, an army scout and an undercover Pinkerton detective before hiring himself out to ranchers to administer justice to cattle rustlers. Estimates vary on how many people he murdered but it's probably in the low 20s, and none more brutal than him shooting a 14-year-old boy in 1902 whose family ran sheep during the range feud between sheep ranchers and cattle ranchers. While he was in prison awaiting his hanging in 1904, he wrote his autobiography.

This section of the 550 is part of a re-routing of the highway that took place in the 1950s. For bit of a detour, the original **Old Lime Creek Road**, is still open and follows the rail line. It's unpaved but very scenic and you'll be spared big trucks, buses and motorhomes. It's a doodle for adventure and dual-purpose bikes.

Not far from Molas Pass you'll begin your descent to the extraordinary town of Silverton.

Gunsmoke in Silverton

Colorado is full of the Wild West towns and gunslingin' characters mythologised on the big and small screen. Names like Wyatt Earp, Doc Holliday, Bat Masterson and Jane Kirkham, one of the few female stagecoach robbers of her time, are all probably familiar to those who've seen a Western or two in their time.

Wyatt moved to Colorado after the infamous gunfight at the O.K. Corral and spent some time in **Silverton** (population: 651). The town's site was first laid out in 1874 as miners moved in and settled. The train arrived from Durango in 1882 when Silverton already had two banks, 29 saloons and a red-light district (Blair St), all completely out of proportion to the size of the town; an R & R centre for miners during their time off. Even if saloons in Silverton look like they did in 1880, the patrons are a lot friendlier. Once anyone heard my Australian accent, they were immediately keen to find out where I was from and what I was doing there. Luckily not a gunslinger in sight ...

The courthouse, Victorian homes and grand hotels are also mostly still there and it's easy to imagine how it must have felt 140 years ago.

Silverton is also the site of the highest Harley-Davidson shop in the world (2048m). Join the thousands who have had their photos taken sitting on the wooden benches outside the dealership.

Take a deep breath

Okay, we're now leaving Silverton, still on the 550 and heading to Ouray, another mining town established just a year later in 1875. This is the most challenging section of Route 550 despite it being just 23.4 miles long.

It sneaks up on you as you leave Silverton until you get to a sweeping 300-degree corner, which, when you climb up from it, presents you with a very narrow road with a cliff on one side and a sheer drop on the other. Don't relax as you pass it because sections of the road get worse after that. Guard rails would seem sensible but can't be maintained due to winter snow. Though the road remains open in winter, be aware that avalanches are common along the 550, and the 59 avalanche chutes found between Coal Bank Pass and Ouray are testimony to this.

The 550 suffers from winter but the road surface is surprisingly good, especially as you climb higher towards the Idarado Mine site past the **Red Mountain Pass** (3358m). You need to be conscious of oncoming traffic as four-wheelers, especially tourists, get shell-shocked by the conditions and hog the road farthest from the sheer drops, giving you little room for safe passing. If you see them coming and you can find some way of accommodating it, it's wise to give way.

The area is known as **Red Mountains** due to the iron residue from years of environmentally insensitive mining, which also polluted the area's rivers. It's probable that the mine owners knew of the consequences but had no idea of the big-picture ramifications of what they were doing. Engineering defeated the environment at the time but it's hard not to admire the feat of railway builders and the workers who completed an incredible 5-mile tunnel under the 4000m-high mountains to Telluride to reduce road travel time for the mine's output.

The snake road continues past Ironton with sweeping, largely blind corners, but the road condition improves as you shadow the deep **Uncompahgre Gorge**, which, unsurprisingly, complicated a rail link between Silverton and Ouray. As you weave down, you'll get lay-offs from which to view Ouray from above.

So is the Million Dollar Hwy a dangerous road? It can be depending on the external conditions and whether you ride with them in mind. The consequences of making a mistake

are more severe than in other places you might come off and the chances of you crashing are more likely with a narrow road and nervous drivers sharing it. As always, you'll be safest if you just ride according to the conditions. It's an open, public road in the land of the free. Just be respectful of it. The best month to travel? September.

Phew, we made it to Ouray

Back in the day, Ouray and Silverton competed with each other during the mining boom to be the town of substance in the area. With no clear winner, **Ouray** (population: 923) has a slightly more civilised history and the entire town is a National Historic District with impressive Victorian-era buildings. Though these days it's full of traffic, you can still imagine what Ouray was like when it was established in 1875. Opening in 1887, the Beaumont Hotel was the finest in the US. It's been recently restored and is well worth a visit, as are the town's hot springs.

The 550 becomes more manageable as you continue north to Ridgway where you'll turn left on Route 62 towards Placerville before you'll turn left again on 145 to **Telluride** (population: 2595). It's a 'Western' town, too, but is now a well-established ski resort with all the attendant benefits and disadvantages for bikers looking for food and accommodation.

Butch Cassidy and his Wild Bunch (aka the Hole-in-the-Wall gang) robbed their first bank in Telluride on June 24, 1889, and the unimposing building that replaced the bank two years later is still on the main street, with a discreet plaque on it to 'commemorate' the event. The haul was half a million dollars by today's standards and there are plenty of stories in the local area about where Butch and his gang buried the money, which has never been recovered.

Telluride is surrounded by mountains with waterfalls visible from the main street, and here you'll find several cafes that make fine places for wining and dining before you head south towards Rico. This section of the Skyway follows Route 145 along valleys but is also hilly and very remote. To your right will be the **Lizard Head Wilderness**, which you can admire from Lizard Head Pass (3116m), a view dominated by Lizard Head Peak (3997m). In between its busy east and west coasts, the area is another reminder of just how vast a space North America really is.

Rico (population: 347) didn't get a train line until 1891, partly because engineering it up Lizard Head Pass was so challenging. The train made the Scotch Creek toll road redundant, which was used to transport mined ore prior to the train arriving, but it's still ridable on dirt/adventure bikes and takes you from

Above Ancestoral Puebloans moved from clifftop dwellings into these alcoves around 800 years ago and the Mesa Verde National Park near Cortez is full of intact examples of the architecture of the period *Opposite* Red mountains along the Million Dollar Highway

What's in a name?

When you ride it, almost the first question you ask is, 'Why is it called the Million Dollar Highway?'

If you stop for a drink in any of the saloons on the route, it's a good way of getting the locals engaged. You may not get the same answer twice, which suggests nobody actually knows, but everyone has a theory.

It obviously cost lots of dollars to build given the terrain through which it passes and some think this is the origin of the name, although it probably cost a lot more to complete the rail line that links the towns in the San Juan Mountains.

Some say it's called that because of the tolls charged by Otto Mears, who built the original track in 1883. You had to be a millionaire to use it. The toll charged at the time is equivalent to US$150 today. Local objections eventually led to the state government taking control of the road in 1887.

Theory three is the road was constructed from gold- and silver-mining tailings and the undiscovered wealth in the base material was worth well over one million.

Another popular theory is the name came from the 'million dollar views' available from various parts of the road. With inflation, it should probably now be called the 'Billion Dollar Road'.

What do I think? I like the story of a motorcyclist sitting in a bar in Silverton who'd ridden the road and was happy to declare he wouldn't do it again for a million dollars.

Above Ouray nestled into the Rocky Mountains *Opposite* The Million Dollar Highway - America's most dangerous road

just past Rico over to the Purgatory area to intersect again with route 550. Only riders with advanced off-road skill levels need apply and access is determined by the weather. There's a lot of snow between mid November to late February which closes the route. Rico itself hosts the San Juan National Forest Visitor Centre that is run by volunteers who can guide you on the great hiking and mountain-bike riding in the area to enhance your understanding of what 'wilderness' really means.

Highway 145 largely follows the **Dolores River** (or, to be more accurate, the 'El Rio de Nuestra Senora de los Dolores'), which is full of trout but you'll need a fishing licence if you're over 15. The river is restocked every year so even hack anglers are in with a chance of catching something here.

From **Dolores** (population: 904) the road straightens out as it heads towards **Cortez** (population: 8855), which has the lowest elevation of the Skyway and is the only town not on a river. It is, however, on a main transport route, which means trucks and other heavy vehicles that are absent on the rest of the Skyway suddenly appear again on the 160 route back to Durango.

There's a shortcut from Dolores to **Mancos** (population: 1221) along Hwy 184 that is described as the 'Trail of the Ancients Scenic Byway'. It's a much better option for riders reluctant to re-engage with the real world of traffic. You'll rejoin 160 at Mancos, and from there it's just 28 miles to where you started your adventure in Durango. What you'll miss though is the entrance to the Mesa Verde National Park, which is 8 miles back from Mancos towards Cortez.

Mesa Verde National Park

While you can conquer the San Juan Skyway in a day, you'll miss things that could burn into your memory forever. One of these is the **Mesa Verde National Park**. Here you will find intact remnants of Indigenous American occupation that date back to AD550. The Anasazi Pueblo (Ancestral Puebloans) lived in pit houses on the mesa tops, but around the year 1200 they moved to alcoves cut into the cliffs. Nobody knows why, but these sophisticated cliff houses were abandoned in the 1300s. Spruce Tree House has 114 rooms and eight *kivas* (partly or wholly sunken spaces used for religious ceremonies). These houses were family accommodation as well as congregational spaces.

The park covers 52,000 acres with more archaeological sites than you could possibly visit, but almost all of them are accessible by motorcycle.

Most of the park is a no-go area for larger four-wheelers so you'll have the narrow roads with sharp curves largely to yourself. A short visit will last at least half-a-day.

BEST EATS

11th Street Station, Durango

You know that thing where a group of you decide to go out but you can't settle on what type of food you want to eat? Well here at 11th Street Station you should have no such problem with its seven food trucks that circle around Ernie's Bar. They all operate independently and there should be something for everyone. Beer and wine comes from Ernie's and the food trucks turn out tacos, pizza, sushi, Thai and gourmet sliders. It's a slice of Durango's multicultural history. www.11thstreetstation.com

Derailed Pour House, Durango

This place is surprisingly cheap for a venue that comes with so many awards and credentials. It's classic American food but taken seriously. Try the Southwest Platter for two: egg rolls, nachos, poppers (thick bacon-wrapped jalapenos, cheese and scallions) with a dill ranch sauce.

The food is legit but the vibe is very casual with big screens playing golden hits from the '70s, '80s and '90s. www.derailedpourhouse.com

True Grit Cafe, Ridgway

John Wayne's *True Grit* (1968) was filmed in and around Ridgway and Ouray, and this cafe is a shrine to both him and the movie. The interior wall of the cafe was the external wall of 'Chambers Grocery' from one of the first scenes of the film.

The owners would never do anything to disrespect the 'Duke' and serves locally sourced 'cowboy cuisine', endeavoring to create a 'ranch-to-fork' experience. Go for either the chicken-fried steaks or the proper steaks. I don't think John Wayne was a vegetarian. www.truegritcafe.com

Columbine Bar & Grill, Mancos

You probably wouldn't go here on date night but it's a great place for a lunchtime stop and is very popular with the locals. It serves American cuisine at good prices and has a range of local beers. It also makes its own desserts so leave a bit of room for some ice cream. Mancos is a small deviation off the highway but is well sign-posted. www.mancoscolumbine.com

BEST SLEEPS

Days Inn, Durango

There are quite a few motels like this to choose from but Days Inn has clean, well-equipped rooms and it's not too far from downtown Durango, which you'll want to explore. You can park your bike outside your room, too. A (very) light breakfast is part of the price, but to compensate there's a brewery next door. www.wyndhamhotels.com/days-inn/durango-colorado/days-inn-durango/overview

Timber Ridge Lodge, Ouray

This swish, inexpensive lodge is a quarter mile north of downtown Ouray and has great views. Motorcycle friendly, here you can park your bike in front of the building and it's close to everything you might want to see or do in town. It's also close to the Ouray hot springs where you can relax your riding muscles in the great outdoors. www.timberridgelodgeouray.com

Circle K Ranch, Hwy 145

If you're riding in the wild west, you might as well go the whole hog and spend a bit of time on a ranch. The Circle K is between Rico and Dolores on the San Juan Skyway and you can pick from motel rooms or lodge rooms. It's a bit more authentic than a dude ranch and the scenery is very atmospheric. Can you ride a horse? Two-hour rides along the Dolores River are available for US$130. There's a weight limit of 240lbs (108kg). www.ckranch.com

Europe and the UK

Route Napoleon & Cime de la Bonette: France

Rural France is full of charm. Here's a route that helps explain the country while climbing to its highest paved road.

SNAPSHOT

France is a mixture of city and country. The rural areas are glorious and this ride gives you a taste of both.

You move from the French Riviera to its most desolate town in one ride and both have unique beauty.

Enjoy the natural pleasure of provincial France and ponder on the influence of Napoleon and what Europe would have been like if his military plans had been successful.

Oh, and eat some snails – seriously, you'll enjoy them.

The French still aren't sure about Napoleon. Yes, he was an important figure in the French Revolution that dragged the country free of its monarchy. He also introduced metric measurements, set up secondary schooling and introduced a civil code that is still the basis of French law today.

He wasn't a bad general, either, engaging in over 70 battles and winning all but eight.

On the other hand, he overturned the French republic and declared himself emperor; was largely responsible for anything up to six million deaths as a result of military conflicts; and reintroduced slavery so that French businessmen could continue to control the Caribbean sugar trade.

He was exiled twice: the first time to Elba and the second (and final) time to St Helena.

He didn't exactly 'escape' from Elba in that he ran the place, but his time there made him think he could take control of France again. He arrived on the shore of Golfe-Juan, 6.5km from Cannes on the Cote d'Azur, with 1100 men and promptly marched them to Grenoble via an interior route to avoid royalist troops.

This route is now the 'Route Napoleon' and runs 324km from Golfe Juan to Grenoble. You'll know you're on the route as it's marked by green and brown eagle road signs, plaques and statues of the French imperial eagle. We're going to use about a third of it before we spear right and head up to the Cime de la Bonette, the highest paved road in France.

How long?
Three days for a return trip from Cannes.

When to go
May and September are good months. It's hot in June, July and August but certainly doable. Snow in winter gets in the way of riding in those months.

Need to know
- Ride on the right-hand side of the road.
- The Route Napoleon is wide and well sealed but the roads to the Cime de la Bonette are narrow in places.
- As a rule, every French village you ride through is more charming than the last one.
- Forget the myth of the French being stand-offish. It's not true in rural France.

Ride rating
Easy to moderate in places.

Distances
- Cannes to Barreme: 106km (66 miles)
- Barreme to Barcelonnette: 84km (52 miles)
- Barcelonnette to St Sauveurs-Tinne: 86km (53 miles)
- St Sauveurs-Tinne to Castellane: 100km (62 miles)
- Castellane to Cannes: 82km (51 miles)
Total: 458km (285 miles)

Temperatures
- These will vary because you're riding from the warmer coast to arguably the highest paved road in Europe.
- June in Cannes: 16°C to 25°C (61°F to 77°F)
- June in Jausiers: 8°C to 22°C (46°F to 72°F)

More information
www.routedelabonette.fr

Route ..
BONETTE - RE...
2807
Plus Haute Rout...

Start with the stars

You might be joining this ride as part of a longer tour of Europe, in which case you'll already have a bike sorted. **Nice** (population: 343,477), though, has an international airport and a very professional bike-hire company called We Rent Motorcycles (www.we-rent-motorcycles.com), so it could easily be a fly-in/fly-out adventure.

They offer a range of higher-end bikes including Harley-Davidsons and BMWs in the €150 a day category, but a little gem in its fleet is a Triumph Tiger 850 Sport for €100 a day. The deal includes unlimited kilometres, breakdown back-up, luggage and insurance (admittedly with a €3000 excess). To rent you need to be over 25 and have had your motorcycle licence for more than five years.

Given the variable nature of the road conditions on this trip, a Tiger 850 would be an excellent pick even without the advantage of it being the least expensive option.

You can pick your hire bike up in either Nice or Cannes.

We aren't going to slavishly follow Napoleon's route but if you want to call in at Golfe-Juan, there's a plaque in the port that shows you where he landed. His first camp was in Cannes 7km away so we'll start from there.

It doesn't cost anything to see how the uber rich live so it's worth spending a few hours wandering around **Cannes** (population: 72,435) to see what all the fuss is about. You may already know it for its private beach clubs, grand shops, high-end restaurants and, of course, the Cannes Film Festival, but it also has an old quarter (Le Suquet) with ruins from the time when the Romans were occupying it.

The La Croisette promenade is worth a stroll as well. Just one street over is the spot where Napoleon and his small army camped for the night. Look for a plaque on the wall of Eglise Notre Dame de Bon Voyage (Church of Our Lady of Good Voyage) on Rue Notra Dame.

Above Cannes, on the Cote d'Azur

Now it's time to shake the gold dust from your riding boots and head north on D6085 signposted to Grasse. As you'd expect, you're not immediately thrust into the wilderness but from Grasse onwards, you'll start to enjoy more open spaces.

Castellane (population: 1462) will be your next stop and it's not a bad place to consider spending the night. It's where Napoleon stopped for lunch on the third day of his Long March and is small enough for you to enjoy a walk around.

If you have the enthusiasm, a climb up to the chapel Notre Dame du Roc that overlooks Castellane is well worth the effort. It takes you to an altitude of 903m and provides serene views.

Certainly relative to Cannes, Castellane accommodation is cheap. I recommend **Camping Frederic Mistral** (www.camping-fredericmistral.fr), which has tent sites for €28 and one- or two-bedroom chalets for €124. It's just 100m to the marketplace and shops, and has secure bike parking.

Game on

The ride from Castellane to Barreme on the D4085 is one of the best sections of Route Napoleon. It crosses two passes, the first being the Col des Lèques at 1146m. You get great views of the road ahead of you and the surface is excellent as you climb, fall and twist your way through beautiful countryside with light traffic. As you get closer to Barreme, the forest comes to the road and provides many fixed objects to hit if you fall off. Keep it in mind.

The traffic gets even lighter when you take a right turn at Barreme on the N202 then left on the D955, which will be signposted Colmars, Allos and Barcelonnette.

This is very much a typical French provincial road that services businesses as well as tourists, with the section from Allos to the D900 to Jausiers often being described as 'torturous'. It's a little rougher than other French roads but is still cruisey by international standards.

Allos (population: 697) used to be agricultural but is now a service centre for the very active ski industry in the area. Lake Allos, close by, is the largest mountain lake in Europe.

Heading north from Allos involves crossing the Col d'Allos pass at 2247m and, while the road isn't perfect, the views are very satisfying.

When you arrive at the intersection with the D900 you can turn left to Barcelonnette or right to Jausiers. **Barcelonnette** (population: 2622) is close and although you'd be going in the wrong direction, if your arrival coincides with Wednesday or

Saturday morning, it's worth going there for the market that takes over the whole central area.

If you turn right, you'll soon be in **Jausiers** (population: 1137), which is at one end of the Cime de la Bonette. One of the reasons we're doing this ride is to do the Cime de la Bonette but its loop comes off Col de la Bonette, which can, understandably, cause confusion.

Cime time

The **Cime de la Bonette** ('Cime' means 'peak') was originally a mule track to service villages and military barracks that are no longer habitated. This started in 1832 but the final road wasn't completed until 1960. It's still impassable in winter due to snow and it's the highest paved road in France and probably the highest, paved through-road in Europe.

Riding it makes recreational drug users feel like they're stoned again and the 'I get high on reality' people understand how 'high' reality can actually take you.

The road is narrow but you'd expect that. There's a bit of foliage at the beginning but it gives way to open fields above the snow line. It's full of curves partly to ease access through the terrain but also to reduce the severity of the climb for the original mules, where weaving was preferable to vertical climbing.

It makes for a perfect motorcycle road. You can see what's in front of you and what's behind you because there's no built or natural obstacles and there's precious little traffic.

As the obvious purpose of the organisers of the Tour de France bicycle event is to torture its competitors, the Cime de la Bonette has been included in the route on occasions (most recently in 2008) and features a 15-degree slope for more than a kilometre. It's the highest point the Tour has ever achieved.

On the way up (or down, depending on which end you started from), you'll see an abandoned stone village with houses that still look remarkably intact. It's a testament to the spirit of humans that anyone thought they could live there permanently. You'll also see a small village at a lower level where people are actually still living. It's the exact opposite of the residents of Cannes.

Towards the peak there's a building complex that looks like it might have been a jail but, in fact, was a military fort. It would have been one of the coldest places on earth.

At the highest point there's a small parking lot and a memorial stone explaining where you are. You might read it on your own but the Clime is so popular with riders that you'll probably be in the company of a few, or a lot, of other riders.

The Cime de la Bonette isn't that long and it's now described as a 'scenic route' so it's worth doing it at least once each way. It's largely devoid of police interest in that you can see them from kilometres away.

Back on the Col de la Bonette, you're now heading south again heading towards St Sauveurs-sur-Tinee on the M64 and then the M2205. It's here you have to make a difficult decision. You can continue on the M2205 and join up with the M6202 that will take you back to Nice (where you can drop your hire bike off) or turn right on the M30 for a ride through one of the

The perfumed rider

Grasse makes more perfume than any other city in the world and has UNESCO Intangible Cultural Heritage Status because of it. Well, you might not want to do this yourself but you might be riding with someone who does.

A number of the factories have workshops which cost between €30 to €80 where, under the guidance of a 'nose' (professional), you'll be helped to blend your very own perfume. You get to keep the bottle you make, of course, and the percentages of the ingredients you choose will be recorded and kept on file so that you can continue to buy it by direct order long into the future. How cool is that - having your distinctive perfume?

There's a bit of variety in the workshops depending on which company you do it with and that's why the price varies. Workshops generally go for two hours.

www.cotedazurfrance.fr/en/to-do/flowers-and-perfumes/create-your-own-perfume-in-grasse

French food

'It's too rich!' scream the objectors, but it doesn't bother the French who eat it regularly and live to an age greater than the OECD average of 81 years. If you're visiting France, eat the following:

BEOUF BOURGUIGNON - combination of beef, bacon, onions, wine and carrots.

QUICHE LORRAINE - bacon, onion, Swiss cheese and eggs.

BOUILLABAISSE - this dish comes from Marseille and it's based on fish but it can be any fish. Common ingredients include tomatoes, onions, garlic, orange peel, fennel, thyme and perhaps a bay leaf.

DUCK PATE EN CROUTE - pate in a pastry dough. It's everywhere.

CHOCOLATE MOUSSE - yep, it came from France: dark chocolate, eggs, liquor, heavy whipping cream and sugar.

COQ AU VIN - it means 'rooster and wine'. It's champignons, red wine, onions, chicken broth and rooster, or hen meat.

ESCARGOT - cooked land snails usually in a butter garlic or mint sauce. Don't say, 'Ooh, I could never eat that!' It's delicious.

CREPES - slim pancakes either savoury or sweet based on eggs.

Oh, and the French drink lots of wine and live to a ripe, old age. Just sayin ...

Opposite top The vegetation thins out as you climb to France's highest paved road, the Cime de La Bonette *Opposite bottom* View over Castellane

Above A French biker horde leaving Les Chaudron's restaurant in Guillaumes *Opposite* The town square in Barcelonnette

From Guillaumes, it's down the D2202 with a right turn onto the D202. If you're fully infected with riding fever, you can take the 202 back to Barreme and use the Route Napoleon back to Cannes but there's a shortcut through French countryside half way along the 202 that will slide you directly into Castellane again so you can renew the friendships you created when you stayed there on your way up to the Cime de la Bonette.

From Castellane, it's an easy cruise back to Cannes for the return of your hire bike, but if you're on a bike with a longer-term deal, rural France is a wonderland of great riding, great people and great experiences. You could spend years there.

As for Napoleon, within 100 days of his march from Golfe-Juan, he was defeated at the battle of Waterloo by components of the Seventh Coalition, which included the British and the Prussians. It was a close-run thing and, had Napoleon been victorious, the world now would be a different place.

He died on Saint Helena, the island of his last exile. Riding around France gives you time to think about his legacy. There's a natural disinclination to think well about men (never women) who are prepared to make decisions that involve the deaths of millions of soldiers but these are often aggressors, which include Napoleon. Leaders who stand up to them have to live with military and civilian deaths as well but are thought of differently. You get plenty of time on the road to think – use it wisely.

Being there

Basically, there's Paris and the rest of France. In Paris, I secured my bike for a week in an underground car park because there was nowhere on top to park it safely. The cars park bumper to bumper and if you want to get your car out, you push your own either forwards or backwards moving the other cars (which are left in neutral without the handbrake on) enough distance away to enable you to escape.

It's different out of the city. France is a big country and in regional areas there are plenty of places to park a bike safely.

France gets bikes. Many accommodations have signs attracting riders and it's a normal way of private transport. It's actually better than that. When I was staying in the Hotel Bel'Air in Jausiers, I came out in the morning and my bike was gone. I enquired politely at the hotel desk if they knew anything about it and they told me it started raining at 2am so one of the staff had moved it to an undercover area.

That's service.

wild parts of the Mercantour National Park. Plan A is better if you want faster riding on good roads but plan B will remind you that not all of France is civilised. The road to Guillaumes is largely a paved, forest road and you pass through the small village of Peone on the way.

Villages like **Peone** (population: 880) and **Guillaumes** (population: 585) speak to the kind of people rural French are. No wealth is obvious, they fit into their natural environment and they're confident. This is occasionally misrepresented as arrogance because travellers from some countries expect the service industry to be subservient. It isn't in France and it never should be.

I was late for lunch when I got to Guillaumes but the chef, (okay, the cook) of Les Chaudrons went back into the kitchen, turned everything on again and made me something to eat. I'm still grateful. A group of riders were leaving as I arrived so I suspect Les Chaudrons is known to local riders.

BEST EATS

Le Main à La Pâte, Castellane
There's a surprising amount of Italian food in this part of France but you're in France, right, so you should be eating French food. Le Main à La Pate is the real deal in terms of ambience and the menu. Highlights include escargot for €16 and the seafood linguine for €20. The steak with pepper sauce is also worth considering for salad-dodgers as it's heavy on fried potato and there's not much greenery.
7 Rue de la Fontaine, Castellane.

Restaurant Les Copains, Barcelonnette
This classic French restaurant is a little difficult to find but well worth the effort. It's small with a relatively limited menu but it's 100% French with lots of local customers. Its menu is home cooking-based but that makes it all the better if you're after authentic regional cuisine. There's no pretension in the decor or service and it's inexpensive by city standards but very beautiful in its own way. Locals tend to arrive by bicycle but motorcycles are welcome.
2 Place Aime Gassier, 04400 Barcelonnette

Halte 2000, Jausiers
Set at an altitude of 2000m in a field with great views of the surrounding hills and mountains, this restaurant is something special. It's only open in summer and it's cash-only, so be prepared. It's very attuned to vegetarians and offers a meat-free degustation menu as part of its service. Carnivores are still welcome. The bigger menu is French/European and, weather-permitting, you should eat in the outdoor area. Prices are moderate rather than cheap but there aren't many places like this so it's an excuse to stretch the budget.
www.facebook.com/halte2000restefond

BEST SLEEPS

Banana's Camp, Cannes
This hostel is really well located in Cannes and, importantly for riders, has secure parking, something missing for much of the accommodation in the city. It's a renovated French villa with all the usual features of a hostel including a shared lounge, garden and bathrooms. It's been recently renovated and is spacious and clean. It has a 24-hour front desk and even a bar.
www.bananascamp.com

Alberge De Pra-Loup, Barcelonnette
This is a comfortable, friendly inn with not many pretensions but it does have a bar, restaurant and outside eating areas with great mountain views. It's on the outskirts of the Parc National du Mercantour where you'll probably want to do some serious riding, so it's very well located for bikers. Relative to the rest of the area, it's also inexpensive and has free, secure parking for motorcycles.
www.auberge-de-praloup.fr

Gites A La Ferme Del Le Var, Guillaumes
More an apartment than a hotel room, this accommodation includes a kitchen with fridge and cooking facilities, a private bathroom and outside barbecue facilities. It's 1.1km from Guillaumes with plenty of space and secure bike parking. Guillaumes is a classic country village with a very good restaurant and food shopping options so it's a good base in case you want to spend more than one night there. Your 'apartment' will have garden- and mountain-views and the fridge will keep your beer cold.
www.gitesdelalevar.com/fr

Above Germany's Hohenzollern Castle

Black Forest High Road: Germany

Germany is more than cake and cuckoo clocks. Just ask the white-knuckle brigade who ride the autobahns, Black Forest High Rd and the Swabian Jura.

SNAPSHOT

Germany is a mix of heavy industry and areas of astounding beauty. The Black Forest High Rd (B500) is very scenic as well as being in a great riding area.

Police interest in motorcycle activity on the B500 encourages you to enjoy the views and save your right hand for other less scrutinised – but just as exciting – roads in the region.

It's a popular tourist destination and accommodation prices reflect this. Look for places to stay outside main tourist towns. Black Forest back roads offer many rewards.

The Mercedes-Benz museum in Stuttgart has a replica of the world's first motorcycle and it's as close as you can get to the real thing. This is where it all started.

If you were a Roman legionnaire in 212BCE, part of your days off each month would be spent relaxing your muscles in the natural spring baths in what is now the German town of Baden-Baden, at the northern end of the Black Forest. You wouldn't have even entertained the idea of going for a walk in the forest because you and your comrades were intimidated by its size and darkness, and native inhabitants may attack without warning.

Baden-Baden fell apart after that for 800 years, as cities in Europe often did, to be rediscovered in the 1100s. Napoleon III made it fashionable again in the 1850s and 1860s as a resort for European nobility.

The locals knew about the Black Forest, though, and started exploring it for hiking. Small businesses emerged to support this but by the 1930s people were travelling by car and a road was needed to get them up into the forest proper.

Partly because the area was developed by middle-class business people and farmers, there wasn't much in the way of heavy industry so the Black Forest High Rd is largely free of big trucks and commercial transport. The road surface loves this and stays in excellent condition. It twists and turns according to the contours of the hills and rises and falls for the same reason. It was made for motorcyclists.

How long?
A three-day loop from Stuttgart should scratch the itch. Make it four days if you plan on also exploring the Swabian Jura.

When to go
May to September is probably the best time, but both April and October are good in terms of reduced crowds. The Black Forest High Rd is open year-round but as well as winter, there could be some snow in the shoulder months too.

Need to know
- It's wise to more or less obey the posted speed limits on the major tourist roads like the Black Forest High Rd as the local police won't give you a second chance. It's ironic that on your way back to Stuttgart on the A81 you'll be legally allowed to ride at 250km/h (155mph).
- Learn in advance the etiquette of autobahn riding (*see* The Need for Speed section) as crashes with huge speed differentials are possible with obvious consequences.
- Expect your credit card to take a hammering.

Ride rating
Easy. The roads generally have a largely bump-free surface and are very grippy.

Distances
- Route without Swabian Jura: 340km (211 miles)
- Route with Swabian Jura: 535km (332 miles)

Temperatures
- April: 5°C to 15°C (41°F to 59°F)
- July: 15°C to 25°C (59°F to 77°F)

More information
www.black-forest-travel.com
www.burg-hohenzollern.com

Start in Stuttgart

We're beginning our ride in **Stuttgart** (population: 635,000), the capital of the state of Baden-Wurttemberg. We're not doing this because it's a must-visit city but it does have an airport and it has a branch of 'Rent-a-Boxer', a motorcycle hire company which, if you aren't on your own bike, might be useful.

It's a car city with Mercedes-Benz, Porsche and Daimler all having a significant presence there; Porsche and Mercedes-Benz originated in the city and both have their headquarters here. The **Mercedes-Benz Museum** is worth a visit as it unfolds its story chronologically and that's actually the entire history of the development of the automobile. Mercedes-Benz (through Gottlieb Daimler and Wilhelm Maybach) invented the first motorcycle and the first car.

A replica of the first motorcycle is on display. It's a replica because they actually had the original but it was destroyed in a fire. The replica is a perfect copy so it's as close as you'll get to the beginning of two-wheeled, powered transport. Are you sitting down? Its high-speed combustion engine produced 0.38kW and it had a top speed of 12km/h.

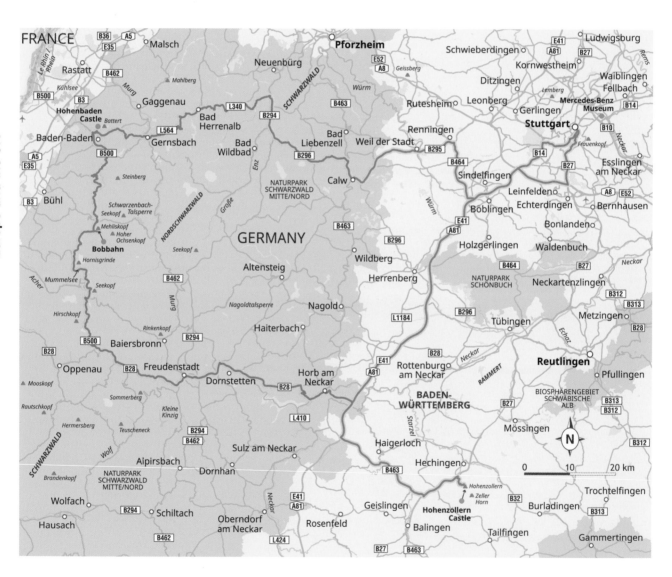

Europe and the UK

You could argue that America gave the car to the world through its development of mass-production but Germany did most of the engineering and design work.

I know – enough talk about cars – but one little story from the museum I liked was a 1924 effort to win the Italian Targa Florio endurance race. Mercedes-Benz cars were always white (and later silver) but they painted the Targa Florio cars red so that Italian fans would confuse them with Italian cars and not sabotage them. The Targa Florio car that won the event is on display.

The need for speed

Getting from Stuttgart to Baden-Baden raises an interesting conundrum. One thing Germany has that most other countries don't is autobahns. These are transport routes with liberal speed limits. A steadily declining number of them have 'no speed restriction' signs on them, which means you can ride as fast as you like. The official advice is 130km/h but it's not illegal to exceed it on derestricted roads.

A couple of quick tips. It's illegal to pass on the right of another vehicle. Check your rear-view mirror before moving to a left lane as the vehicle approaching you from behind might be travelling 100km/h faster than you. Use the right lane when you can unless you're keeping up with the left lane traffic and, when the vehicle behind you flashes its lights, it means you should move to the right as it's about to overtake you. Oh, it's also illegal to run out of fuel on an autobahn so plan in advance.

While it's tempting to stretch the legs of your chosen mount without having to worry about the police, many autobahns are notorious for traffic jams as a result of roadworks, overcrowding and crashes. From Stuttgart to Baden-Baden, the temptation will be to take the A8 before turning down the A5. You might fluke a good run but you might be unlucky and it's not scenic.

Here's plan B. Take the A8 west for a short distance before turning left onto the A81 south and turn right at the Boblingen/Sindelfingen district signposted to Sindelfingen and Calw. When you get to **Calw**, acknowledge that it was the town of the German writer and spiritualist Hermann Hesse, and turn right for a short distance and then turn left on the 296 and right at the 294, narrowly missing the village of **Bad Wildbad.** What a great name for a town. I don't know what goes on there but I'll bet it's interesting. Turn left off the 294 onto the 564 and you'll arrive at Baden-Baden, already being well-acquainted with the Black Forest. This route takes longer and it's a bit slower but it's the right choice.

Top A legendary Gullwing Mercedes-Benz at the company's museum in Stuttgart *Bottom* Hohenbaden Castle Ruins

Above View over Mummelsee, one of the better lakes on the Black Forest route

Technik Museum Speyer

If you're heading to the Black Forest High Rd from the north (Mannheim/Ludwigshafen), stop in at **Speyer's Technik Museum** (www.speyer.technik-museum.de). It covers a huge range of transport history including a very lively motorcycle collection with some very unusual exhibits.

The museum recently took over the entire inventory of the Friedel Münch Museum with 26 restored Münch motorcycles built between 1967 and 1999.

Friedel Münch broke new ground using a 1000cc, four-cylinder car engine that he wished to call the 'Mammoth' but was denied due to trademark issues. No matter - everyone in the world knows these bikes as the 'Münch Mammoth'.

Friedel's upgrade of the original bike featured a 2L engine producing 260hp with an electronically limited top speed of 250km/h - just the thing for the autobahn.

Only 15 of these bikes were finished and one is on display at the museum.

Also out of left field is the NSU Delphin 111 land-speed record bike. Looking like a giant fish, it broke the 300km/h barrier at the Bonneville Salt Flats in 1956.

The rider, Wilhelm Herz, built a version IV upgrade of the bike, which he believed would break 400km/h and, thanks to his son Heinz, a replica of it is on display.

Bye-bye Baden-Baden

Baden-Baden (population: 55,527) is a pretty town but it's a tourist hot-spot and now relies heavily on casinos and gambling for its income. So unless that's your interest, ride through it and start your adventure with the B500.

There are the ruins of **Hohenbaden Castle** just above Baden-Baden but you may be too interested in the road to stop there. You'll be missing a walk and a free entry to the ruins, which, if you have time, you'll enjoy.

If you ride a bike, though, you probably should stop at **Mehliskopf** just a little up the road and have a ride on the Bobbahn, which is a mechanical bobsleigh. You get into a cart and are towed to the top of a very big hill before being let loose to control your descent with a handbrake (or not). It's cheap thrills and there's a cafe and bar at the end of it.

Next stop is **Mummelsee**, which is one of the better lakes on the Black Forest route with plenty of food and drink options for you to enjoy while you watch the tourists mucking around on the pedalos or enjoying the wood-fired bread being made before your very eyes. It's a standard stop for riders and you'll have plenty of bike company. There's a path around the lake if you want even more exercise and it's a chance to experiment by ordering currywurst, a German version of fast food involving sausages. But if you want a more authentic version, check out Volkswagen's currywurst (*see* 'Volkswagen Currywurst' section).

Mummelsee is only about 30km along the Black Forest High Rd but it's 1000m above sea level and, allegedly, was carved out of the earth during the last Ice Age. The locals believe mermaids live in the lake. Sounds believable to me.

Now the famous road starts to stretch out in front of you with its beautiful surface and sweeping corners. The devil, however, is in the detail. If you have a satellite navigation system on your bike, it will tell you that the speed limit can vary between 70km/h, 50km/h and, occasionally, 30km/h. It's easy to understand why speeding motorcycles in the past have shocked authorities but the road is much more forgiving than the current limits. A BMW S 1000 R can do over 160km/h in first gear and has five left after that. There are only a few fixed speed cameras on the Black Forest High Rd route (they look like grey post boxes) and they're near Baden-Baden but police with mobile speed cameras patrol the area. You play your cards and take your chances.

The good news is this over-policed section of the B500 isn't the only game in town. The Black Forest High Rd runs between Baden-Baden and Freudenstadt. It then morphs into a group of other highways before heading down to Triberg, where it becomes the B500 again and ends up at Waldshut-Tiengen near the Swiss border. The total distance from Baden-Baden to there is 233km. It's a beautiful ride by any other world standard but there are many small towns to interrupt the flow of the ride and it's certainly not the best way to get back to Stuttgart if that's where you want your ride to end.

If you decide to finish with the B500 at Freudenstadt, it will spare you from having to visit the 'House of 1000 Clocks' near Triberg. Here's a wild guess: nobody reading this book has the slightest interest in cuckoo clocks. Correct me if I'm wrong.

On the other hand, who doesn't love a good castle? You can visit Hohenzollern Castle on your way back to Stuttgart.

Castle on the hill

To get there, follow 28 briefly until you can turn right on 28A then right on the E41 and left on 463 before left again briefly on 27 to Hechingen, the closest town to the castle. Sounds complicated, but it's very well signposted so you won't miss it and the distance is 60km on very pretty Black Forest roads.

Hohenzollern Castle's history is a complicated mix of European politics, but the reason to visit is to wonder at its construction and ponder on the lives of those who built it, stone by stone. The castle you're looking at is actually the third on the site but it's easy to understand why they kept rebuilding it. What a location.

The first iteration was in the early 11th century. It was completely destroyed in 1423 after a 10 month siege. The second version was built from 1454 to 1461. It was larger and better built but it fell into decline towards the end of the 18th century.

The current castle was assembled between 1846 and 1867 as a memorial to the Hohenzollern family. The last Hohenzollern in residence was there briefly in 1945.

It's totally understandable if readers from the 'new world' find it difficult to get their heads around how one family group first mentioned in dispatches in 1061 can move through recorded history for almost 1000 years. The current castle is still owned by the same family.

If you're like me, you'll speculate on what it would be like now as a private residence. At last, room for all your bikes – but you'd need at least 100 staff to maintain it, not to mention the mechanics. A militia would be useful, too, in the event of an attack, but its position on top of the only hill in the area would be a strategic advantage. At night while trying to go to sleep you could read the letter from George Washington thanking his Hohenzollern relative Baron von Steuben for his service in the American Revolutionary War.

It truly is an extraordinary place and well worth a long stop.

Volkswagen currywurst

The 'currywurst' (pork sausage) you had at Mummelsee was probably good but, almost unbelievably, the Volkswagen car company in Germany also makes it.

It's manufactured by a team of 30 in a section of the Wolfsburg VW Plant and sold in the 17 canteens and restaurants in the Wolfsburg factory with ketchup and French fries.

It's also sold in the workers canteens in the other six VW factories in Germany but non-employees can buy it in selected supermarkets.

It's pretty easy to identify as the sausages have an official part number branded onto the sausage skin: Volkswagen Originalteil 199 398 500 A.

The proceeds of the sale of VW currywurst outside of the manufacturing plants is used to subsidise the price of food in VW's staff canteens.

This isn't enough for you? VW also makes its own ketchup (part number Volkswagen Originalteil 119 378 500 B).

With production of around seven million sausages each year, currywurst is VW's largest-selling official part.

One last blast

If you have a little extra time before returning your hire bike to Stuttgart, Hohenzollern Castle is on the edge of the Swabian Jura (or Swabian Alb), which is a beautiful riding area with hills rather than mountains and quieter roads. The Park Hotel (*see* Best Sleeps) near Ulm is a motorcycle hotel with lots of local information on riding routes. From Ulm to Stuttgart is less than 100km of classic German roads.

If you're heading back to Stuttgart from Hohenzollern Castle, backtrack along 463 until it intersects with the A81 and turn right. The A81 is a derestricted autobahn and gives you one last legal chance to see what your bike feels like if you ride it flat out.

Being there

Coming from a country where it's possible to have your bike crushed by the government and actually go to jail for exceeding the speed limit excessively, you eventually learn to ride with some degree of legal caution. In parts of the Northern Territory of Australia, the speed limit is 130km/h but in most other jurisdictions, 110km/h is as fast as you're legally allowed to ride.

At that speed, a BMW R 1200 GS will use about 4.7L per 100km and, eventually, you become accustomed to working out how far you can go between fuel stops.

If you carry that thinking onto an unrestricted German autobahn where the sky is the limit, you could be in for a surprise.

I started out with half a tank and sitting on 160km/h before the red mist descended because I was being passed by cars. Cars! The honour of motorcycling was at stake so I drifted up to 200km/h where I was at least keeping up with the traffic in the far left lane. It can't have been more than five minutes of this before the fuel light came on. What? I knew from experience that my own R 1150 GS used 6L/100km at 120km/h but here I was about to run out of fuel on an autobahn. How much fuel does a BMW R 1200 GS use at 200km/h? The answer is obviously a shitload.

Then I remembered it's actually illegal to run out of fuel on an autobahn. The road authorities rightfully consider it's something you can predict so it's your fault and they don't want any stoppages on a road where speed differentials are so great. The fines aren't huge unless your stoppage causes a crash. In Australia you can just push your bike into the scrub, hitch to a petrol station and come back with 4L so you can limp on. Autobahns aren't like that - there's nowhere to hide.

I slipped over to the right lane and, shamefully, sat behind a motorhome doing 90km/h until I could find somewhere to refuel.

I always assumed the recommended top speed on autobahns of 130km/h was about road safety but now I think it's got something to do with unexpected fuel consumption. Live and learn.

Below The authorities know motorcyclists get tempted on the Black Forest High Road and motorcycle warning signs are everywhere *Opposite left and right* Baking bread the hard way at Mummelsee where you can also get excellent German beer.

BEST EATS

Waldschanke am Hungerberg, Baden-Baden

Nice pub-like atmosphere in a nice park with very good views of Baden-Baden from the outside seating area. There's indoor seating as well. The food is traditional German, which is probably what you want and it's cheap. There's a good range of local beers as well.
Hungerberg 6, 76530 Baden-Baden

Star DeLuxe Pizza and Kebap Haus, Freudenstadt.

There are around seven million Turkish people living in Germany and about half of them are permanent residents with their families. Germany used Turkish labour between 1961 and 1974 due to domestic shortages and they're now one of the biggest migrant groups in Europe.

This low-key restaurant has German influences in its menu but lots of Turkish-inspired dishes as well. It's very popular with the locals but you can usually get a seat. Cheap and very cheerful.
Ludwig-Jahn-Str. 34, 72250, Freudenstadt.

Hohenzollern Castle Beer Garden, Hohenzollern

Sometimes ambience and atmosphere can be as important as the food, and the beer garden in the Hohenzollern Castle provides this in spades.

The weather has to be right, of course. Beer garden classics are all on the menu but the Hohenzollern Bowl and the Prussian Burger are well suited to vegetarians and carnivores. Hohenzollern makes its own beer and the location makes the whole experience special.
www.burg-hohenzollern.com/castle-gastronomy.html

BEST SLEEPS

Hotel Athos, Baden-Baden

This is an old-school hotel run by a Greek family in a well-located part of Baden-Baden with walks through a municipal garden to get to most of the town's attractions. The hotel has, naturally, a Greek restaurant but it also has (limited) undercover and open parking and single rooms start from €85.
www.athos-hotel.com/m

Park Hotel, Swabian Jura

You have to like a hotel that promotes itself especially for motorcycle riders, and Park Hotel does just this. Rates are very reasonable. The Swabian Alb region is known for its winding routes through small villages and scenic forests. The hotel knows everything there is to know about the best routes and is happy to share the information.
www.lobinger-hotels.de/en/parkhotel/freizeit/rad-motorrad-hotel

Natur-camping Longenwald, near Freudenstadt

Got a tent on the back of your bike? This campsite has 100 pitch sites with power so you can charge your electronic devices and is 3.5km away from Freudenstadt at the end of the Black Forest High Rd.

It doesn't have mobile reception and internet connection is intermittent but it's a beautiful spot with an outdoor pool usually open from May to September. Keep in mind it's at an altitude of 720m, so it can get a little chilly at night. A tent site for two adults is €40 a night.
www.camping-langenwald.de

The Amalfi Coast: Italy

If you want to combine a great ride with a great holiday, head for the Amalfi Coast in Italy. Oh, you'll need to take your wallet and you must be prepared to ride a scooter.

SNAPSHOT

If the Amalfi Coast road was for motorcycles only, it would be one of the best rides in Europe. Unfortunately, people who drive cars have found out about it and it can become very crowded, particularly in summer. There are times of the day and times of the year when it's less crowded, however, so you need to take advantage of this.

Set between the Lattari Mountains and the Tyrrhenian Sea, the coast road takes you through villages of rare charm and beauty, forcing you to make it into a holiday as well as a road trip.

In countries like large parts of coastal USA and Australia, the idea that you might have to pay to go for a surf or put a towel down at a beach is unimaginable. It would be considered as the privatisation of public space and would be grounds for a change of government.

A recent attempt to do this on Australia's Bondi Beach saw an ex-prime minister's wife and a celebrity chef – along with 40,000 signatures on a petition – condemning the idea.

TV chef Adam Liaw asked why one of the world's best beaches (Bondi) would 'authentically recreate the experience of spending time on a much worse beach (Amalfi) in a country (Italy) known for having very bad beaches'.

Beach jealousy notwithstanding, the Amalfi Coast in Italy, where it's common to pay for beach space, has something Bondi can never have: a spectacular 53km-long road that twists, winds, rises and falls in the very small space between the Lattari Mountains and the Tyrrhenian Sea.

American writer John Steinbeck travelled it with his wife and a driver in 1953. He claimed it was 'carefully designed to be a little narrower than two cars side-by-side' and full of terror.

'We didn't see much of the road. In the back seat my wife and I lay clutched in each other's arms, weeping hysterically'.

Steinbeck was in a Fiat 500, but even for motorcycles it's a very narrow road.

How long?
If you've made it to the Amalfi Coast, you're now on a holiday. Exploring the coast road itself can be done easily in a day but internalising the 'vibe' could take you up to a week.

When to go
April to June and October are your best chances of getting great summer weather without the crowds. From a hospitality perspective, many hotels and restaurants close towards the end of October and don't open again until later in March.

Need to know
- As the Amalfi Coast is so small, you don't have to change accommodation to access the main attractions - there'll always be time to go to the one place each night.
- Be thankful you're riding a motorcycle. New rules to reduce traffic include only being allowed to drive your hire car on even-numbered days if your numberplate ends in an even number and on odd-numbered days if your numberplate ends in an odd number.
- You need to ride the coast road, of course, but even with a scooter it will sometimes be best to use buses or a water taxi to get around.

Ride rating
Intermediate. Your skills at low-speed manoeuvring will be put to the test as will your ability to handle a narrow road with lots of traffic. The locals are exceptionally good drivers in these conditions, although most local cars have scrapes on one or both sides.

Distances
- The Amalfi Coast road runs for 53km (33 miles) between Sorrento and Vietri Sul Mare.

Temperatures
- May: 12°C to 22°C (54°F to 72°F)
- August: 18°C to 29 °C (64°F to 84°F)
- September: 15°C to 26°C (59°F to 79°F)

More information
www.visitamalfi.info/en

Above In season, it's almost impossible to even park a scooter

Getting there

If you're in Italy on your own bike, no problems. Amalfi is an easy 276km ride from Rome. The 'strada statale 163 Amalfitara', as the Amalfi Coast road is formally known, runs 53km from Sorrento to Vietri sul Mare (near Salerno). The direction in which you choose to travel actually makes a difference. If you ride it from Salerno, you hug the cliff, not the abyss. If you like to live dangerously, start from Sorrento. However with that said, once you're actually there you'll probably ride it in both directions anyway, so no need to sweat the decision.

A fully laden BMW R 1300 GS has roughly the same width as Steinbeck's Fiat 500 and exactly the same problems with passing and overtaking. If you arrive at either Salerno or Sorrento by bus or train, you can get a SITA bus to wherever you've decided to stay and rent a scooter from the myriad options available. Anything more than 125cc is overkill on this road.

If you decide to spend a few days in the area (which you should), an alternative to the expensive ocean-front accommodation is to head for a village in the nearby hills. **San Lazzaro** (population: 32,353) is a short and very entertaining ride from Amalfi up into the Lattari Mountains. It has inexpensive accommodation, great regional restaurants, is accessible by bus and has a scooter rental business in the middle of the village that charges €55 a day for Yamaha 125 scooters.

It also has a magnificent lookout and a million steps that can take you to Amalfi on foot, but potentially at considerable cost to leg muscles you may not have used for a while.

If you're without your own bike when leaving, take a ferry from Amalfi to Sorrento for not many euros, which will give you brilliant views of the coast and mountains.

We're all going on a summer holiday

If you haven't worked it out already, the coast road is extremely busy in the Italian summer. By 'busy' we mean you can sit in traffic jams for long periods as the road narrows through the main villages of Positano, Praiano, Amalfi and Ravello. It's quicker on a scooter, of course, but the locals in this area are so good at tight driving that there's often no room even for scooters to slip by the cars and buses.

Your options for a cleaner run are either late April to early June, or October to early November. Its moderate climate also makes it a good ride in winter, too. If you have to go in the peak period, you'll find the road far less busy just after daybreak and, surprisingly, just after lunch when the locals relax for an hour or two.

Below The impressive town of Positano *Opposite* Ruins at Pompeii

Pompeii

Depending on which route you choose to take, Pompeii is as little as 38km from Amalfi. It was probably first settled in the 7th century BCE and suffered a number of conquerors before it became a Roman city around 80BCE.

You know it because nearby Mt Vesuvius erupted in AD79, burying the city and its inhabitants under a layer of ash and burning fragments of pumice stone.

It was rediscovered sometime around 1750, but serious archeological work didn't produce results until the 1870s when it was also opened to the public. Its significance is that it's a snapshot of life in AD79 frozen in time. Much work has gone into discovering the meaning and use of the huge number of revealed buildings and it makes it easy to construct a mental picture of what it would have been like to live there at that time.

Allocate the better part of a day to visit. There's secure bike parking at the western end of the archaeological site near the Zeus Pompeii Ristorante Pizzeria Bar and you can enter from there. The audio guides you can hire at the same spot are very useful.

Ready, set, go!

We're travelling the road starting from **Sorrento** (population: 16,609). The coast road route was established between 1832 and 1850, largely following the donkey-and-cart tracks that linked the villages in the area. When you initially leave Sorrento, the road seems to be much like many others in this part of Italy. That all changes when you hit the coast on the other side of the Sorrento peninsula. Here you get some sense of how little space the road-builders had to play with. Often, the Lattari Mountains just drop into the sea, meaning the road had to be carved into the rock itself. Most natural valleys along the route host villages but the architecture on display reinforces the space constraints; houses rub shoulder-to-shoulder and stack themselves back up the mountainside until the laws of gravity make further building impossible.

The road surface is very well maintained and offers pleasing grip. Stone and brick barriers run along most of the sea-side of the road, which may assist if you slide off but you know it will always hurt – so caution is required.

Where it can, the road follows the easiest contours which means hundreds of bends and twists. Forward vision is often limited as cliffs block your view, particularly on left-handers if you're riding from Sorrento. Oncoming traffic that you often can't see will inevitably include buses so you need to allow for a squeeze against the stone barrier to let them through. Parts of the route open up a little, however, and allow you to press on with a little more confidence. This is particularly the case after you've passed Minori.

The first proper town you'll come to is also the route's most impressive: **Positano** (population: 3942). You can bypass it but why would you? Instead, weave and dive down the road leading to the beach area (Spiaggia Grande) taking note of the vibrant shops and businesses along the way. As you corkscrew your way down, keep an eye out for the many motorcycle parking lots. Incredibly, in peak season, most of them are full and it's usually impossible to find a park, even for a small scooter, near the beach area. There are no problems out of season.

So you've paid to park your bike and you'll pay again when you get to the beach if you want a chair and an umbrella. There are a couple of small, free public areas that you'll be able to find easily, as that's where the local crowds will be.

Positano is exceedingly beautiful and the view up to the mountains from the beach shows it in all its glory. It's an even better view from the water and a ferry ride from the harbour perhaps to Capri or Amalfi will showcase not just Positano but the rest of this fabulous coastline.

Above Roadside stalls sell local products including Amalfi lemon drinks *Opposite left* The road from San Lazzaro to Amalfi *Opposite top right* A private beach in Amalfi *Opposite bottom right* Parking at Sorrento

Amalfi lemons

The Amalfi Coast road, especially from Sorrento to Amalfi, has plenty of side-of-the-road stalls selling drinks based on Amalfi lemons. The lemons are grapefruit-sized and probably sweeter than the lemons you're used to. They're protected as well: you can only call your lemons Amalfi lemons if they're actually grown there. You'll see t-shirts, signs, statues and monuments worshipping Amalfi lemons all along the coast road.

There usually isn't much room beside the stalls but it's perfect for bike parking on the hotter days. On offer will be the lemons themselves but also lemon granita, which is super refreshing.

The lemons are probably used most in limoncello, which is traditionally an after-dinner liquor served cold. It's actually kept in freezers but its alcohol content is so high it won't go solid. Enjoy but approach with caution.

Another popular use of Amalfi lemons is Delizia al Limone, which is a sponge cake lightly soaked in lemon syrup then filled and covered with lemon cream. Delish.

Within walking distance (not in motorcycle boots) to the west is the nicer beach of Fornillo, which is also blessed with summer beach bars.

Just 7.6km past Positano is the less frenetic and less expensive former fishing village of **Praiano** (population: 2026). It has hotels and camping facilities along with its Marina di Praia, a small but beautiful beach at the end of the untamed Praia Valley. If you're into sun worship, this beach is the only one on the coast that gets the last rays of the sun before it sets.

Piracy was long the scourge of the Amalfi Coast and there's a medieval remnant of the defence against it in the village of **Torr a Mare**, situated on the end of a rocky promontory near the town.

Amalfi

The coast road between Positano and Amalfi is usually crowded as it links the two most popular villages on the route, so your riding pleasure moves to survival mode and entertaining yourself by observing the locals.

The traffic will slow as you approach Amalfi simply because the road narrows and all the people here are holding everything up

by walking across the road between the beach and the central business district, such as it is. In case anyone from the Amalfi council is reading this, a walkway overpass would be a really good idea. There may be building constraints, though, as the entire Amalfi Coast is listed as a UNESCO World Heritage Site.

Amalfi (population: 5102) has a glorious history being Italy's oldest maritime republic. It's located where the Valle dei Mulini spreads out into the sea. Most of its history happened in the period up to AD1000 when it was a proper republic, a powerful trading centre and, eventually, a duchy. As is the way with power, it declined after internal conflicts, occupation by the Normans and, eventually, natural disasters. In 1343 a seaquake destroyed around a third of the city with most of the seafront washing away. Then it largely disappeared from world view and existed mostly as a small fishing village until it was rediscovered as the beautiful-but-overrun, overpopulated place it is today.

Some indications of past glory survive in the cathedral, parts of which date back to the 9th century. It's been mucked about with architecturally-speaking ever since and is an interesting mix of various styles based on who was the dominant power during its multiple reconstructions.

Despite this, there isn't much of a sense of history in Amalfi. It's essentially a tourist town with plenty of nice hotels and restaurants, a popular beach, plenty of shops and the charm of houses-on-hills that dominate the entire coast. Having said this, the **Amalfi Civic Museum** is worth visiting just to see the Tabula Amalphitana, the ancient code outlining the maritime trade laws of the Amalfi Republic when it was at its most influential.

For riders, leaving Amalfi opens up the cleanest section of the coast road. There's less traffic as you pass through Minori, Maiori, Cetara and the official finish of the road at Vietri sul Mare. The road still twists and turns but is less dangerous in relation to traffic because vision is better and you're able to still glimpse brilliant vistas of the coast as you enjoy sweeping corners on a great road surface.

Oh, you've arrived at Vietri sul Mare. Have a coffee or something a little stronger, turn around and head back to Sorrento – the adventure continues …

Being there

Staying in the Lattari Mountains village of San Lazzaro as we did rather than in an expensive tourist hotel in Amalfi was an immersion in authentic regional Italy.

Airbnb is a scourge in many countries as it's reducing long-term rental options for people who can't afford to buy a house, but it's very seductive for travellers in a foreign country who want to stay in one place for a week or so.

The village is mostly locals with just a smattering of tourists, so you live as the locals do. We arrived in the middle of a LGBTQIA+ rally in the town square that is directly outside the local Catholic church. The keynote speaker was due to start at 5pm, which coincided with the church bell tolling to denote the hour. The bell ringer, clearly not a supporter of the protest movement, didn't stop. He rang the bell for a full 15 minutes having locked the church doors so he couldn't be interrupted. It was the talk of the town that evening.

We had an apartment on the third floor of a three-story building with the owner and extended family occupying the other two floors. We joined their conversations as we arrived home each afternoon and followed their recommendations for authentic cooking in the village.

Within the week, we were on nodding terms with the grocery shop staff, on first name terms with the coffee shop owner in the town square, and on friendly terms with the hire-bike operator and the woman who ran the tourist information kiosk.

BEST EATS

O'Puledrone, Sorrento
Are you after an adventure, not just dinner? This restaurant is run by a fish cooperative that will take you out on a three-hour fishing trip for €70, and the chef at the restaurant will cook what you catch and serve it up with a carafe of local wine. Fresh fish is also available without the fishing expedition from €25 upwards. From April to October it opens noon to 3pm and then 6.30pm until it feels like closing.
www.opuledrone.com

C'era Una Volta, Positano
This is an authentic trattoria that cooks and serves traditional regional food. It's located at the top of the town, which is a little inconvenient, but it runs a free shuttle to and from the town centre in summer. It's inexpensive, too. Pizzas are available from €5 and the house wine and beer is cheap. Open for lunch and dinner.
www.ristoranteceraunavolta-positano.com

Ristorante Leonardo's, San Lazzaro
Leonardo's is a delightful old-school restaurant in the hills of the village of San Lazzaro. The restaurant has a panoramic view of the Amalfi Coast, an amazing local menu, wine by the carafe and pleasingly eccentric waiters. It's worth the ride up into the hills.
www.ristoranteleonardos.eu

BEST SLEEPS

Accommodation booking websites will let you know what's available on the Amalfi Coast road but, as you'd expect, much of it is expensive. As you move slightly away from the coast, prices fall off a cliff, even though you're on a cliff and have great views of the coast.

Plazzo Lauritano, Agerola
How about a twin room with a terrace and breakfast thrown in for under €100 a night? Agerola is the hill district behind Amalfi but it's close to the city centre and all the amenities of the town, all without the cost of being on the waterfront. It's also a bit quieter if your priority is a good night's sleep.
www.palazzolauritano.com

Domus Gaia, Amalfi
This is close to Amalfi and features a double room with terrace (great views) and a private external bathroom. There's free bike parking but it's 100m from the accommodation. By Amalfi standards, that's pretty good.
Via Giovanni Amendola 34 Palazzo B, Amalfi.

Opposite Once the road starts hugging the coast after leaving Sorrento, the views become spectacular

Above The Causeway Coastal Route hugs the Northern Ireland coast

Causeway Coastal Route: Northern Ireland

If you've ever wondered why the Northern Irish have dominated motorcycle road racing for the past century, the Causeway Coastal Route will provide most of the answers.

SNAPSHOT

What makes the Causeway Coastal Route special is that it loads most of what riders dream about into one package: plenty of corners, spectacular scenery, lots of things to do and see on the way, plenty of pubs and restaurants, and every conceivable service necessary for a successful ride.

It also involves interacting with the locals, which has its own delights even if you don't always understand what they're saying.

It's a stress-free adventure on one of the world's great roads.

Saint Columba loved Ireland. When he banished himself from it in AD563 over a war he was responsible for, he settled on the island of Iona between Ireland and Scotland. This was the closest island to his home country from which Ireland couldn't be seen. This was his most severe penance.

Another yet-to-be-canonised lover of Ireland was William Bald. He and the 'Men of the Glynnes' built the Causeway Coastal Route between 1832 and 1842. Prior to that, the northern part of Ireland could more rightly be considered 'East Scotland'. At its closest points, Scotland and Ireland are only 12 miles apart and it was far easier for the citizens of the North Antrim Coast to do business with the Scots than it was to travel to Belfast, the capital of what's now Northern Ireland.

Bald fixed that with his new road that hugged the coast tightly and linked the extreme north with the rest of Ireland. While Columba became a saint, Bald and his men are now simply remembered by a humble memorial sculpture at the end of the promenade in Larne that celebrates 'The Antrim Coast Road', the original name for this most excellent ride.

What makes it special? It has plenty of corners for one, and with lots of great scenery and interesting diversions along the way, plus myriad pubs and cafes no more than 20 miles apart, it's a dream ride.

Officially, the Causeway Coastal Route runs between Belfast and Derry, a distance of 195 miles. *Lonely Planet* voted it number one region for 'Best in Travel' in 2018. For riders, it will arguably be one of the 'best in travel' contenders while motorcycles continue to exist.

How long?
While the Causeway Coastal Route isn't particularly long, there's so much to see and do on the journey that you'd sell yourself short if you didn't devote at least three days to it. The attractions distract from the ride itself but when you decide to return to Belfast, you'll be able to focus exclusively on the ride.

When to go
Summer is best but school holidays run from July/August when the route gets very crowded. Hence you'll probably enjoy the ride more if you do it in early June or in September.

Need to know
- If you're arriving in Northern Ireland from anywhere in Great Britain, no paperwork is required.
- You ride on the left-hand side of the road and obey normal road markings on two-lane roads.
- Some patience is required if you travel in school holiday periods as overtaking opportunities can be irregular and there will be plenty of slow-moving traffic.

Ride rating
Easy at normal touring speeds allowing for it mostly being a two-lane road with a very good surface.

Distances
- Belfast to Derry is 195 miles (313km) making it roughly a 400 mile return-trip.

Temperatures
- July: 12°C to 19°C (54°F to 66°F)
- September: 10°C to 17°C (50°F to 63°F)

More information
www.tourismni.com

Getting there

If you're short of time, the most convenient option is to fly into Belfast and rent a motorcycle from the myriad motorcycle rental outlets. Visit Flyride Ireland (www.flyrideireland.com) to get an idea of what bikes are available. You can expect to pay around £100 pounds a day.

Many riders will visit Northern Ireland as part of a bigger ride in the UK and can take advantage of inexpensive ferry crossings on the Stena Line from Liverpool. This takes you to Belfast but you can also leave from Cairnryan in Scotland on a P&O ferry, which will take you to Larne where the interesting riding on the Causeway Coastal Route actually starts. The Cairnryan/Larne crossing takes two hours.

King of the castle

If you arrive at Larne you'll need to backtrack towards Belfast for 14 miles to make sure you include a visit to the very well-preserved castle at **Carrickfergus**. It was built in 1177 and it dominated Carrickfergus Bay (now Belfast Lough). It was strategically important until after WWII, but was given back to the new Government of Northern Ireland by the British Army in 1928.

Europeans tend to take castles for granted, but if you're from elsewhere, you'll find them endlessly fascinating. If you were in one of its loch towers in 1912, you would have seen the RMS *Titanic* leave the loch on its maiden voyage when construction had finished in Belfast.

Are you after a motorcycle connection? Prince William, an avid motorcycle rider, had the peerage title of Baron Carrickfergus (which had been extinct since 1883) bestowed on him on his wedding day in 2011.

If your start point is Belfast, the castle is a mere 11 miles up the Causeway Coastal Route.

Also between Belfast and Larne is the **Gobbins Cliff Path Walk** (www.thegobbinscliffpath.com) on Islandmagee, which takes you 3 miles along the very edge of the wild Irish Sea. It takes three hours and is physically demanding but if you've packed your bike appropriately (ie brought along walking shoes) and can secure your riding gear on your bike, it's certainly worth considering. The walk has been open since 1902 but now features infrastructure to assist progress that allowed the walk to be reopened in 2016 after the safetycrats had closed it for many years.

Above Carrickfergus Castle, 11 miles from Belfast

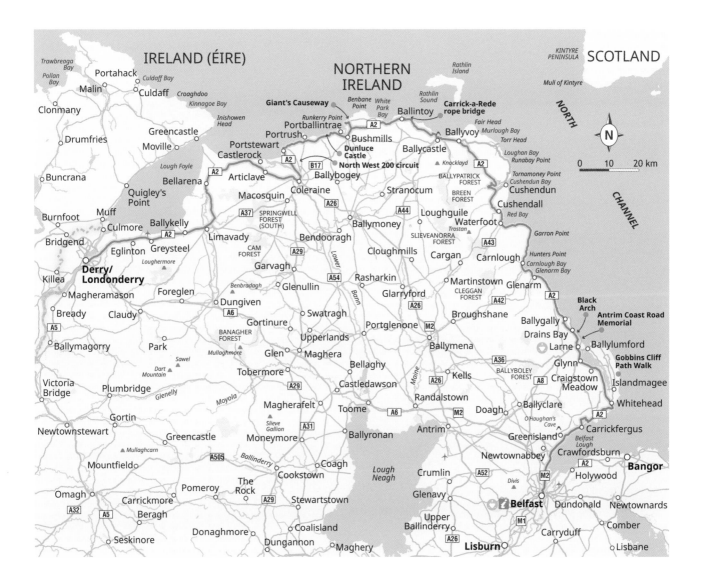

NW200

Motorcycle racing on public roads (closed, obviously, during the racing) has always been popular in Northern Ireland and the biggest meeting of the year is the North West 200 where up to 150,000 spectators watch the region's finest riders race on a triangular circuit that abuts the Causeway Coastal Route.

It started in 1929 on the 8.9 mile (114.4km) circuit, which is one of the fastest in the world given the length of its straights. Top speeds of 200mph (320km/h) are common.

As road racing is entirely on public roads where you can hit fixed objects if you fall off, it's more dangerous than circuit racing and 19 riders have died since the event commenced. Robert Dunlop, brother of Joey and father of Michael and William Dunlop, was killed in a crash during NW200 practice in 2008. Robert had 15 victories there over the years and Joey had 13. There's a monument to both Robert and Joey at nearby Ballymoney.

The NW200 is usually held in May and it's worth thinking about making it part of your Causeway Coastal route tour. It's the next best thing to the Isle of Man TT (*see* p. 98).

Heading north

The rider in you will light up when you pass through the Black Arch, a short tunnel near Larne that is the first hint of the amount of explosives William Bald had to use to create the Causeway Coastal Route back in 1832.

From here the route becomes open, and although it's largely straight, it follows the coast to provide a peaceful introduction to the rest of the ride. The villages of Ballygalley, Glenarm, Carnlough and Cushendall remind you that housing estates aren't the only places in which people actually live. All have great cafe and pub facilities, and ocean views are guaranteed.

Ten minutes after Cushendall is Cushendun, but it's a lively 10 minutes as the road goes slightly inland and the twisties start. If you're up for it, there are two loop roads between these towns that expose more of the Antrim countryside and multiply the corners on well-sealed, little-used roads.

Cushendun (population: 1280) itself has a fine beach if the weather suits a swim and it's a short walk to the Cushendun Caves that were used in the filming of *Game of Thrones*. In fact, there are 15 filming sites conveniently located to the Causeway Coastal Route if that popular TV series captured your imagination. At the moment, the *Game of Thrones* sites are tourist attractions but, as New Zealand is slowly discovering with its *Lord of the Rings* sites, trying to build sustainable tourism on the back of contemporary popular culture isn't as easy as it looks. Regardless, if you're going to ride the Causeway Coastal Route in the near future, *Game of Thrones* references will be hard to avoid.

Torr head

The ride from Cushendun to Ballycastle provides two options. One is to head up to Torr Head via the Torr Head Scenic Route, and the other is to stay on the Causeway Coastal Route. If you're coming back from Derry the same way, you can cover both roads.

The Torr Head diversion is well worth the effort. It's a well-sealed but very narrow road that climbs and weaves through the coastal mountains. Despite it having a broken white line down its centre, it's too narrow for most buses and caravans, so it's largely traffic-free. Keep an eye out though for local farmers and their wayward flocks.

Torr Head (population: 150) is the closest point in Northern Ireland to Scotland, with the distance from the head to Scotland's Mull of Kintyre being just 12 miles. The head was the site of an 1822 Lloyd's shipping signal station, which was severely damaged by the Irish Republican Army (IRA)

Above Ruins of an old fort along Torr Head

in 1921 during the War of Independence. The coastguard quarters were also destroyed to prevent them from being used as barracks for the British. The signal station has since been restored and the ruins of the other buildings on the head make interesting viewing.

Slightly further down the road is the very pretty Murlough Bay where you can ride almost to the beach. Does it look familiar? Yep, another *Game of Thrones* location, as was Ballycastle where the Torr Head road rejoins the Causeway Coastal Route.

Ballycastle (population: 5628) is a busy town, but it's only 6 miles to one of the North's major attractions: the Carrick-a-Rede rope bridge, which, in various forms, has been used by fisherfolk for centuries to get to a very small island where nets can be strung to catch mostly salmon (yes, yes, another *Game of Thrones* location!) The bridge is a long walk from the car park and, like the upcoming Giant's Causeway, it requires riders to have walking shoes to replace their boots, and some way of securing their riding gear to their bikes. The rope bridge is over an 8m drop into the ocean and can be sobering for those with issues about height.

Giant's Causeway

Just 7.3 miles from the Carrick-a-Rede rope bridge car park is the UNESCO World Heritage–listed **Giant's Causeway**. Science tells us it was formed 50 to 60 million years ago from volcanic eruptions, but it's best to go with local knowledge that says it was formed by a fight between a giant in Scotland and a giant in Ireland who built it so that they could settle the argument about who was the stronger. The Irish giant prevailed by cleverness rather than strength but the result was 40,000 interlocking basalt columns, which are indeed strange and fascinating to behold.

Like the rope bridge, it's a longish walk from the car park to the Causeway so don't attempt it in your riding gear.

You might like to consider not paying the car-park fee at the event centre and going the extra 200 yards to park at the Causeway Hotel on the site. The parking fee (around 10 quid) is the same but it's reimbursed by the hotel if you buy food or drinks afterwards and, after the walk, you may need a drink.

If the drink you're craving is a whiskey, the old Bushmills distillery is only 10 minutes from the car park. Distilling may have started as early as the 1400s in the area, but a licence

wasn't issued until 1608. It's probably the oldest distillery in the world and it's very respectful of its heritage. Unlike Scotch malt whisky, the Irish product avoids peat smoke and is distilled three times rather than twice, enhancing – it's claimed – its smoothness. Oh, and you can tell the difference because the Irish put an 'e' in the spelling of whiskey, which the Scots avoid. If you need to take a gift from your trip back to a loved one, there's a 12-year-old Irish single malt whiskey that is available only to people who personally visit the distillery .

Your second-last castle fix on the Causeway Coastal Route is just 2.4 miles past Bushmills: **Dunluce Castle**. Built on a headland in the mid 1550s, it's an astounding example of how fragile a peaceful life was at the time. Access was only by a drawbridge and, once the residents of the town that grew up around the castle had retreated to it, it was very difficult to attack. There are sheer cliffs surrounding it and the brickwork of the castle runs to the very edges of these cliffs, meaning scaling the cliffs was just part of the effort required to enter it. Legend has it the castle kitchen was built out over the ocean and collapsed during a storm, drowning almost all of the kitchen staff.

You can park your bike near the entrance and, for a change, you can interrogate the castle comfortably while still in your riding gear.

The elephant in the room

From Portrush, near Dunluce Castle, it's a 36.7 mile ride to Derry, the official end of the Causeway Coastal Route. The road is slightly less interesting in that it largely deviates from the coast but **Derry** (population: 85,279) is well worth a visit as it's the only remaining walled city in both Northern Ireland and Ireland alike. The 1-mile walk around the walls is rewarding, as is a visit to the Tower Museum, which lets you in on the history of the town as well as providing an excellent viewing post.

The city prompts a few things to think about regarding the division of Ireland. It's actually two countries: the Republic of Ireland (to the south) is independent and Northern Ireland is still attached to the United Kingdom. Trouble between the nationalists (largely Catholic) in the Republic and the unionists (largely Protestant) in Northern Ireland have featured prominently in world news for the past 100 years or so. The scars left by 'The Troubles' still hurt both sides. Derry was

known by that name until 1613, but King James I of England changed it to 'Londonderry'. Locals tend to call it 'Derry' now but most maps still refer to it as 'Londonderry'.

Regardless of your sectarian disposition , Northern Ireland is now a peaceful and friendly place to visit. The issues around reunification are yet to be fully resolved and the water has been muddied recently by the UK leaving the European Union. All this occupies the minds of the locals but doesn't get in the way of a fascinating ride for visitors along the Northern Ireland coast.

Whether you finish your ride at Portrush or go on to Derry, getting back to Belfast should be the reverse of your initial ride. This time, however, you can concentrate on the road rather than the attractions. The Causeway Coastal Route is busy in peak tourism seasons but is a good ride in winter and always quiet early in the morning, whatever the season. It allows you to set your own pace and treasure the legacy William Bald left when he completed building the route.

Being there

I find myself writing this from Joey's Bar in Ballymoney in Northern Ireland. Joey's daughter, Donna, has just poured me what could be the perfect Guinness and it would be selfish of me not to share the pleasure.

Just to refresh your memory, Joey Dunlop had 26 victories at the Isle of Man TT and died a national hero when he crashed his 125 in Eastern Europe at age 48. When he wasn't racing, he'd fill his race van with food and clothing for orphans in Romania and deliver them himself.

There isn't a living being in Northern Ireland who doesn't know his name and revere him.

I'm riding a Triumph Tiger 1200 and what I'm enjoying most is its agility. Its slim seat line at the front makes it feel lower than it actually is and what you're looking at forward of that isn't overwhelming. If Triumph had told me it was an 800 I wouldn't have had any trouble believing it.

It doesn't feel like a particularly big bike but it has all the benefits of a massive engine in a manageable package.

I would have liked Joey Dunlop to give me a second opinion. I signed something at Triumph when I borrowed it that said I wouldn't let anyone else ride the bike, but if Joey was still alive and asked for the keys so he could do a quick lap of the nearby NW200 track, I would have given them to him in a heartbeat. I'm pretty sure Triumph would have understood.

BEST EATS

You aren't going to starve to death on the Causeway Coastal Route. There are villages every 6 miles or so, all with charming ale houses and kitchens. Pub food tends to be inexpensive and filling, particularly if you're prone to the occasional Guinness Pie.

Mattie's Meeting House
Located a mile inland from Ballygally between Larne and Glenarm, Mattie's is a local institution that has a history going back to the 1800s. It's a fine place for a local dish and it's simple food done well. The pints aren't bad, either. It's more for the locals than the tourists, so it's a great place to find out what a real Irish pub is like.
www.matties.co.uk

Harry's Cushendall, Cushendall
This is a slightly upmarket restaurant with pub prices that prides itself on the freshness of its local products - it's especially known for its seafood chowder. It's not a big restaurant so it's wise to book in advance.
www.harryscushendall.co.uk

Maud's Ice Cream
This is Northern Ireland's most famous ice cream and there's invariably a queue to get into the shops. It won the Champion of Champions award and the National Ice Cream Alliance competition recently. Maud's ice-cream parlours are in Ballycastle, Ballymoney, Portrush and Portstewart on the Causeway Coast route. The Turkish Delight flavour is pretty special while the Poor Bears Delight recently won first place at the legendary Irish Food Awards.
www.mauds.com

Harry's Shack, Portstewart
This is located right on the Strand Rd in Portstewart. There's plenty of room inside the shack but, if the weather is good, you might also consider sitting on the beach and listening to the waves. Harry's is most famous for its fresh seafood and the way it's prepared; unlike the fish and chips you mostly get in the UK, Harry's is crisp and crunchy.
118 Strand Rd, Portstewart; +44 (0)2870831783

BEST SLEEPS

Visiting Northern Ireland is a good opportunity to join Hostels International (HI) and take advantage of their low-cost, secure accommodation all over the globe. Hostels International (Northern Ireland) has options in Belfast, White Park Bay and Bushmills, which would cover your accommodation for riding the Causeway Coastal Route. Hostels can be anything up to one third of the price of a conventional hotel with much more in the way of facilities, including laundries and drying rooms, which will suit riders. Prices range from the basic shared dorms to double rooms, all with en-suites. Yearly membership is £10 and you'll save

Above Cushendun Caves *Opposite* Carrick-a-Rede rope bridge

that the first time you book in. There's no age limit on joining. Visit www.hini.org.uk/membership for more details.

White Park Bay Youth Hostel, Balintoy
Spectacular clifftop location overlooking the sea and within walking distance of the major attractions of the area. It has a secure car park for your bike and a self-catering kitchen if you want to save even more money.
www.hini.org.uk/hostels/white-park-bay-youth-hostel

Bushmills Youth Hostel, Bushmills
This is a modern hostel in a small, ancient village and is just a five-minute walk to the famous Bushmills Distillery. Features of the hostel include en-suite rooms and free wi-fi. There's also a beautiful, walled garden for outdoor eats.
www.hini.org.uk/hostels/bushmills-youth-hostel

Carnately Lodge, Ballycastle
This really nice lodge is a bit cheaper than accommodation in the centre of Ballycastle but it's only half-a-mile away and has the benefit of more peaceful surroundings. There's secure bike parking onsite, free wi-fi, Netflix in rooms, a games room and complimentary drinks and snacks on arrival. I recommend paying that little bit extra for the excellent breakfast.
www.carnately-lodge.business.site

Q&A
Elspeth Beard

Elspeth Beard became the first British woman to ride around the world. She left London in 1982 and arrived back there in 1984 having travelled 35,000 miles (56,000km). Her book on the trip, *Lone Rider*, was published in 2017. It's available from larger bookshops and online outlets.

What got you into riding?

I first rode on a bike when I was 16 when a friend was taking his Husqvarna down to Salisbury Plain and asked me along. Shortly after this I bought a Yamaha YB100 simply as a cheap and efficient way of getting around London. The following year I upgraded to a Honda CB250N. I soon got bored with the Honda and, in 1979, I bought a second-hand 1974 BMW R60/6 with about 30,000 miles on the clock. It was with this bike that I realised the travelling potential of a motorcycle.

What gave you the confidence to undertake your world ride when you were so young?

With my BMW I felt an immense sense of freedom and, over the next couple of years, I gradually travelled further afield, starting with a tour of Scotland, then Ireland, and then a two-month trip around Europe in the summer of 1980.

The following summer I met up with my brother in Los Angeles where we bought an old BMW R75/5 and rode together across to Detroit. All these trips gradually built up my confidence and also taught me how to look after myself and my bike. It was a combination of events in my life the following year which prompted my hasty departure.

Did you have a favourite part of the ride?

My favourite places would have to be northern Thailand, Nepal and Ladakh. As well as the beautiful mountain scenery, the people were always so friendly and welcoming.

You've still got the restored version of your R60/6. Do you still ride it?

Yes but these days I only take her out for a gentle Sunday ride or to take her to be exhibited at bike events I'm attending.

If you had your time over, would you do it again?

Absolutely. It was pivotal and gave me the courage and confidence to take risks in life and push myself farther to take on many other challenges.

How do you think it changed you?

The trip completely changed my life and made me the person I am. Being pushed to your limits you learn so much about yourself and I realised I was capable of dealing with anything. It gave me the confidence to take on anything life can throw at me without any fear.

Opposite Elspeth Beard and her trusty BMW R60/6

North Coast 500: Scotland

The North Coast 500 (NC500) in Scotland is a ride along the primitive roof of Great Britain. Take advantage of it while it's still young, wild and free.

SNAPSHOT

The NC500 is a relatively new initiative to link older roads across the top of Scotland so that you can ride around the northern edge of the country. As the name of the road suggests, it's roughly a 500 mile journey in a remote part of Great Britain.

The trip is characterised by rugged coastal scenery, narrow roads and charming villages. It gets busy in the middle of summer but is deserted, for good reason, in winter. It's on the bucket list for riders who like a bit of challenge in their adventures.

Those from the New Worlds who've taken advantage of developments in DNA testing to trace their family history are often surprised to find plenty of Irish and Scottish blood flowing through the family veins. In Scotland, the exodus was due largely to social engineering by the British after the failure of the 'Highlands Army' to defeat the English Army during the 1745 Jacobite Rising.

The Jacobites wanted to restore the House of Stuart to the British throne and Charles Edward Stuart led them to a crushing defeat at Culloden in 1746. The Brits immediately introduced the Traitors Transportation Act to get rid of the rebel leaders but then embarked on a program to destroy the social infrastructure of the Scottish Highlands from where many of the Jacobites had been recruited.

Clan chiefs were stripped of their estates and a 1746 Act of Parliament made it illegal to wear Highland dress (clan tartan). Ancestral lands were cleared for sheep grazing, making emigration the only option for survival for many. The polite historical term for the forced dispossession of Scots was 'the Clearances'. Many Highland Scots went to the United States and Canada. Up to 25% of Canadians today have Scottish blood lines. Australia got its fair share as well when transportation started in the 1770s and among these, plenty were non-convict settlers in both Australia and New Zealand.

Why is this important? It helps explain why in a country so densely populated as Great Britain that there's such a vast expanse of uninhabited, near-wilderness in the far north.

Opposite Roads are often narrow on the NC500. Note the 'passing place' just before the T-intersection

How long?
Three days would allow you to dwell on the pleasures, but five days would be better.

When to go
May to September will give you the best weather but it gets busy in the summer months. Many of the restaurants and hotels go into hibernation over winter and the roads are often closed by snow.

Need to know
- Be aware that locals are starting to get frustrated by tourists who don't understand the etiquette of 'passing places' on single lane roads - of which there are plenty on the NC500. Neither do they like visitors going too fast or too slow. They like motorcycle visitors, however, because they spend more money in the smaller villages and they don't get in the way on the NC500 route.
- Midgies (small flying insects) are a curse in the summer months and bite without mercy, especially around dawn and dusk. Come prepared and bring repellant.
- Scottish English can sometimes be difficult to comprehend. Scots in the far north will understand your question but you may not understand their answer.

Ride rating
Easy at normal riding speeds.

Distances
- The NC500 has a total distance of 516 miles (830km).

Temperatures
- May: 7°C to 10°C (45°F to 50°F)
- September: 10°C to 13°C (50°F to 55°F)

More information
www.visitscotland.com/places-to-go/inverness

Road warriors

As it was easier to get to the remote villages along the west, north and east coasts of Scotland by boat, the country's road network has historically been patchy. Prior to Culloden, the small number of roads built were mostly for military movements with some of them using building material taken from Hadrian's Wall.

Scottish engineer Thomas Telford (1757–1834) got serious after 1800 and added 900 miles of roads and 120 bridges to make the remote parts of the country more accessible. These roads are still the framework of the current road network.

The North Coast 500 isn't an ancient road in itself but a construct of the Tourism Project Board of the North Highland Initiative. It was launched in March 2015. This doesn't mean the roads aren't old: it's just that they've never been linked like this before and never marketed as a single route. The NC500 is now a 516-mile established track around the north coast of Scotland. It certainly wasn't conceived just for motorcycles but we can take advantage of a truly unique ride that suits bikes far more than any other form of transport.

That's because large sections of it are single lane roads with 'passing places' dotted along their edges. Long sections of

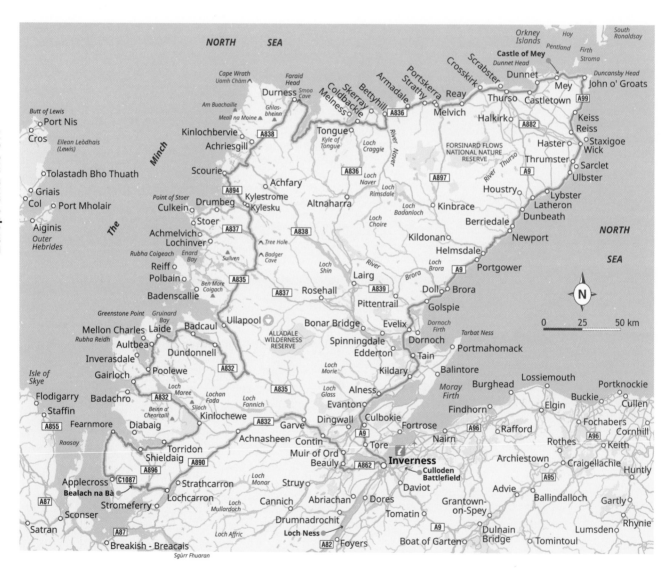

the NC500 won't facilitate overtaking or passing if you're in a motorhome or towing a caravan, or even if you're in a conventional sedan. Motorcycles are thinner and capable of taking small windows of opportunity to overtake.

Inverness

The NC500 starts and finishes from Inverness Castle. **Inverness** (population: 46,984) is the capital of the Highlands and it's worth dropping in at the Visit Scotland iCentre located below the castle for maps and up-to-date information on the NC500 route.

You can fly into Inverness and hire a bike for the trip from a range of bike-hire companies. **NC500MotoExperience** (www.nc500motoexperience.co.uk) is fairly typical with bikes including a BMW F750S for £160 for a single day (reduced to £140 for subsequent days) or £850 for a week. This covers all riding gear including a helmet.

Chances are you'll be riding up from England as part of a bigger trip but you'll end up in Inverness regardless. Twenty minutes past Inverness on the A9 is **Dingwall** (population: 5360), which is a large village convenient to the NC500 route and with less expensive accommodation options than Inverness.

The only big decision you'll have to make is whether to ride the NC500 clockwise or anti-clockwise. You can also choose to ride straight up the middle of the Highlands to Tongue where you'll meet the NC500 route somewhere near its halfway point. You experience more of the real Highlands this way and get a better sense of how remote they really are. It's possible in the 38 miles between Lairg and Tongue that you won't see another vehicle.

The majority of travellers take the clockwise route and one advantage of this is that most of the traffic is heading in the same direction.

Heading west

The formal NC500 route heads west out of Inverness on the A862, turns right at Beauly and veers left at the Muir of Ord. It's possible to get lost on the NC500 but, generally, it's very well signed. Make note of the villages along the route as they'll be signposted as well. Once past Muir of Ord, head towards Garve, then follow the A832 to Achnasheen where you'll turn left onto the A890 to Lochcarron. Turn right soon after on the A896 and follow the signs to Applecross. It's also well signposted as part of the NC500 route.

You're not going to Applecross for the nightlife. You're going because the route takes you over the legendary **Bealach na Bà**. This is one of the best riding experiences of the whole NC500. You climb to 626m in short order along a snake road with plenty of hairpin turns and great views. This road was made in 1822 but didn't get a bitumen topping until 1955. It's marked as being not suitable for motorhomes, caravans, buses and big trucks, so here you'll get some relief from traffic on, admittedly, a narrow and potentially dangerous road. Superb fun on a motorcycle, though.

Around Inverness

If you have additional time after your NC500 ride, there are plenty of other interesting short rides from Inverness.

Two of particular interest are the Culloden battlefield and Loch Ness (yes, *that* Loch Ness!)

The Culloden battlefield is only 6 miles from Inverness Castle and is well signposted. Turn left on Old Edinburgh Rd, which becomes Old Perth Rd after a roundabout and then Old Culloden Rd after another roundabout.

The battlefield area has been returned to how it would have looked in 1745 when 5000 Jacobite Highlanders faced off against 9000 government troops. The Jacobites, many of them Scottish Highlanders, were soundly beaten and the repercussions of this are still being felt in Scotland today.

A highlight of the visitor centre at the battleground is an auditorium experience where all four walls are used to recreate what the battle would have felt like for the soldiers. There's no voice-over and the images are graphic, but so would have been the battle.

A walk around the moor area reveals burial sites of the clans involved, with flags marking various military positions. You'll understand it better after you've seen the battlefield exhibition in the visitor centre.

Loch Ness is around 20 miles south of Inverness Castle on the A82. It is the second largest loch in Scotland by surface area but because of its 755ft depth (230m), it has the highest volume of water.

There are nine villages around the loch with the village of **Drumnadrochit** housing a 'Loch Ness Centre and Exhibition', with information about the legendary Loch Ness monster.

Loch Ness is perfectly constructed to sustain the monster narrative. Along with its depth, the water visibility is very low because of the high peat content of the surrounding soil. You can't see into the water and it's very deep - of course a monster lives at the bottom of it.

Depending on the season in which you do it (it's often closed in winter), you'll find some travellers who didn't read the signs and block the pass with large motorhomes or caravans. It's a narrow road and, if drivers get it wrong, there are often interruptions where reversing to lay-bys will hold you up. It's not an altogether bad thing, though. The views here are spectacular.

Issues if you don't stay on the narrow road include steep slopes along the road's edges. Some of the turns are tight enough for a first-gear crawl and you should be pleased with yourself if you make it to the top viewpoint without occasionally having to put your foot down on the road. The descent is just as awe-provoking as the ride up.

Applecross (population: 544) is remote. Apart from one road in and one road out, the only access is by sea. In fact, this part of the coast road that leads to Shieldaig wasn't completed until 1976. Applecross does have a pub, a few shops and a campground and is full of Highlands hospitality. The coast road from there to Shieldaig is a single track and it's sometimes difficult to remind yourself you're actually in the UK. William Wallace might still be out there somewhere. **Fearnmore**, which you'll pass through, may be the most remote village you've ever seen.

You're now heading to Gairloch after turning left when you get to Kinlochewe on the A832. **Gairloch** (population: 620) is another western Scotland community that has traditionally only been accessible by sea. Cod and haddock fishing kept it alive but the fishing boats now land lobsters, prawns and crabs, which you can buy fresh and local. You can also access boat tours to greet an array of marine life including whales. The route along Loch Maree is some of the best scenery in Scotland.

From Gairloch, the one major road is signposted to **Ullapool** (population: 1500), the dominant settlement in the northwest area. It's been there possibly forever and shows up on maps from the 1500s but the current iteration was designed by the aforementioned Thomas Telford in 1788 to support herring fishing. It's also currently a terminal for the Stornoway ferry and, courtesy of its harbour, it's a favourite of yachts, smaller cruise ships and tour boats. The infrastructure in the town ensures great seafood dining with it being well known as a fish and chips destination. It's a reassuring stop on the NC500 in that it feels like civilisation.

While you can stay on the A837 to Kylesku, the NC500 loop via Lochinver is worth taking, again, just for the seafood at the port. You'll also see a wrecking yard full of (mostly) cars that have come to grief on the NC500. It's a reminder that you have to concentrate. The route will take you to Kylestrome and, from there, you'll head up towards Durness on an inland route that

will give you plenty of time to reflect on what 'remoteness' feels like and how single lane roads with 'passing places' should work.

Road etiquette

'Passing places' are paved, off-road sections of a single lane road where you can pull over and allow oncoming traffic or traffic behind to pass safely. The locals are experts and pass seamlessly by each other by intuitively knowing when and where they should use the passing places. The NC500 has become very popular over the past 15 years, meaning it's often crowded with visitors in large vehicles who don't understand how the system works. It's frustrating for riders and locals alike. Even though the roads are often single lane, there's plenty of space for bikes and local cars to overtake or pass. This route was made for motorcycles. Etiquette demands if you see someone behind you travelling faster than you, pull over and let them pass. Similarly, if someone is approaching you, look for a passing place to allow them through. The road from Kylesku to Durness twists so much in the mountains that it's difficult for even bikes to pass larger vehicles safely. If you're riding, come to terms with occasional frustration.

During 2016, the first full year of the official NC500, deaths and serious injuries increased by 45%. You need to take the route seriously.

The far north

By the time you've arrived at Durness, there'll be a certain sameishness from there to Thurso, but if you've got plenty of time, there's much to see and do. The villages are smaller and more remote but that's because they're on the very tip of Great Britain and you should expect them to be less developed. Nature has sculptured the coast with deep sea lochs including the Kyle of Tongue where, if you're running short of time, you could turn right for a Highland gallop back to Inverness. The wildness of the north coast changes a bit as you head towards **John O'Groats**, which has the flavour of a conventional tourist town.

On the way from Thurso it's worth calling into the **Castle of Mey**. It has a rich and interesting history but is famous because it was bought by Queen Elizabeth II's mother in 1952 and restored to something like its former glory. There are conflicted views on British royalty but it's hard not to like the Queen Mother. When Rover decided to stop producing its P5 model (upper class, but still relatively modest), the Queen Mother bought enough P5s to see her through her lifetime. No Rollers for her.

Top The route starts and ends at Inverness *Bottom* Bealach na Ba is one of the best riding experiences on the route

On the NC500 to Wick, keep an eye out for brochs on the coast. These are Iron Age roundhouses found only in Scotland and date from between 600BCE to AD100. Most are ruins but all are deliberately situated with good surveillance views of the coast. There's a preserved example at **Dunbeath**, along with plenty of ruined medieval castles and crofts.

After Brora, civilisation starts to reassert itself as the NC500 heads back towards Inverness and the villages become more frequent. On this section you'll be crossing a number of firths, coastal inlets that tend to be long without being very wide. If you were in Scandinavia, they'd be called fjords. Civilisation builds progressively until you find yourself once again outside Inverness Castle.

Do it sooner rather than later

While the development of the NC500 has unquestionably brought more tourists to the remote Scottish Highlands, not all the locals are happy. Their previously deserted roads are now being damaged by convoys of rental campervans and the visitors are spending their money in the larger towns rather than, as originally planned, in the charming smaller villages. Worse yet, in peak holiday season, insensitive visitors without knowledge of passing etiquette are hugely increasing travel times for the locals. The other side of the coin is drivers who travel too fast; many locals say the route should be renamed the 'Indy 500'.

As it increasingly becomes a victim of its own success, some restrictions in use in the future would seem inevitable. The shame of it for motorcyclists is that we are genuinely welcomed. We spend more time in smaller towns because there's a limit to what we can carry and we don't block up the roads – a car and a motorcycle can overtake and pass safely even on the narrowest piece of bitumen.

There's a thought for the North Highland Initiative: Scotland's NC500 – locals and motorcycles only!

Being there

Scotland has wrestled with independence for centuries. Sometimes it won, sometimes it didn't. The 1706 Union with Scotland Act was one of the motivations for the attempts to return Scottish royalty to the English throne, which ended with the Battle of Culloden, the last pitched battle on English soil.

There was a Scottish independence referendum in 2014 in which 1,617,989 Scots said 'yes' and 2,001,926 said 'no'. Case closed? Not quite.

With Brexit in 2016, Britain decided to leave the European Union (EU) which outraged the Scots. When you're a stranger in a strange land, you need to find some talking points to get the conversation going in pubs and around campfires at night. While I was there we covered the weather and I immediately moved it on to Brexit.

On the NC500 route, most businesses I spoke with said that if they'd known about Brexit, they would have voted 'yes' to independence so that Scotland could have remained in the EU.

I've spent time in Wales and that proud group would love to be independent but they understand they don't have an economy to support it. Arguably, Scotland does.

Scotland tried to have a new referendum in 2022 but it now relies on the permission of the British Parliament. But from the information I could gather first-hand, Scotland would like to remain in the EU.

If you're on the NC500 ride and you're stuck in a pub due to bad weather, just raise Scottish independence as a topic and sit back and relax. Everyone else will do the talking for you.

BEST EATS

Seafood Shack, Ullapool
Fresh, local seafood cooked to order from a catering trailer with outdoor seating. The menu changes daily depending on what the local fishing boats have caught. Open seven days from midday to 6pm in the summer seasons.
www.seafoodshack.co.uk

Ben Loyal Hotel, Tongue
Not only will you get great views across the Kyle of Tongue but here the kitchen uses local produce and Tongue oysters are always on the menu. Venison with plum and juniper compote is also popular. The restaurant is open from April to the end of October from 6pm to 8.30pm.
www.benloyal.co.uk

The Cabin, John O'Groats
This is the most northern takeaway on the mainland. The fish and chips, burgers and rolls are great value for money. Seating is outdoors with views. It's open from 11am to 6pm but closed on Fridays, and like most places, in winter too.
John O'Groats Harbour, Wick; +44 1955611400

Batty's Baps Sandwich Bar, Dingwall
Here's a chance to explore Scottish delicacies including haggis, black pudding, white pudding, tattie scones and local, skinless sausages. It's a friendly eatery with very reasonable prices. Open for breakfast and late lunch.
www.battysbaps.co.uk

BEST SLEEPS

Inverness Youth Hostel, Inverness
This (relatively) inexpensive youth hostel is located just a short walk from the city centre and has private en-suite rooms as well as spacious, shared accommodation. Your bike will be safe and you'll be close to where all the action is. It's another reason why you should join Hostelling International (HI).
www.hihostels.com/hostels/inverness-youth-hostel

Ben Loyal Hotel, Tongue
Tongue is about half way around the NC500 loop and Ben Loyal has self-contained pods for riders who want to stay the night. These have a king-size bed and their own bathroom, all within stumbling distance to the best food in Tongue.
www.benloyal.co.uk

The Crofters Snug, John O'Groats
This accommodation actually says 'bikers welcome'. It's 6 miles west of John O'Groats and has pods, with one offering specal appeal: Sheperd's Hut, which sleeps two in a king-size bed and has an en-suite along with a log-burning cooking stove. From April to October it has a two-nights minimum but there are plenty of attractions in the area.
www.thecrofterssnug.co.uk

Top Ardvreck Castle ruins at Loch Assynet *Bottom* A beach at Durness which has a zipline crossing for the adventurous *Opposite* The lonely highlands road from Lairg to Tongue

Five Passes: Switzerland

This route is a tasting plate for the riding glory of the European Alps. They're 1200km long separating the Mediterranean states from the rest of Europe and are arguably the home of the best rides in the world.

SNAPSHOT

There are eight passes in the Andermatt region and here we cover five of the best for riders. Don't let the constant exposure to beautiful mountains and valleys distract you from the amazing roads.

It's a collection of passes that will show you what the rest of the Alps has to offer and confirm your new desire to explore them all.

Enjoy the corners, enjoy the mountain environment and enjoy the villages you'll stay in afterwards.

The European Alps: up, up, up, up, up; down, down, down, down, down. Repeat 88 times. Weather permitting, you could spend months here exploring myriad passes without doing the same one twice. It's arguably the epicentre of motorcycle riding joy and feels like it was designed specifically by some revhead deity who knew in advance that, one day, motorcycles would be invented and used for this pleasure.

The mountain range comprising the Alps is 1200km long (750 miles) and stretches across France, Switzerland, Monaco, Italy, Liechtenstein, Austria, Germany and Slovenia. The routes across the mountains (the passes) were developed partly to help the Romans in their military conquests but also to facilitate trade. Most were only usable by pack animals until well into the 19th century, and were important in linking northern and southern Europe.

If you accidentally pass through a time portal while you're out riding and you find yourself in the Alps in the early 1900s, make sure you're on a trail bike! But thanks to the development of large-scale road paving from the beginning of last century, particularly paving using asphalt and utilising the Scottish process of John McAdam (a raised centre to allow water to run off), access to the Alps opened right up.

How long?
One day for the ride but three days to savour the experience.

When to go
June to October, although it's warmest in July.

Need to know
- Be prepared for sudden changes in grip. The road surfaces are generally good but lots of snow in winter takes its toll and degrades the road surface on a regular basis throughout the year. The older passes, including Furka, have good repairs.
- A combination of new freeways and tunnels bypassing the main routes means far less traffic, so it's largely left to motorcyclists to enjoy.
- Fuel can be irregular so fill up in advance.
- The passes are usually only open for the period June to early October.

Ride rating
Easy for touring; intermediate for spirited riding; and advanced for scratching.

Distances
- 230km (143 miles)

Temperatures
- May: 4°C to 10°C (39°F to 50°F)
- July: 10°C to 17°C (50°F to 63°F)
- September: 8°C to 14°C (46°F to 57°F)

More information
www.andermatt.swiss/en

Opposite Alps roads twist and turn to keep the gradient to a minimum which makes it perfect for motorcycling

An Alps taster

There's a route in Switzerland where five passes are linked and can be explored in one day's riding. There's not much else like it in the Alps and it provides an excellent introduction to what else is in store for you in the famous mountain range.

The passes are the Grimsel, Susten, Nufenen, St Gotthard and Furka.

Being at the centre of the St Gotthard Mountains, the village of **Andermatt** (population: 1600) makes for a convenient starting point. Because of this, however, accommodation tends to be a little more expensive compared to the surrounding areas. Most people speak German here, and it has a rich history where its fortunes have waxed and waned over the centuries. Like the national flag, it lies almost at the centre cross of Switzerland – from north to south and from east to west – and all the services you might want are here.

The five passes are linked in a rough figure eight, so to ride them all and end up from where you started requires you to complete one pass twice. Don't fret: the Furka Pass is a completely different experience if you ride it both ways, so aim to make this the pass you ride twice.

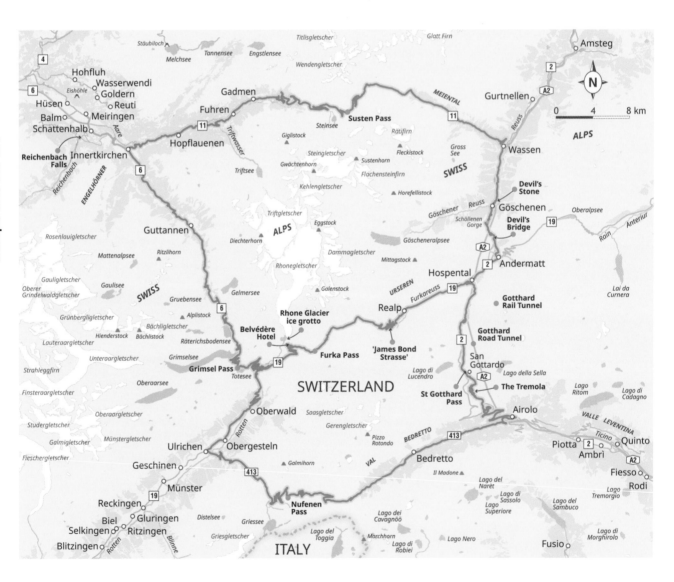

Above The abandoned Furka Pass Belvedere Hotel which featured in the James Bond movie, *Goldfinger*

All the pass roads have this in common: cars and trucks can't climb vertically so the roads twist and turn to allow traffic to not be too stressed in climbing and descending. For bike, it means constant corners, many of them tight.

The **Furka Pass** (elevation 2429m) has a very good road surface but as it's the second highest pass in the region it's affected by winter weather and is arguably the pass with the most variations in road conditions. A combination of snow, wind and rain attack the road surface so it requires frequent maintenance resulting in irregularities in the road surface.

Head out from Andermatt on Hwy 2 and turn right at the Hospental roundabout (signposted 19) to Brig to access the Furka Pass proper. Now start climbing and take a little time to enjoy the Alps scenery.

You may be bemused to pass a spot called 'James Bond Strasse', where some of *Goldfinger* was filmed. It was a scene where Bond in his Aston Martin DB5 races Tilly Masterson in her Mustang and James eventually uses one of the many DB5 accessories to blow her car's tyres out. You'll appreciate the poetic license of this when you experience how narrow the road actually is. Also on the Furka Pass is the now-closed Belvedere Hotel, which also featured in the film. Here you can park your bike and walk 200m to visit the **Rhone Glacier ice grotto**, a 100m-long tunnel re-drilled every year that will beguile riders with its mystical shades of blue. See it soon, however, as global warming is progressively shrinking the glacier.

The peak of the Furka Pass is a bit misleading in that there's a hotel and parking area where you think it might be, but it's actually just a little bit farther on. The hotel initially looks shabby in summer, which is an indication of just how severe winter is in this area and how damaging it can be to infrastructure. If you arrive around lunchtime, the goulash is highly recommended.

Most riders find ascending more comfortable than going down, as gravity helps you wash off speed rather than having to rely on braking. The Five Passes ride makes you practice both. There's not much traffic (apart from other bikes) on the Furka Pass as its 11% gradient climb and descent discourages trucks and buses. The road is also very open so you can plan passing manoeuvres with confidence. If it's your first time on an Alps pass, you'll be shocked when you arrive at Ulrichen still on the 19 and realise there are another four passes to go.

The left turn at Ulrichen will be signposted to Nufenen and Airolo and is hard to miss. You'll start climbing again on the Nufenen Pass.

The road to Airolo

The **Nufenen Pass** (elevation 2478m) is the best road surface along the Five Passes, and that's courtesy of it only being open to bikes and cars since 1969. As is the case with all the passes, the scenery is spectacular, but in terms of riding, it's almost too good. It's the highest mountain pass with a paved road in Switzerland and if you like clean and neat, you'll love it.

As with all of the passes along this route, there's a cafe-restaurant-bar at the top, and the views from the car park area are excellent.

The Nufenen Pass also has little traffic in summer so it's a relatively safe place to explore the outer edges of your bike's tyres, but the descent from the summit is severe so it's possible to arrive at corners sooner than you think. Be warned.

Airolo (population: 1501), where you'll arrive at the end of the Nufenen Pass, is a surprise town in that it hosts a variety of road and rail tunnels that have relieved traffic on the Saint Gotthard Pass and made it attractive again for car and bike tourists. These tunnels through the Alps are amazing engineering feats that have radically shortened travel time for businesses, while, at the same time, taken heavy traffic off the passes. Each tunnel claimed to be the world's longest at the time of its construction, starting with the Gotthard Rail Tunnel in 1882, the Gotthard Road Tunnel in 1980 and the relatively recent Gotthard Base Tunnel, completed in 2016.

To get a glimpse of how it was trying to cross the Gotthard Pass back in the day, check out Curbside Classic's 'Gotthard pass 1963 to 1965' on YouTube to see how busy it was prior to the tunnels. Take note of the insane passing moves to get by Citroen 2CVs, Fiat 500s and Volkswagon Kombis.

Opposite top A drinks break on the Furka Pass near the old Belvedere Hotel *Opposite bottom* Riding the Tremola between Airola and San Gottardo

Museo Nazionale del San Gottardo

You wouldn't expect to find a museum of this quality in San Gottardo but it's well worth a stop along the Tremola from Airola to get some background of this area you're experiencing as you ride the Five Passes.

The museum (www.museonazionalesangottardo.ch) is spread over. spread over a number of displays and includes great vintage film of what it was like to try and cross the passes before tunnels were introduced. Among its permanent rooms is a brief history of the area, covering from around the year 1200 before focusing on the technology that has largely made the passes redundant to commercial operators and tourists - liberating the roads for motorcyclists, as if made just for us.

The museum has a restaurant but otherwise there are food vans offering an array of local street food.

Gotthard glory

You have a variety of options to leave Airolo to get back to Hospental, Andermatt and the Susten Pass route: a motorway, a highway or most memorable of all, the Tremola – an amazing, hand-laid cobblestone road that constantly reminds you of the varied history of transport in the Alps.

The **Tremola** climbs from Airolo to San Gottardo to join the **Saint Gotthard Pass** (elevation 2106m) route back to Hospental. You can also do it via the two other aforementioned routes but the Tremola is a once-in-a-lifetime experience. Despite its impracticality as a road surface (cobblestone blocks of granite), it's still maintained in its original build format and is a unique, if slow climb. Follow the green signs for 'Passo San Gottardo' that will take you along Hwy 2 until you leave it on a slip-road, which takes you under Hwy 2 and onto the Tremola. You'll be able to rejoin the highway when the Tremolo finishes.

The Tremola is heavily used by local farmers so it's a slow trip. Livestock movement is common, so you need to watch out for that as well, all while remembering that stone blocks aren't as grippy a surface as asphalt. It's a rare treat, though. Make a note of the rainbow spread of the rocks and ponder how that was devised and achieved without the aid of computers.

The end of the Tremola is **San Gottardo**, a small village, which as well as offering some good hotels and restaurants, it has the excellent Museo Nazionale del San Gottardo (*see above*), a worthwhile stop to give you a good idea of both the environment and the history of this area you're riding.

From San Gottardo back to Hospental, Andermatt and on to the Susten Pass is another great ride along very good road surfaces. By now, you'll have become used to Alps scenery but you'll never get tired of the road – sweeping corners, switchbacks and unending curves to keep you ride-fit.

Susten Pass

Stay on Hwy 2 through Andermatt for a further 6.6km where a treat awaits at **Goschenen** (population: 448): the Devil's Stone and the Devil's Bridge. According to local tales, citizens of Goschenen in the 13th century asked the devil to build a bridge across the River Reuss, which was at the bottom of the Schöllenen Gorge. The devil agreed on the condition that the first soul that crossed the bridge would be his. When the job was completed, the locals sent a goat across. Outraged, the devil flung it into the Reuss and followed it to get a rock big enough to destroy the bridge. He had a rest on the way back and a nun sat beside him and carved a cross on the rock, meaning the devil couldn't touch it again. As a result of all this, the bridge is still there and so is the rock. It all sounds believable.

If you want some exercise, the bridge is only a 30-minute walk from Andermatt station. After this bypass, return to Hwy 2 and turn left onto Hwy 11 when you get to Wassen. The road will be signposted to Innertkirchen and Meiringen

Susten Pass (elevation 2260m) was built from 1938 to 1945 and is notable for its 300m-long tunnel near its highest point. There's also a good restaurant by the tunnel if you feel like a break from the constant cornering.

When you get to Innertkirchen, a left turn onto Hwy 6 will take you to the last of the five passes: Grimsel. You may be tempted though to continue 6km straight ahead to the resort town of **Meiringen** (population: 4621) where you can take a cable car to enjoy spectacular views of the Alps. The equally spectacular Reichenbach Falls are also located there. As you'll be constantly reminded, (warning: spoiler alert), these are the falls where Sherlock Holmes fatally finished his career. Another option is to park your bike at Innertkirchen station and take the scenic rail trip to Meiringen – a memorable ride with scenery through the train's massive windows.

Highway 6 takes you directly to the **Grimsel Pass** (elevation 2164m), which is as much fun as the other four and also has a welcoming restaurant at its peak. Look out for the motorcycle art in the middle of the road.

After the steep descent, take a left turn at the hotel that will take you once again over the Furka Pass and back to Andermatt.

By this time you'll have covered 230km of climbs and descents, most of which features corners. It will have taken you four hours or so, stops notwithstanding. You'll probably feel like a rest after that but if you do the same trip the next day, it will feel fresh and new again. It's the magic of the mountains.

Being there

The Swiss are neat, orderly people. I'm not sure how they do it but it's probably the cleanest country in the world. There's no roadside litter and, well, everything is organised.

Foolishly, I rode there once in winter and got trapped in a hotel by a snowstorm. I'd arrived late and parked my bike where I thought it would be out of the way but all the buildings near the hotel were covered in snow and there were few obvious parking spots.

I ambled out the hotel the following morning after what I thought was a well-deserved sleep to discover I'd parked in front of the garage door of one of the local residents. He'd been waiting for two hours for me to move the bike so he could get his car out to go to work and was apoplectic.

He screamed at me in German for about three minutes before I could try to tell him I didn't understand a word he was saying, but that just made it worse. The veins on his forehead were at bursting point and, had I not been twice his size, I'm sure he would have tried to extract physical revenge.

It got worse. I couldn't stop him shouting at me but the situation became so comical I got the giggles. I thought he was going to have a heart attack. So if you're reading this, my upset Swiss comrade, please accept my apologies!

BEST EATS

Artist Restaurant, Furkablick, near Furka Pass

This might not be your standard restaurant experience. It's the only game in town, though, near the top of the Furka Pass and the food is excellent. The goulash is recommended. The hosts are wonderful and the view from the elevated, outdoor deck is the stuff of dreams.

It's near the top of Furka Pass. Seriously, you can't miss it. If you agree, your 'reading' will be recorded and become part of the art project. Fame at last!
www.furkablick.com

Berggasthaus Susten Pass Hospiz, Wassen

This beautiful wooden building is located just after the tunnel at the top of the Susten Pass. It provides good regional food, drinks and accommodation. It's very motorcycle-friendly with

Above The view from the verandah of the Artist Restaurant, Furkablick, on the Furka Pass

specific parking for bikes. It goes without saying that the views are spectacular.
www.sustenpass-hospiz.ch

Grimsel Pass Hotel
This is a bit flash but if you can make it to the breakfast buffet (7.30am to 10.30am) you probably won't have to eat for the next 24 hours. Choose from various local cheeses, meats, yoghurt, muesli, fruits, honey, homemade jams, egg dishes (freshly cooked to order), regional breads and juices. There's accommodation as well with an extensive evening menu.
www.hotel-grimselpass.ch

BEST SLEEPS

Hotel des Alpes, Airolo
A nice, clean hotel in the middle of Airolo with its own restaurant and pizzeria, and close to many other dining options. It's popular with bikers riding the Five Passes, and you can park your bike at the entrance, which is off the road and relatively secure. Be careful if you're booking online as there are four 'Hotel des Alpes' in the area and it's easy to get them confused.
www.hoteldesalpes.com; 123 West Grant Ave

Gotthardbackpacker, Wassen
Great building in a beautiful village on the Five Passes route. Dorm beds for €35 and double rooms for €100. There's a self-catering kitchen but otherwise there's both a restaurant and supermarket 150m away. Secure bike parking. Beautiful.
www.gotthardbackpacker.ch

Hotel-Restaurant Alpina, Innertkirchen
The Hotel Alpina is on the road to the Susten and Grimsel passes. It's traditional Swiss-style and the rooms have satellite TV and wi-fi. The bathroom facilities are shared, so this is a more affordable option to others. It has a pub and a restaurant where you'll find both fondue and game meats on the menu.
www.alpina-ritzli.ch/hotel_restaurant

The Mountain Course: Isle of Man

Here's your chance to join motorcycling's Immortals — you're going to ride the Mountain Course on the Isle of Man.

SNAPSHOT

The Isle of Man (IoM) is the spiritual home of motorcycling as well as being a fascinating ride destination in its own right. We're going there to ride (at much slower speeds) the same 37.7-mile Tourist Trophy (TT) Course used by road racers from 1911 to today, but there's plenty more to see and do outside of racing.

If you take your own bike the scenic four-hour ferry ride here is in itself a highlight.

If motorcycling has a spiritual home, it's a small island in the middle of the northern Irish Sea.

Isle of Man tells a very big story. There's evidence of human occupation as far back as 6500BCE and its storied past has seen it being fought over by the British, the Romans, the Irish, the Scots and the Vikings.

 How long?

A week would allow you to do justice to the IoM's many charms but you could ride the TT Course a couple of times and still be able to explore the isle's highlights in as little as three days.

 When to go

The warmest and driest months on the IoM are from early April to late September. The dates when motorcycle racing are on - late May to early June, and late August - see the isle flooded with visitors as accommodation and hospitality resources are pushed to the limits. It's the most expensive time to visit but also the most exciting. Visiting the IoM outside race periods will allow you to ride uninterrupted laps of the TT Course and save a few quid at the same time.

 Need to know

- Ride on the left-hand side of the road.
- The IoM has its own currency but accepts British pounds and euros. Try not to take too much IoM currency with you when you leave as exchanging it anywhere else but in Great Britain can be difficult.

The Vikings established a parliament called Tynwald there towards the end of the 9th century, making the IoM the place with the oldest continuously governing body in the world.

Some joke that motorcycle racing commenced the very moment the second motorcycle was built. But 1905 was the year when the IoM formalised motorcycle racing, and 1907 was when the TT was run for the first time. England at the time had a blanket speed limit of 20mph (32km/h) but the Tynwald wasn't so conservative and welcomed motorcycle racers from around the world. The TT has run there almost continuously since and hence the IoM is regarded as the world capital of road racing.

'Road racing' means just what it sounds like: racing on public roads. For most of the year, the 37.7 mile-long Snaefell Mountain Course, on which the TT is run, is just part of the IoM road infrastructure and is used by farmers, delivery vehicles and locals going about their business. During the two-week TT period, usually late May and early June, the road is closed off every second day for practice and racing. You'd think the 80,000 locals would hate the disruption but it's quite the reverse: most of them line the course as spectators during the racing and small-talk in the shops and pubs is usually about which rider has set the fastest time.

Racing on the IoM is almost as old as motorcycling itself and the values it has demonstrated continuously for over the past century are the values woven into the genetic framework of all riders. Muslims go to Mecca, Catholics go to Rome and bone-deep motorcyclists go to the Isle of Man.

- If you intend to hire a motorcycle, plan well in advance as hire stocks are limited.
- Watch out for livestock on the isle's rural roads, which can appear when you least expect it.
- Be prepared for a little rain. In August, for example, it rains on average for 14 days although it tends to be patchy. The locals say that 'the fierce winds that plague the isle keep the clouds moving'. Take some warm clothes.

 Ride rating
The TT Course is easy in most sections but moderate in some of the climbing areas, including the climb up Snaefell Mountain. It's used as a public road when racing isn't happening. Racers will tell you it's off the ratings chart and terrifying at nearly 200mph (322km/h).

 Distances
- The IoM is just 32 miles (52km) long and 13.5 miles (22km) wide so everything is easy to get to.
- The TT Course that you're going there to ride is a 37.7 mile (60.7km) circuit and takes 1.5 hours to complete.

 Temperatures
- January: 5°C to 8°C (41°F to 46°F)
- July: 13°C to 19°C (55°F to 66°F)

 More information
The Isle of Man Welcome Centre (www.gov.im/welcomecentre) is located at the sea terminal in the capital Douglas, and is a font for all tourism wisdom.

Left When racing isn't taking place, the Mountain Course on the Isle of Man is open to the public

Legend of the mountain

When you ride the Snaefell Mountain Course, you won't be racing. But you will be riding the exact 37.7 mile route used by the legendary racers. If you start from the actual race start/finish line, you'll pass through many villages on your way up to Ramsey near the top of the IoM where you'll start the climb up to Snaefell Mountain's 620m peak. Once up there, you'll cruise along the top of the range before descending past Governor's Bridge to the finish line and pit area.

Traffic willing, the journey will take about 1.5 hours. You will have enjoyed the scenery but mostly you'll be consumed by shock and awe that anyone races there at all. The best racers can lap the circuit in under 17 minutes.

Riding the waves

The IoM is situated in the Irish Sea almost equidistant from England, Northern Ireland and Scotland. If coming from England, and you have your own bike, you will probably take advantage of regular ferry departures from Liverpool and Heysham on the west coast. The ferry services are run by the IoM Steam Packet Company (popularly referred to by the locals as the 'Steam Racket Company' due to increased fare prices around the TT weeks).

It's a very entertaining four-hour journey and, with your bike secured in the hold, it gives you a chance to introduce yourself to Manx ale in the upstairs bars all while taking in the ocean scenery and checking out the souvenir shops.

If you're on foot, fast ferries run from Liverpool and if your intention is to hire a bike on the IoM (*see* Motorcycle Hire), you can also fly into the IoM airport located at Ronaldsway.

Once on the island, the Manx bus service is extensive and will take you just about anywhere. The routes wind around the small villages so progress can be indirect and slow, although there's always something to see out the windows.

For an adventure, Douglas to Port Erin in the south is serviced by a steam railway built in 1874, which remarkably still uses the engines and carriages dating from that time.

Timing is everything

Whether you decide on the peace and quiet of visiting during non-race periods or the spectacle and glamour of racing, you'll still get to ride the Snaefell Mountain Course. The best time to visit the IoM is between April and August and it's a beautiful place even without the racing. It's also considerably cheaper without the racing with vastly improved access to all IoM's

charms and facilities. The most exciting time to go, though, is either during the TT fortnight (late May/early June) or during the equally impressive Festival of Motorcycling (Manx GP and Classic TT) usually held in the last two weeks of August.

The population of the IoM swells by around 20,000 during these events and costs jump accordingly, but the company of an army of like-minded visitors and plenty of entertainment is an intoxicating mix. There's nothing else like it in the world.

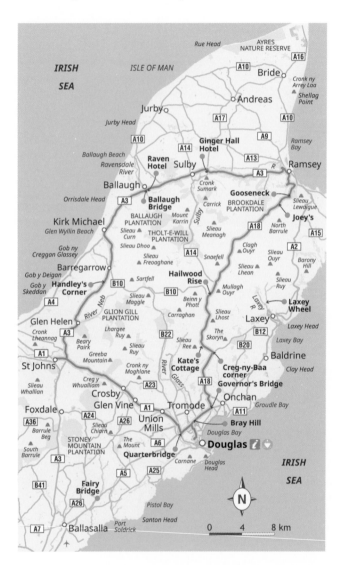

Opposite top That chariot is actually attached to a motorcycle - it's a sidecar *Opposite bottom* The Creek Inn at Peel is a very popular lunch and dinner spot for visiting riders. Try its seafood platter

Above The fairytale main street of the IoM capital, Douglas *Opposite* The lighthouse on the northern tip of the Isle

Where champions roll

MotoGP riders who visit the IoM - including world champs Valentino Rossi and Mick Doohan - are extremely respectful of the road-race fraternity. Joey Dunlop's untimely death in 2000 (at a circuit in Estonia where he was leading a 125cc race) robbed road-racing of a genuine star but others, including Joey's nephew Michael Dunlop, have risen to the challenge.

To give you an idea of what's involved, here's Australian TT champion Cameron Donald's outline of his 'normal' TT week:

For me, it involved 16 laps of practice and 25 laps of racing around a 60.7km circuit with more than 250 turns per lap on closed public roads. That works out at 2488km of riding three different motorcycles through approximately 10,250 turns all at an average speed of over 200km/h.

The TT was originally a round of motorcycling's World Championship that started in 1949 but it lost this status in 1976 as a number of prominent riders believed the course to be too dangerous. Given the speed of modern bikes and the impossibility of protecting riders in the event of crashes, they were probably right.

Racing on the IoM has survived as the world's most prominent road-race meeting and its heroes are a roll call of the world's best: Geoff Duke, John Surtees, Mike Hailwood, Giacomo Agostini, Phil Read and John McGuinness, just as a sample.

You'll still be able to ride the Snaefell Mountain Course but you'll have a lot more company. There's a tradition called 'Mad Sunday' that takes place on the first Sunday of race week. It has a significant element of craziness about it because the population has peaked and there's no racing on the Mountain Course, meaning visitors can ride it and get a real sense of what the racers experience.

The less-populated area of the circuit, the section across the mountain, has no speed limits and is designated for one-way traffic. Think of it as a motorcycle production race with 10,000 entrants of varying ability. The police close the circuit to clean it up every time there's a significant crash, which means riders bunch up at Ramsay in the pubs and garage forecourts. When the road opens again, everyone races to the next crash.

Start your engines

Before you start to explore the rest of the isle, you should get a lap of the TT course under your belt.

From Douglas, ride along the foreshore to the south and turn right at the Quarterbridge Hotel. This will take you up Bray Hill to the racing pit area and start/finish line. Tellingly, this is located opposite a cemetery where a large number of the 280 riders and spectators who've died are buried since the Mountain Course was first used in 1911.

Because it's a street circuit, it runs through villages where stone houses are built right up to the road's edge and stone fences line most of the rest of the course. It's a very unforgiving route on which to crash. The IoM's worst year was 2005 when nine riders were killed, along with one spectator and one race marshal. Since 1937 the only year when races were held without a fatality was in 1982 so it's an event only for the most daring of riders.

Because you're not racing (unless you're here for Mad Sunday), the road will seem like a safe, scenic tour. But it's easy to imagine how unsafe it must feel at 185mph.

The TT is held in a clockwise direction so set off down Bray Hill and this time turn right at Quarterbridge. It's hard to get lost on the route as it's marked by milestones – 37 of them from start to finish. Some of them (Crosby, Glen Helen, Ballaugh Bridge etc) are named for the villages the course passes through but there are also a few commemorating famous racers, all legends and past competitors including 'Joey's' after Joey Dunlop 'Handley's Corner' for Wal Handley and Hailwood Rise in tribute to Mike Hailwood.

The first section of the course, which includes the villages of Union Mills, Crosby and St John's, is relatively heavily populated. Hence, understandably, there are posted speed limits in urban areas and these are enforced. When you slide right at St John's and head up towards Ramsay, civilisation thins out slightly and agriculture takes over. You'll find yourself riding through fields and villages including Glen Helen, Barregarrow, Kirk Michael and Ballaugh.

When you get to Ballaugh you'll find a hump in the road at Ballaugh Bridge over the Ravensdale river. During racing events, the riders regularly get air there and if you make an effort you'll get a bit of hang time as well. A good place to watch the racing is the Raven Hotel just past the hump.

The road starts to straighten out after Ballaugh and there's a speed trap on the way to Sulby that is used during racing because it's possible to ride flat-out here to record top speeds. James Hillier has the current record of 206mph recorded in 2015 on a Kawasaki H2R.

In this area, the Ginger Hall Hotel is worth a visit. It's a good source of inexpensive accommodation and it's right on the TT course but the bikes pass here so quickly it's difficult to see them.

Ramsey (population: 7845) is the second largest town on the IoM and makes a nice place to stop for a break with plenty of restaurants and accommodation with pleasant views of the Irish Sea. You'll turn right here and head just out of town for

Motorcycle hire

If you're only able to visit the IoM for a short time, say a couple of days, hiring a motorcycle on the Isle makes more sense than taking your own bike. Among a handful of rental companies, **Isle of Man Motorcycle Adventures** (www.motorcycleadventures.im) is based near the TT grandstand and start/finish line.

Here you'll have a choice of seven different bike brands available for hire, and range from the relatively inexpensive Honda CB500F (£175 a day) through to the more expensive Honda CBF1000 or Suzuki 1250S Bandit. Among the more attractive options is the Honda XL700 Transalp (£185 per day), a great, all-purpose bike very suited to the IoM roads. Discounted prices apply for longer-term rentals; if you want the CB500F for a week, it's available for £660. If you plan to visit IoM during the TT or other race events, the earlier you can book a bike the better.

The bike hire company offers pick up from your port of entry and transport to your pre-booked accommodation where your hire bike will be waiting. It also offers guided tours.

the right turn, which will take you up Snaefell Mountain. This is where the racing gets serious with long stretches of open road and consistent high speeds. The Gooseneck, just after you turn onto the mountain road, is a good place to watch racing as bikes have to slow down for a first gear corner and you can actually focus on them.

The road from here is slightly dystopian with not much sign of habitation and you'll get an acute sense that you're on your own in a strange world. There are few signs of human settlement as you ride without speed limits back towards houses and shops. There's a left turn at Kate's Cottage (built in 1869) as you head down the hill towards the pub on the Creg-ny-Baa corner and, after a well-earned Bushy's ale, there's an increasing sense of returning to civil society until you get to the finish line past Governor's Bridge.

'Yes', you can tell your friends, 'I've ridden the IoM TT Course'.

Wait, there's more

There's much more to the IoM than the Mountain Course and since you're there anyway, take advantage of it.

Douglas (population: 26,677) is a charming, fairytale town with a great promenade, which if you wish you can see from the slow comfort of a horse-drawn tram. Farther south is **Castletown** (population: 3109) with its Castle Rushen, built in 1265. Take your time through seaside villages of **Port St Mary** (population: 1953) and **Port Erin** (population: 3530), noting how ancient the whole isle looks and feels. Stay on the west coast as you cruise up to **Peel** (population: 5374) where you can park your bike at the Creek Inn, get some exercise exploring the Viking-built Peel Castle and then reward yourself with a fresh seafood lunch.

Pub meals over the whole island are generally of a high standard. If the isle has a traditional dish, it would be local smoked kippers, although 'queenies' (queen scallops) were declared the Manx national dish at the recent IoM Food and Drink Festival.

To get to the tip of the isle from Peel involves rejoining a section of the TT course but you can turn left just after Sulby and head up to the lighthouse on the tip of the Point of Ayre. Unfortunately, this will take you past the IoM garbage dump, although a reward at the end of the road is a rare, sandy beach.

To complete the Isle circuit, head down to Ramsey and then stay on the east coast rather than take the TT circuit turn up Snaefell. You'll pass the village of **Laxey** (population: 1705), which also has another great pub and it will give you a chance to visit the **Laxey Wheel**, the largest working waterwheel in the world.

Oh, and don't forget to say 'good morning' and 'good afternoon' to the fairies as you cross **Fairy Bridge**. Racing legend Joey Dunlop would visit Fairy Bridge to pay his respects as soon as he arrived on the Isle. The locals believe it brings good luck and TT riders (now including yourself) need all the help they can get.

Being there

The IoM police force is one of the most liberal in the entire world. It allows visitors to engage in all manner of what would be identified as 'misbehaviour' almost anywhere else. You can do a burnout in the main street of Douglas while the coppers talk to each other over a coffee on the footpath. You'll only get into trouble if your behaviour has the potential to harm others.

There are limits, though. I ran into a colleague there a few years ago, Big John, who objected to a fine he'd received for speeding in a town area. The issuing officer told him he was quite entitled to contest it the following morning in front of a magistrate. The court is part of the IoM jail and Big John turned up at the appointed time to be laughed at by the bench and have his fine doubled.

Furthermore, he was to be escorted through the jail to the cashier's office and, if he couldn't pay the fine immediately, he was to be held in the jail until he could. Part of this process was to handcuff him for the walk of shame past the other prisoners, but he's not called 'Big John' for nothing and the court authorities couldn't find cuffs big enough to fit his wrists. This is how he came to being escorted through the prison in leg irons. Imagine that in the 2020s - leg irons!

The moral of the story is that while the IoM police are admirably tolerant, it's best not to argue with them. If you're doing 150mph across the mountain on Mad Sunday, they won't blink. If they tell you to go home from Douglas Promenade at midnight because you've had too much to drink, though, just do as you're told.

The day after Big John went to jail, five of us decided we didn't want to be at the Gooseneck to watch the next race and decided we'd try to get to Creg-ny-Baa on the other side of the course while the road was still open between races. We didn't have long, so we were riding across the mountain in a pack at 130mph when we were waved down by a policeman. Amid much brake lock and smoke, we came to a terrified standstill expecting the worst before he asked us where we were going. We told him Crag-ny-Baa and he told us we'd better get a move on because they were going to close the road again in 10 minutes. Fancy being stopped by the coppers doing 130mph and told we'd have to ride faster! Who doesn't love the IoM?

Above A slower country pace, alongside stone bridges and plenty of greenery

BEST EATS

The Creek Inn, Peel
Lovely pub with great, local food in the traditional IoM style. The seafood platter is particularly interesting and very fresh. You can sit outside in summer and watch the more athletic climb up to the 11th-century, Viking-built Peel Castle.
www.thecreekinn-peel.foodanddrinksites.co.uk

JAKS Bar and Smokehouse, Douglas
Great location overlooking the bay and a great vibe. It's a bit pricey but in the capital you'd expect that. It's known for its steaks but there are plenty of shared platters available at reasonable prices. Plenty of sport and music on the big screens, too.
www.jakspub.com

Harbour View Bistro, Ramsey
This pub has Ramsey's best view of the waterfront and its seafood is delivered fresh off the boat. Try the Queenie linguini for a genuine experience of Manx quisine. Reasonably priced for the location and quality. It's a local institution.
www.harbourviewbistro.im

BEST SLEEPS

Peel TT Tent Village, Peel
If you're going to the IoM for the TT, book a tent here. The tent will be ready for you when you arrive and it will have everything you need in terms of bedding, except you'll need to bring your own sleeping bag (otherwise they're available to purchase). Services include charging points, wi-fi, a food area and a bar. Tents are available for two,

four or six people. It's easy walking distance to Peel's pubs and restaurants. They also have a similar tent village near Douglas.
www.duketravel.com/isle-of-man-tt/peel-tt-tent-village

Penta Hotel, Douglas
There's an argument that if you've made the effort to get to the IoM, you probably need to stay on Douglas Promenade, which runs the length of the capital beside the bay. Douglas was developed as a holiday destination for wealthier British tourists so it has lots of accommodation along the beachfront from which to choose.

Located at the north end of the promenade is the Penta Hotel - while it looks grand, it is among the least expensive of the available offerings and has very clean rooms with great views. It has a relationship with the Regency Hotel, a short walk away, which has a restaurant and bar among other facilities guests at the Penta can use.
www.penta.im

Maughold Venture Centre Bunkhouse, Maughold
This classy bunkhouse is located near Port e Vullen and is close to Ramsey via the Manx Electric Railway. It has bunk rooms if there's a gang of you, but can also cater for couples and individuals.

It's cheap and cheerful and a good option during TT weeks (from £30 per person, including breakfast) when other accommodation prices on the isle can be outrageous. Safe bike parking, too.
www.venturecentre.im

Lake District: England

While 15.8 million tourists visit the Lake District in northwestern England each year, they concentrate themselves in the lakes and hiking trails, leaving the winding mountain roads, steep passes and postcard villages to be terrorised by ever-grateful biker hordes.

SNAPSHOT

The World Heritage–listed Lake District is a popular holiday destination in England but the tourists tend to only stay in the major centres, meaning the roads are left to us riders. Some of the passes are particularly difficult for cars, especially those towing anything, often leaving the roads deserted – which of course only enhances the ride.

The roads are mainly narrow and twisty but are generally in good condition and the scenery – classic English countryside featuring the highest mountain in England and beautiful adjoining valleys rich in stone-fenced farmland – is always pleasing to the eye.

In the summer months it can be a slightly expensive area to visit as its popularity surges, but it's manageable if you stay away from the major visitor hotspots.

Remarkably, the jury is still out on how many lakes there are in the Lake District. If you get asked the question during a pub trivia night, the accepted answer will probably be 'one': Bassenthwaite Lake. If there were more than one, wouldn't it be called the 'Lakes District'?

In fact, 92 bodies of water have been identified in the 912 square miles that the Lake District covers, and these are variously called meres, tarn or water. This doesn't mean they aren't technically lakes; as 'water', for example, is a Cumbrian dialect name for 'lake'. For the record, a tarn is a small lake and meres are ponds (or lakes, just to add to the confusion).

The important thing for riders is that these bodies of water are largely formed by run-off from the huge fells in the area meaning the road network is twisty, mountainous, narrow and unsuitable for big trucks and buses. Fells? That's what the locals call the area of uncultivated high ground above the timberline of the mountains.

Opposite Leaving the Honister Slate Mine at the top of Honister Pass in England's Lake District *Overleaf* Derwent Water, the third largest lake in the region

 How long?
Though you can easily do this ride in a day (130 miles; 209km), the combination of road conditions, traffic and safety precautions means it can stretch out the time it takes to complete, as do the frequent stops to admire the landscapes.

 When to go
April to October provides the best weather, with summer (June to August) being the driest. This of course makes them the most popular months, so aim for the shoulder months.

 Need to know
- You ride on the left-hand side of the road but many roads are single-lane routes so you need to be familiar with the protocol of 'passing places'.
- Lake District's best riding is on its more remote roads, which are narrow and steep if you ride the peaks.
- Distances aren't great but it can take longer than you anticipate due to road conditions and traffic.

 Ride rating
If you avoid the major passes, the Lake District is an easy ride - but where's the fun in that? The two steepest passes, Hardknott and Wrynose, require patience and experience, particularly if you're on a heavy bike. Moderate skill levels are enough if you can stay focused on the task. Check weather conditions before you ride as the passes can close without much warning.

 Distances
- Kendal to Keswick via 'the Struggle': 37 miles (60km).
- Keswick to Eskdale: 43 miles (69km).
- Eskdale back to Kendal: 41 miles (66km).
- Note that distances are shorter if you take the major routes suggested by Google Maps.

 Temperatures
- July: 12°C to 18°C (53°F to 64°F)
- October: 5°C to 12°C (41°F to 54°F)

 More information
www.lakedistrict.gov.uk
www.visitlakedistrict.com

Hiding in plain sight

Protecting the Lake District from even more tourism is its location. Five hours north of London and 1.5 hours away from the nearest airport (Leeds Bradford), it's bit of an effort to get here but it's worth it. After the Peak District, the Lake District was England's second area to be declared a national park in 1951, and was designated a UNESCO World Heritage site in 2017. It features England's highest mountain, Scafell Pike (978m), as well as a rich history of both post–Ice Age settlement and Roman and Viking occupation. Remnants of this history survive, as does an extraordinary rock circle claimed to be older than Stonehenge.

Understandably it's of great interest to tourists, which means accommodation can be expensive. However if you locate yourself in the larger town of **Kendal** (population: 28,944) on the outskirts of the District, you'll find cheaper places from where to base your stay. This is an old market town with remnant buildings dating back centuries with a focus on agriculture and transport, and also has all the facilities you might want in a city including the popular Shakespeare Inn (*see* Best Eats).

The best of the lake

You can do this trip easily in a day and it will give you some clues as to where you might return if you have more time. Leaving Kendal, you'll follow the A591 to the area's largest tourist attraction, **Windermere** (population: 4826). Its lake is the longest in the district and it's full of classic tourist attractions including boat rides, tours and fine dining restaurants. It's a pleasant ride but this is the most highly trafficked part of the district so expect to enjoy the scenery more than the ride itself.

We're turning right just past there at Ambleside onto Kirkstone Rd, which the locals call **'the Struggle'**. It's a steep, undulating climb on a narrow road but bikes like the Triumph Tiger 1200 I rode weren't troubled. It would have been a lot more of a struggle in the more adventurous days of BSA Bantams.

While you're climbing this route, think back to how it was once done: by foot; with a horse-drawn wagon; riding a bicycle; or herding sheep. You may also ponder why the roads in the Lake District (and in much of England) are so narrow. They were initially tracks for horses and carts, and some of them date back to anno Domini. Early paved roads were invariably single lane with occasional 'passing points' and nobody imagined at the time how private transport would proliferate. The very British solution to the problem was to paint a line down the middle, creating two tracks without having to actually widen the road.

What this means for riders is it's often hard to work out where a particular road is going. Just over the crest in front of you, does it swing right or left? Because of the stone fences and hedges helping to obscure the view, it's easier to follow the telephone pole line. Of course, this doesn't tell you anything about oncoming traffic however! Hence the narrow roads here require respect.

When you get to the top of 'the Struggle', turn left onto the A592. There's a reward at the top: the **Kirkstone Pass Inn**, the third-highest pub in the UK (527m) and worth a visit if it's open. **Kirkstone Pass** is the area's highest rideable pass and has a remoteness that makes you forget instantly about all that traffic in Windermere. It's a feature of the best rides in England: it can be annoyingly congested in places and then almost frighteningly isolated five minutes later. Patterdale is only 15 miles from Ambleside but you may not see another vehicle from the inn to Patterdale's outskirts.

Donald Campbell

Speed demon Donald Campbell went to meet his maker in 1967 while trying to break his own water-speed record on Coniston Water in the Lake District. The Campbell name was known world-over firstly because of the exploits of Donald's father, Malcolm. Donald is the only person in the world to hold both land- and water-speed records in the same year (1964).

The Lake District run was an attempt to lift the world water-speed record from 297mph to over 320mph. Campbell died on the second run and it's popularly believed that the crash happened because he hadn't left enough time for the wake from the first run to settle. He was doing 300mph at the time when he met his unfortunate demise. His remains and the wreck of the boat weren't recovered until 1997. Among the items found was a St Christopher medal, the patron saint of travellers.

Dog day afternoon

Patterdale (population: 497) is quintessential rural England. If you happen to be here on the August Bank Holiday you'll be treated to the Patterdale Dog Day: a fun-filled day of sheepdog trials, a gundog show, fell races and a sheep show.

Follow the A592 to the left of Ullswater and then turn left onto the A5091 to Troutbeck. Here you'll turn left again onto the relatively dull A66, but look for the signs to the **Castlerigg Stone Circle** before you get to Keswick. There are more than 300 stone circles in Britain but few as old as Castlerigg. Most are Bronze Age burial sites but Castlerigg is from the earlier Neolithic period. It was constructed around 3000BCE for reasons largely unknown. Park your bike by the farm fence and amble through a working sheep grazing area to this stone circle rich in mystery. It obviously meant something significant 5000 years ago, but what? It's eerie and hard to get out of your head as you resume your ride to Keswick.

Top The A592 is so close to busy Windermere yet so remote *Bottom* Part of the Castlerigg Stone Circle

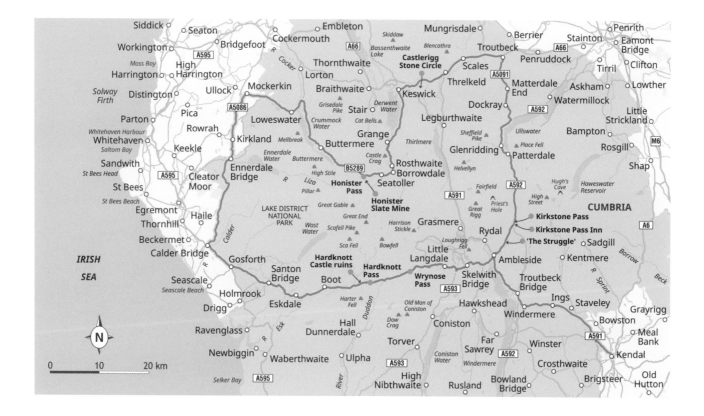

Head south on the B5289 with the peaceful Derwent Water, the District's third largest lake, on your right. The road to Rosthwaite is a spicy mix of twists and turns with a good surface and relatively clear forward vision. Pass through Seatoller from where **Honister Pass** awaits. It's the home of the Honister Slate Mine, the only slate mine left in the UK and its cafe makes the most of passing tourists being a rare sign of civilisation in an otherwise lonely landscape. This leg of the route is good practice for the Hardknott and Wrynose passes that will be your next major climbs.

Stay on the B5289 through Buttermere until the left turn-off to Loweswater and then left again at the A5086. You could stay on this 'major' road until you need to turn left again just after Gosforth but there's a back road not far down the A5086 that takes you over Ennerdale Bridge down to Calder Bridge and then just a short distance to the Gosforth turn-off. You're following the signposts to Eskdale Green and Boot that places you on Hardknott Pass road.

Lakeland Motor Museum

Located just a few minutes ride from Windermere, between Newby Bridge and Haverthwaite and adjacent to the A590, the **Lakeside Motor Museum** (www.lakelandmotormuseum. co.uk; admission £11) is one of the best in Britain. It displays over 140 motorcycles and cars along with 30,000 other exhibits that help to contextualise the vehicles.

The bike and car displays are in front of faithful recreations of shop windows that match the era of the vehicles. Female fashion from the late 1800s to the 1970s will bring back memories for some visitors, as will the WWI display.

Of particular interest to riders is an Isle of Man TT display and a collection of Vincents. Other highlights include the replicas of Donald Campbell's speed record breaking Bluebirds, both water and land vehicles, along with plenty of his memorabilia.

It's a fascinating place to spend half a day, particularly if the weather is stopping you from riding.

Road to perdition

Plenty of paper maps don't include **Hardknott Pass** road and if you research it you'll find lots of warnings about attempting it. Prominent signs include 'narrow route' and 'severe bends' along with 'unsuitable for all vehicles in winter conditions'. That's a challenge right there, isn't it?

The Romans built this pass road in AD110 and established a fort called **Hardknott Castle** at the top to protect supply routes to Hadrian's Wall and to discourage the Scots. It's a big fort and its foundation ruins remain along with indications of where the rest of buildings were located. It has a huge parade ground, suggesting large numbers of troops were housed there. Given its isolation and how cold it must have been in winter, one wonders what the soldiers did in their free time. It puts your complaints about your heated grips not being warm enough into perspective.

The road is paved the whole way and the lack of vegetation makes it easy to follow but it's certainly narrow and twisty with an above-average number of tight turns with wrong cambers. If it's raining, the road turns into a channel for flowing water, amplifying the difficulty.

The road was actually repaved after WWII when it had been used to test the climbing ability of tanks and their tracks tore up the original surface.

The reward for your effort is spectacular views and an experience of isolation you might find hard to replicate in the UK. This is particularly impressive in that it's only 15 miles from Boot to Ambleside. It doesn't read like far but, depending on conditions, it can easily take an hour.

The adventure doesn't finish with Hardknott Pass. **Wrynose Pass**, which follows it, has a seemingly narrower road but with more passing places. It's possible for a motorcycle and a car to pass each other, but in most places, not two cars. This means paying attention to passing places that you can pull into in advance if you see approaching vehicles. Don't assume anyone in a car is a good driver: they'll be mesmerised by the surroundings and will invariably take up more room than they need. Like Hardknott Pass, Wrynose has relatively open vegetation so you can see what's coming in front and behind. You can thank the harsh winter conditions for that.

The loop we're doing on this ride actually goes around **Scaffel Pike** (978m), England's highest mountain. You can see it from almost wherever you are on this journey but it doesn't look much higher than where you're riding.

Phew, we've reached Ambleside again, where we turned off all those hours ago to take on the Struggle. You've done four major passes and lots of country roads but there are still plenty more rides in the Lake District that deserve your attention. You could stay here for weeks.

Being there

It's getting late. It's getting dark. I've been riding for nine hours. I'm booked into the Kendal Hostel but nobody knows where it is. The locals stare at me blankly and one tells me there isn't a youth hostel in the town. I tell them the name of the street that it's supposed to be on and I still get blank stares. 'There isn't a street by that name here'.

It's now dark enough for me not to be able to read my map and the youth hostel details without going into a pub for the light.

Oh, I'm actually in a town called Keswick, not Kendal. My bad.

Kendal is 30 miles away and I'm annoyed with myself for making such a stupid mistake. I do what I always do in that situation and take it out on the bike. I channel Malcolm Campbell as I rip through the unsuspecting traffic and set a new record for the trip.

When I finally front the desk at the Kendal Hostel, they've never heard of me.

'You didn't book through one of those online booking agencies, did you? They never tell us what's going on'.

The Road Gods smile on me. They have a spare room. Tomorrow is another day.

BEST EATS

Shakespeare Inn, Kendal
The Shakespeare Inn is a mid-19th-century former coach stop with a small number of rooms available in what used to be the stables. Its menu is full of locally sourced produce and it has a focus on traditional fare including Sunday roasts. Its cask ales are excellent.
www.shakespearekendal.co.uk

Fresher's Café, Ambleside
Basic cafe menu but beautifully cooked, and a really nice vibe with both inside and outside dining where the views are perfect for the occasion. Have the full English breakfast (available until 3pm) for under 10 quid. Awesome. Motorcyclists specifically welcomed.
www.fresherscafe.co.uk

Bridge Inn, Buttermere
You can use the money you save by staying in the Buttermere YHA to indulge yourself at the Bridge Inn in the same town. It's a traditional English pub serving Cumbrian dishes with local ingredients. Try the Herdwick Lamb Hotpot which has near-zero food miles for the lamb used.
www.thebridgehotel.uk

BEST SLEEPS

YHA Buttermere, Buttermere
A beautiful, old building in a beautiful valley full of walking trails. Private rooms and dorms available along with landpods and tent camping spots.
www.yha.org.uk/yha-buttermere

Kendal Hostel, Kendal
Situated in the middle of a relatively large market town, this family run, independent hostel provides a good base for an on-foot exploration of a classic ye olde English village with all its period architecture and great use of stone as a building material. The hostel is clean, cheap and convenient, and has a great kitchen and dining area. The safest place to park your bike is where the hostel hangs its washing.
www.kendalhostel.co.uk

The Inn at Ravenglass, Ravenglass
This is a charming pub with great views of the estuary across the road. It has very limited rooms but they're quiet, comfortable and moderately priced. The Inn serves great food (try its seafood platter) and beer as well, with an emphasis on local catch seafood.
www.facebook.com/innatravenglass

Above The Kirkstone Pass Inn at the top of Buttertubs Pass *Opposite* Three Shires Inn

Yorkshire Dales: England

When you least expect it, the strangest routes can leapfrog to the top of your riding list. The Yorkshire Dales in Northern England? Yep, and some argue that it contains the best 5.5 mile (9km) stretch of road in all of Great Britain.

SNAPSHOT

Known mostly everywhere except England for being the place where *All Creatures Great and Small* was filmed, the Yorkshire Dales offers great riding without the crowds. It's a microcosm of rural England and all the more charming for it.

Motorcyclists know about it, though, and as many as 200 of them gather at Devil's Bridge on weekends to have breakfast and work out riding routes on the gypsy ribbon of roads available.

If you were around in 1978 and turned on your most probably black-and-white TV set, you would have seen *All Creatures Great and Small*. Based on the adventures of veterinarian James Alfred White, it was set in the Yorkshire Dales during the 1930s and '40s

Fast forward to 2020 and a new series of the same show once again swept the world. For many of us, that's all we know about the Yorkshire Dales. It's a charming series about a charming place: the upland area of the Pennine Hills that, since 1954, is mostly part of the Yorkshire Dales National Park.

The area comprises almost unnaturally green pastures divided up by dry stone walls and full of grazing sheep and cattle. If you like stone fences, a 1988 survey claims there are 4971 miles (8000km) of them still in use. Apart from the colour green, it's the thing you most notice about the area. Some of the Yorkshire Dales walls are more than 1000 years old and still serving faithfully.

Along with its physical beauty, this is a road network that seems to have been made with only motorcycles in mind. Most of the roads off the major network are narrow, winding and largely free of traffic. The Yorkshire Dales are no secret in England and it's why there's actually a start and finish place for bikes where anything up to a couple of hundred riders meet on weekends.

How long?
Our route can be done in a day but you'll learn more if you spread it out over two.

When to go
April to October provides the best weather, with June, July August being the driest. The Yorkshire Dales isn't fashionable with the whole influencer set so riders can enjoy it whenever they decide to go. It's cold and bleak in winter, though.

Need to know
- Ride on the left.
- Be conscious of potential livestock and slow-moving tractors that appear on the road from around any random corner.
- The roads tend to be narrow, so pick your overtaking spots carefully and give oncoming traffic plenty of room.

Ride rating
Easy at posted speeds but intermediate if the red mist descends with open conditions encouraging you to ride at higher speeds.

Distances
- Kirkby Lonsdale to Tan Hill Inn: 46 miles (74km).
- Tan Hill Inn to Reeth: 16 miles (26km).
- Reeth to Ribblehead Viaduct: 25 miles (40km).
- Ribblehead Viaduct to Ingleton: 7 miles (11km).

Temperatures
- July: 11°C to 18°C (52°F to 64°F)
- September: 9°C to 15°C (48°F to 59°F)

More information
www.yorkshiredales.org.uk

Above The magic roads (and stone fences) of the Yorkshire Dales

Sausage & bacon butty, please

Welcome to the Devil's Bridge on the River Lune on the outskirts of the village of **Kirkby Lonsdale** (population: 1968). The village was once such a popular market town that it hosted 29 pubs. Eight remain and walking around town is a good way of orienting yourself to the day's ride. It's possible Kirkby Lonsdale was created as a support town to the Devil's Bridge built in 1370 to provide a crossing

If cuisine is your thing then there are definitely better places in Kirkby Lonsdale to have breakfast (including the **Royal Hotel** opposite the market place) but none will have the ambience of the green van (*see* Being There) just over Devil's Bridge. A local by-law says only motorcycles are allowed to park there on Sundays and bank holidays, and the tradition behind this meeting place is well over 50 years old. Bikes rule.

Most of the bridge crew, particularly the sports-bike riders, will take the A65 when they leave and head towards Hawes as they turn left on the B6255. Hawes will be a base camp for quick rides over the legendary **Buttertubs Pass**, which was made even more famous recently when former *Top Gear* presenter Jeremy Clarkson declared it to be 'England's only spectacular road'.

We'll get there eventually, but instead we're leaving the Devil's Bridge briefly on the A683 before turning right on a slip-road signposted 'Casterton/Barbon' on the way to Dent. This immediately takes you into a summary of the Yorkshire Dales: narrow roads, stone fences, livestock and scenes that demand photography if they're not already seared into your memory.

Streams from fairytales babble along the side of the road as you wave at farmers, avoid sheep and marvel at deserted railway bridges that would, in any other part of the world, be major tourist attractions. When you arrive at the first T-intersection, turn right following the signs to Hawes.

Here the terrain starts to level out with very little natural vegetation as you enjoy uninterrupted views of far horizons. It's good riding in that you can see what's coming with every corner and there are no surprises awaiting as you exit at your chosen speed.

Hawes (population: 803) was recorded as a market town as far back as 1307 and it's still a market town. Things change slowly (or not at all) in this part of England. It's a lively village and

Top The bleak but beautiful Stonesdale Lane on the way to the Tan Hill Inn *Bottom* The road signs are as old as the towns

popular with riders as it's the access point to the area's best road, **Cliff Gate Rd**, the home of Buttertubs Pass. Dedicated bikers ride Cliff Gate Rd to Thwaite, then ride it back the other way, have lunch in one of the many eating houses in Hawes and then do it all again. But for the moment we have other plans ...

Buttertubs Pass

If you left Devil's Bridge around 10am, you'll be starting to feel a little peckish. We're heading to the **Tan Hill Inn** for lunch, Britain's highest pub and one of its strangest. But more of that later.

To get there, cruise through Hawes and turn left up Brunt Acres Rd, turn left again at Bellow Hill and then right soon after at Quarry Rd. Veer right at the Shaw Ghyll Caravan and Camping site and you'll be starting the B6278 Cliff Gate Rd. Hawes to the Tan Hill Inn is only 13 miles but 5.5 miles of it is on Cliff Gate Rd, which includes **Buttertubs Pass**. It seems much longer when you ride it.

Cliff Gate Rd is narrow but well-formed. Even before you get to the pass, the road twists and climbs with occasional 12m drops on either side to entertain you if you make a mistake. The area is green and pleasing to the eye but it's best not to become too distracted as gradients are steep at between 7% and 20%.

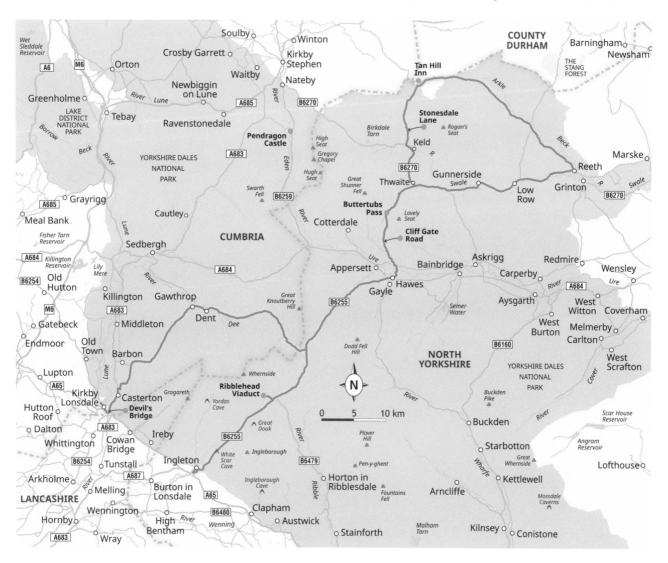

Like much of the Yorkshire Dales, Buttertubs Pass is very open with great vision in relation to oncoming traffic, of which there seems to be very little even in the busy period of the day. Jeremy Clarkson may have been engaging in hyperbole but it still should be considered a national treasure for riders.

After your adventure on the pass, you'll arrive at a T-intersection where you'll turn left onto the B6270. Ride through Thwaite and Keld, and then turn right at Stonesdale Lane to climb to the Tan Hill Inn.

Stonesdale Lane must be one of the loneliest roads in the world. You may see a couple of bikes on the route but that will be your only contact with civilisation. The words 'bleakness' and 'isolation' are often used to describe this area and it was officially condemned in the *Doomsday Book* (published in the year 1086) as being a 'wasteland' and not worthy of further investigation. William the Conqueror sent his accountants to find out what he owned and how much tax he should be getting but, in the North Pennines, they concluded that nothing of worth could exist there.

According to the history of the **Tan Hill Inn**, it's entirely possible an ale house escaped their attention. In 1586, William Camden's guidebook to Britannia noted a 'solitary Inn' more-or-less in this location and the existing inn dates back to the 1700s.

The inn thrived in its early days because of coal mining in the local area but it's prospering now as a welcome relief on the 'Pennines Way' – an incredible walking/cycling track that stretches for 268 miles across the country's northern uplands. In the coal mining days it was originally called the King's Pit and today and you can still buy a beer called by that name at the current pub.

'Putting the bite back into bitter, Kings Pit is a golden, amber ale, pleasantly malty with an underlying nutty bitterness. An aromatic ale laced with sweet undertones of toffee and a touch of citrus. It's medium-bodied, producing a fine, foaming head emanating a beguiling, hoppy aroma, leaving you with a satisfying, dry finish.'

Go on, tell me you don't want a pint of that right now.

The food is also excellent in the old English tradition and the Tan Hill Inn serves probably the biggest beef Wellington in the Commonwealth.

It's all downhill from here

Once you've dragged yourself away from the Tan Hill Inn, take another remote road down to **Reeth** (population: 724) to enjoy more of the wild aloneness of this part of Yorkshire. It's a little more civilised than Stonesdale Lane but not by much.

The 'dale' part of the Yorkshire Dales is the valleys between the hills and, in the best traditions of British road building, you won't be climbing passes unless it's absolutely necessary.

Reeth used to be best known for providing 10% of England's lead, but it's now a village that relies on tourism from walkers and riders – of both the pedal and motorised kind. It's the largest town in upper Swaledale and boasts some lovely cafes and pubs.

Don't relax too much, though, as you're about to take the B6270 along the north side of the River Swale back to just before Thwaite, where you'll turn left to approach Buttertubs Pass from the opposite direction. If you didn't love it before, you'll be entirely convinced by the time you get back to Hawes where you can finally have a break and explore the myriad shops, restaurants and pubs in this busy but interesting town. If you arrive mid-afternoon, you can sit at one of the tables outside the Crown Pub in the market area of the main street and watch the sports-bike heroes returning from battle and heading back to civilisation.

Hawes is where you can taste the original Wensleydale cheese, a product that was always famous but made spectacularly more so when it was promoted by outfit-riding Wallace and Gromit in their clay-animation movies. When Wallace said it was his favourite cheese, some say the pair saved the industry. It's a crumbly cheese with a honey aroma but it's also made with fruit including cranberries. Buy a block and some dry biscuits and enjoy them with your pint as you watch the passing parade.

Pendragon Castle

In our current 'post-truth' world, myths and legends are making a spectacular return to popular culture. If you want to believe something, why can't it be true? Who cares what scienticians think?

Located in in Kirkby Stephen, **Pendragon Castle** was claimed to have been built by legendary King Uther Pendragon, father of King Arthur in the 5th century. The story goes that Uther died there when he was poisoned by Saxon rivals.

While today the castle is a ruin, it's hard not to be moved by the sense of history you get from standing among the original stones as you contemplate what is legend and what is fact.

Opposite top The stone walls and barns have stood the test of centuries and each shelter has its own story *Opposite left* A modest property in the Yorkshire countryside *Opposite right* Having conquered 'The Struggle', Triumph's Tiger 1200 has a well-earned rest

Leave Hawes travelling east on the B6255, keeping an eye open for signage to turn right to the Ribblehead Viaduct. If you get to the Station Inn on B6270, you've gone just a little bit too far.

Irrespective of how you feel about trainspotters, the **Ribblehead Viaduct** is extraordinary. It's 400m long and has 24 arches, with every fifth arch being reinforced to help the rest carry the weight of trains from Settle to Carlsile in Scotland. It's a stone bridge over a gully, but of proportions tremendous enough for you to think it must be an AI-construct, not a work of human creation.

In actual fact it was the last main railway in Britain to be built mostly with manual labour. It was a feat involving some 2300 men, of which around 200 died in the process. Some of these were industrial accidents but others were from diseases such as smallpox in the workers camps as well as fights in pubs. Construction started in 1869 and it's still in use today. Remarkable.

Return to the B6255 and cruise down to **Ingleton** (population: 1755) where there's a fine youth hostel if you want to save a little on accommodation. Alternatively, if there's still plenty of daylight, travel the extra 19 miles to Kendal in the Lake District region where a whole new riding adventure awaits (*see* p. 107).

Being there

Okay, I couldn't in good conscience put Devil's Bridge Snacks (www.devilsbridgesnacks.com) in the 'best eats' section as the menu at the van is limited and the coffee is probably to die of rather than to die for. It is, however, a sensational place to meet before a ride, and eating while standing is better for digestion.

Known mostly for its bacon butty, the van focuses on local products. The eggs are local free-range, the buns are sourced daily from the Lunesdale Bakery and the beef patties are from Dales Butchers.

It was established in 1955 when all the bikes in the parking lot would have been British. The original owners retired and Kerry (ex-chef at the Royal Hotel in Kirkby Lonsdale) married Mel (Saturday girl at Devil's Bridge Snacks from 1990) and they took over the business.

The gatherings there on weekend mornings and on public holidays is legendary, to the point where only motorcycles are allowed to park there. The van is open seven days a week, though, and is busy even weekdays.

I chatted to a group there and proceeded to run into them twice during this ride, the second time at a pub in Reeth where I convinced one of them to emigrate to Australia. We're mates now.

BEST EATS

Foresters Arms, Carlton-in-Coverdale
There are plenty of stone pubs in England but this one is particularly beautiful and has the added advantage of being owned by the local community who bought it in 2011. Its menu is classic old England but that's probably exactly what you want. The beer is the same. Try Thrakston's Old Peculiar ale from the keg; you can't get it in many places.
www.forestersarmscoverdale.com

Tan Hill Inn, Reeth
You have to go there. It's Britain's highest pub and is the cultural epicentre of what is locally judged a wasteland. The current iteration dates back to the 1700s. The kitchen keeps busy with mostly traditional English food but what about this steak? Eight ounce Onglet steak marinated in chimichurri (grilled up to medium-rare) accompanied by flat mushrooms, thyme, garlic, cherry vine tomatoes, hand-cut chips, house salad, onion rings and garlic mayonnaise. Yes, it's 22 quid but you won't be hungry again for the next 24 hours.
www.tanhillinn.com

Cross Keys Inn, Cautley
Here's something you weren't expecting: a temperance inn! Yes, it's a pub with no beer but don't let that put you off. It serves fresh, local food and has a good range of vegetarian options. The history of the inn features Quaker connections and is all the better for it. While it doesn't sell alcohol, it doesn't mind if you bring a bottle or two to have with dinner. It's located 4 miles from Sedbergh on the A683 on the left.
www.cautleyspout.co.uk

BEST SLEEPS

YHA Malham, North Yorkshire
A great youth hostel that's well located if you want to do a bit of walking while you're in the Yorkshire Dales. Malham Cove (as seen in Harry Potter movies) is a five-minute walk away. All the usual youth hostel features (plus camping pods, an on-site shop, restaurant and bar). Free wi-fi is a bonus as it's not as common in the UK as you'd expect.
www.yha.org.uk/hostel/yha-malham

Kings Head, Skipton
A fine pub located in a classic English village with good surrounding walking trails. It has six rooms, each named after an English monarch. The rooms are under 100 quid a night, which is very good value in the Yorkshire Dales. It's a proper taste of the English countryside and the food is first-class too.
www.kingsheadkettlewell.com

The Royal Hotel, Kirkby Lonsdale
Got a little cash to spare? It's actually not that expensive (£130 to £175 per night) but you get great value-for-money at this Georgian townhouse hotel. England is full of them but this is another delightful village to stroll around. As you'd expect, the Royal has a restaurant and a bar and serves a very nice full English breakfast and high tea, too. The rooms are also a touch of class. Go on, indulge yourself.
www.jamesplaces.com/royal-hotel/

Above left Start your ride with breakfast at Devil's Bridge Snacks at Kirkby Lonsdale, a local biker institution *Above right* Stock up on sugar hits at the Sweet Shop in Kirkby Lonsdale *Opposite* Not villages but farms also make from stone

Asia

Kerala: India

The thought of riding a motorcycle in India can be foreboding but there's a jewel in the south waiting to be fully discovered that might change your mind.

SNAPSHOT

Kerala has been named by *National Geographic Traveller* as 'one of the 10 paradises of the world' and is arguably the best sorted of all the states in India. Its communist government has made it the least impoverished state and the general well being of its population is reflected in a calm, confident attitude that makes riding a motorcycle in its regional areas a very pleasant experience.

It's still India, though, and its fascinating mix of vibrant public life is on full display on this very well-managed tour.

Most riders who have India on their bucket list are usually thinking about riding a Royal Enfield to the base camp at Mt Everest. It's something that you can actually imagine. Riding anywhere else in India is unimaginable. It's huge. Where would you start and where would you finish? How would you cope with the constant exposure to extreme poverty? It's possible for some travellers to just manage an air-conditioned bus ride from their plush hotel in Delhi to Agra to see the Taj Mahal but it would be a quick visit and you'd be grateful the bus had tinted windows to shield you from the reality of a country with a current population of 1,428,627,663. The '1' in that number refers to a billion. Ride a motorcycle there? Unless you're an intrepid rider used to navigating India's challenging traffic conditions, it's a resolute no thank you.

India isn't just one giant blot of humanity, however. Way down south on the Malabar Coast is Kerala, a state long sought out by travellers for its more relaxed, rural charms. It has the highest human development index in the country, the highest literacy rate (96.2%) and the highest life expectancy. It's the least impoverished state in the country and the highest achiever of sustainable development goals. A coalition of popularly elected communist and left-wing parties have been in and out of government since 1957 and currently dominate the political agenda.

Kerala is also the home of Kerala Bike Tours, which, among other things, offers a 12-day, 11-night guided motorcycle tour featuring jungles, beaches, a million corners and lots of local tea.

It's possible to ride in Kerala without a guide but Daniel Benster and his partner, Niaz Va, know the state inside out and it would be much trickier to construct a tour like this without their knowledge and contacts.

How long?

Kerala Bike Tours offers a 12-day, 11-night guided tour with airport pick-ups and drop-offs.

When to go

Between September and March is the most comfortable time for riding in Kerala when there's less humidity. Kerala is a popular tourist destination in the December/January period and can be a little crowded, although not too many tourists will be following the Kerala Bike Tours route. Avoid June to August as it's the monsoon season.

Need to know

- Prices for the Kerala Bike Tours start from around US$2800 per person for a shared twin room.
- Ride on the left-hand side of the road.
- If you're riding in summer, a mesh jacket will be cool as well as provide protection if you come off your bike.
- The roads you'll be riding are generally two-lane and narrow. Be conscious of approaching buses and trucks, particularly if the road is climbing or descending in the mountains where turns are sharp.

Ride rating

Intermediate. This is a relatively low-speed tour that suits the conditions but it has lots of twists and turns, and road conditions can vary requiring rider concentration. Other traffic on the road, which varies from bicycles to large trucks will have an affect on the road conditions. In particular, loose gravel and dirt can build up on corner apexes on hairpin bends.

Distances

- The total distance is just under 1000km (581 miles) with daily rides ranging from 60km to 250km.

Temperatures

- September : 24°C to 27°C (75°F to 81°F)
- March: 24°C to 29°C (75°F to 84°F)

More information

www.bookmotorcycletours.com/kerala-bike-tours

www.keralatourism.org

Asia

Above Tea plantations in the Western Ghats of Kerala are very productive thanks to monsoon rains

Fly/ride holiday

You'll probably enjoy this ride best if you encourage a few of your friends to join you. The minimum number is four for 12 days and 11 nights. Kerala Bike Tours (KBT) will pick you up from the Cochin International airport and take you to the starting point accommodation where you'll be briefed on the trip and be introduced to your bike. KBT owns all its own Royal Enfield 350 and 500 Bullets, and each has its own name so bonding is inevitable.

Royal Enfield (RE) was a British manufacturer but established a licence agreement with Madras Motors in India to assemble 350 Bullets for the Indian Army in 1955. Indians loved them and the tooling to produce them was eventually sold to Madras Motors and, from 1962, all Bullets have been manufactured there.

The giant Indian manufacturer Eicher Motors eventually took control of Enfield India and Royal Enfield now has an ever-expanding range of newer models – but many Indians still love the older-style Bullets. The 350 Bullets are still being produced and hold a dominant place in the market share. They're good for 120km/h but vibrate after 90km/h, which is fine for most Indian road situations as you'll never want to go faster than that. Daniel, one of KBT's owners, has a romantic attachment to them and will wear his fleet out before switching to newer bikes. Royal Enfield has been around since 1901 so it could take some time for any change to take place.

The 'Spice Coast of Kerala' tour we're doing is just under 1000km with daily rides ranging from 61km to 250km.

Hit the road, Jack

It takes a while on the first day of riding to get out of the built-up areas and into the forest. But it's worth it when you arrive at the **Thattekad Bird Sanctuary** and have the chance to take a river cruise to see what one of India's leading ornithologists says is the 'richest bird habitat on peninsula India'.

Above The ride gang is introduced to their bikes. Initial misgivings gave way to a passionate love affair

Accommodation is in beautiful wooden huts, and the peaceful ambience and great local food reinforces the 'luxury' tag attached to the tour.

It gets even more impressive the next day when you climb into the Western Ghats through the Sholayar forest. 'Ghats' are mountain ranges leading to the Deccan Plateau and run in the east as well as the west of the peninsula. The Western Ghats get plenty of rainfall from the monsoons, which partly explains why Kerala is so green and why tea plantations prosper.

This night, we stay in a hilltop plantation house with panoramic views and it's impressive enough to encourage a rest day so you can sleep there the following night. In the rest day, you can visit one of the tea factories on the plantation. If you're unimpressed by tea generally, your view will probably change afterwards.

At night, the plantation is full of wildlife, including leopards and elephants.

It's a fair 250km ride the next day crossing over to the state of Tamil Nadu to the hill station of **Ooty** (population: 98,238). Hill stations are towns of higher elevation and largely developed by European colonialists as refuges from the summer heat in lower-lying areas. Ooty is a fine example and our accommodation that night was at the Taj Savoy which was a reminder of British colonialism at its best and worst. The support staff (all Indians, of course) wore dinner-suit serving attire and we were treated like members of the royal family which, obviously, we weren't. The service was impeccable, but I like to think there was a degree of irony in the way it unfolded. As we left the following day, the Savoy had baked us a farewell treat wishing us a safe ride, which was a tender touch.

Before you get too excited, we stayed at the Taj Savoy because the normal accommodation at Ooty wasn't available; but the usual hotel is much better situated if you want to explore the town on foot.

Climb every mountain

Getting to Ooty involved riding through the plains of Tamil Nadu after a 40 hairpin bend descent that eventually leads to another climb up the Nilgiri Hills to 2000m. Hairpin bends are a feature of this ride as it's the best road design to allow underpowered and overloaded vehicles to move up and down the Ghats. It is, of course, perfect for riders who love corners and the angles of the hairpins suit RE bikes – no real speed involved but plenty of tight leaning,

From Ooty it's just an 80km ride to the tiger reserve of **Masinagudi**, the buffer zone for Mudumalai National Park, where you'll check-in to a jungle resort, Bamboo Banks, full of native wildlife. You'll be able to watch the cook prepare your meals and have an experience of genuine India. The sleeping units aren't Taj Savoy standard but the Taj Savoy doesn't have spotted deer, wild boar, monkeys and wild elephant.

'Wild' here means exactly what it says. You can go for an amble on the resort grounds and run into any manner of potentially hostile creatures. The pre-ride briefing from KBT instructs you that elephants are moody and best left alone. There are tigers

in the jungles,too. It shouldn't stop you walking but you need to be conscious of your surroundings.

Monkeys are generally passive but have their own clan agendas. On one of our two nights in Bamboo Banks, a troop of them tore through the accommodation buildings, overturning tables and chairs and generally creating havoc. They don't really care about you so it's safe to just stand back, watch and enjoy. Amazing. Oh, don't let them into your rooms as they'll steal things they can't possibly use but mostly they'll just be after food.

You'll spend two days at Bamboo Banks so you can either relax, go for a motorcycle ride through the Mudumalai Tiger Reserve or rev up one of the quad bikes on the property for a race on the dirt circuit they've created. Be warned – quad bike racing is probably the most dangerous thing you'll do on this trip.

Day eight is all about the riding. On your way to Sterling Resorts Anaikatti you'll climb to 2000m before descending via 117 hairpin bends, which are all numbered on signs to help you monitor where you're up to. You need to keep your eyes open for elephants, which can just decide to sit in the middle of the road and can't be convinced to move. There are around 500 deaths a year from elephant attacks in India. It's estimated there are 30,000 elephants left in the wild here and they are becoming more aggressive as their habitat shrinks due to population growth and competition for resources. Give way if you see them, keep your distance, have an escape plan and don't turn your back on them to take selfies. This ride returns us from Tamil Nadu to Kerala.

After a night in a resort by a river, it's another ride through beautiful plantation country and small villages to a 'secret' beach resort and a long swim in the Arabian Sea. You'll stay on the beach the following day for rest and recuperation.

The Kerala coastline spreads for 595km and over a million locals are involved in the fishing industry. The clean, sandy beaches are usually lined with coconut trees and are a major tourist attraction, although KBT's Ayurvedic Beach Resort is relatively secluded. If massages are your thing, ayurvedic massages are a 3000-year-old Indian practice that focuses on the skin rather than your muscles. It's characterised by the heavy use of essential oils, and relaxation is the goal. After 1000 kilometres on your RE, it might be just what you need.

Left A stunning Kerala sunset *Opposite top* Most roads in India are busy 24/7 *Opposite left* Lunch - pick up some rice and select your sides *Opposite right* Street shopping is a popular activity in Kochi

Above **Marari Beach** *Opposite left* **Each hairpin turn is numbered on the downhill section of the ride to Ooty** *Opposite right* **The tour's excellent accommodation in Kochi**

Royal Enfield

Royal Enfield (RE) is one of the world's oldest motorcycle companies with its 350 Bullet being the longest-running model in continuous production. When the Redditch-based company unloaded the Bullet to India in 1955, it probably thought it was the deal of a lifetime - money for old rope. Little did RE know how India would embrace the bike and eventually restore the company's position as a market leader.

Starting with a hand-built collection of out-of-date technologies, RE in India is now dominating the middle-weight class and is number one in the UK and Korea, number two in Thailand, and number three in France, Italy and Australia. Its growth in some markets is now 45% a year.

A new model of the Bullet 350 was unveiled in mid 2023 that looks much like the old one but has thoroughly modern engineering and build quality. Royal Enfield already sells around 12,000 Bullets each month into the Indian market and has high hopes for the revamped model.

Royal Enfield expanded its range of models with a 450cc, liquid-cooled Himalayan also being launched in 2023. The new models have exciting styling but the Indian market will probably stick first and foremost to the traditional 350 Bullet.

Siddhartha Lal, managing director of Eicher Motors which owns RE, confirmed the importance of the Bullet at its launch.

'This motorcycle is unwavering - it does not change. It is our north star that keeps us honest and real'.

Royal Enfield will prosper. I wish I could buy shares.

City lights

The Kerala Bike Tours adventure winds up in the city of **Kochi** (population: 2.1 million). You may know it as 'Cochin' but the local government reverted to its traditional name in 1996 as part of the process of de-colonisation, necessary after almost 500 years of occupation: first by the Portuguese, then the Dutch and finally the British.

The Portuguese arrived soon after Vasco da Gama established a sea route in 1498 and built a fort there in 1503 as well as establishing a trade centre for spices including sandalwood, cloves, cinnamon and pepper. The area is still called the 'Spice Coast'.

Much remains of Portuguese architecture in the Old City (Fort Kochi) but the Portuguese were ousted by the Dutch in 1663 who were, in turn, replaced by the British in 1795. The British remained there until India gained its independence in 1947.

Saying goodbye to your Enfield – which, by now, you've grown to love – is a hard task but the Old City offers plenty of distractions and is a fascinating place to spend a few days. *Lonely Planet* recently listed it as number seven in its top 10 cities in the world to visit. Replace your riding boots with something more comfortable and take one of the walking tours on offer with a local student guide. Lash out on the fresh seafood as well – it's the best in India.

With its communist government and prosperous economy, Kerala isn't typical of the rest of India. One of the things the KBT experience will do for you, though, is give you the confidence to explore farther afield. The rest of India may not be as forbidding as you initially thought.

Do it sooner rather than later. While you've been reading this, the population of India has grown by 3321 ...

Being there

Aha, a police road block with about 40 of Kerala's finest appearing to be leaving cars alone but pulling up motorcycles.

I'm sure the bike will have proper registration but where did I put my international riders licence? I may have been going a little fast as well on my 500cc superbike so I'll need an excuse. Maybe an excuse will be superfluous as the police on these jungle roads probably don't speak English.

I'm approached by the biggest, meanest-looking copper who proceeded to shake hands with me. Nobody had told us but it was Motorcycle Safety Week. We'd been stopped so that they could congratulate us on our safe riding gear - full face helmets, armoured jackets, padded riding jeans and riding boots. It made sense in that most of the other riders on these roads were in flip flops, shirts and sarongs. India has the most people killed in the world in motorcycle crashes each year - around 100,000 - but that has to be viewed in the context of its immense population and how many locals actually ride bikes.

Deaths are one thing but the number of injuries from non-fatal crashes must be phenomenal. I'm a fan of mesh jackets in hot climates as they let the breeze through while still providing safe coverage. It's easy for abrasions to become infected in tropical climates so it's worth avoiding if possible.

That's a thing about Kerala: even the police are courteous and helpful.

BEST EATS AND BEST SLEEPS
Kerala Bike Tours takes care of all this and the accommodation and food is excellent.
www.keralabiketours.com

Q & A
Heather Ellis

Heather Ellis is an Australian motorcycle adventurer and author of two books based on her travels: 'Ubuntu' and 'Timeless on the Silk Road'. The books are available through Amazon but signed copies for Australian readers are also available directly from Heather via www.heather-ellis.com.

What got you into riding motorcycles?

I grew up as a bush kid so outdoor activity was second nature to me. I spent some time at my aunt and uncle's sheep station in South Australia where I was introduced to Honda's Z50 when I was seven years old. I eventually bought a Honda XL185 and progressed to a Yamaha XT250 when I was working at the Ranger Uranium Mine in Kakadu in the Northern Territory. I did quite a bit of riding there.

What sowed the seeds of your ride through Africa?

As an emerging teenager, I devoured Wilbur Smith novels. Many of them were set in Africa and I became fascinated by the place. Another big literary influence was Robert Ruark's *Something of Value*, which explored the Mau Mau uprising in Kenya in the 1950s.

I went backpacking for two years in 1991 and saw a lot of the UK, Europe, Egypt and Israel, which just increased my hunger for travel. My parents weren't too pleased when they heard my plans to ride through Africa.

How did you decide on what bike and gear to take?

I asked my mates who all thought Yamaha's TT600 would be the best bike for the trip so I bought it new. I kitted it out with leather panniers, which were great. I could lie the bike on its side resting on a pannier and the rear wheel was off the ground, enabling me to fix punctures and replace tyres. I had a workshop manual and learned about maintenance on the way.

Those with a bit of experience of TT600s would probably have suggested a smaller, lighter bike. They don't have an electric starter and can be difficult to coax into life.

Ha! It's true I had to remove quite a bit of foam padding from the seat. I used the bladder from a wine cask to make the seat a bit more comfortable. I had to start the bike while it was on its side stand but I never really had any trouble with it. Occasionally I'd flood the carburettor but all I had to do was wait 10 minutes before trying again. I've still got my TT600 and it's my bike of choice for my next big ride. You could say we 'made the bond'.

Your Africa adventure is captured in your first book, 'Ubuntu: One Woman's Motorcycle Odyssey Across Africa'. What prompted your subsequent ride across Central Asia?

I'd always planned to ride home to Australia from the UK via Russia, Central Asia and China but wanted to have some Russian language skills to do the trip as few people in these areas speak English. I booked a Russian language course at Moscow University and this required a three-month visa, which required a HIV test. It came back positive.

I was healthy and the diagnosis was a shock. The antiretrovirals we have today are as good as a cure and control HIV to undetectable levels, but these were not discovered until a year later in 1996. The doctor said I had perhaps five years so while I was writing the first draft of *Ubuntu*, I decided to stick with my original plan and that's the basis of the second book, *Timeless on the Silk Road*.

I didn't need a HIV test for a one-month visa, which I got in Turkey. I made it as far as Vietnam before illness overcame me and I flew back to Australia where I ended up the Cairns Base Hospital. I was put on the new antiretrovirals which saved my life.

If you could talk now to your 18 year old self, what advice would you give her?

Get a bike and ride around the world! Do it while you're young without possessions and responsibilities. It's probably not for everyone but it suited my country-girl disposition and attitude.

What's next?

By 2026, my youngest two children will be well over 18 and I'm going to have my TT600 rebuilt for a ride from South to North America. I'll be 63 and chapter three of my life will begin ...

Opposite Heather Ellis and her Yamaha TT600 with villagers on the road to Epulu, Democratic Republic of Congo

Ha Giang Loop: Vietnam

Vietnam is an extraordinary country of dignified, generous citizens who love their homeland and welcome visitors to share in its treasures. In the north, a guided tour is a good idea. Here's one of the best.

SNAPSHOT

Vietnam is one of the last, great, riding wildernesses. It's not wild in the sense of road conditions and accommodation but riding there is unlike riding anywhere else in the world. It's an intoxicating mix of scenery, local lifestyle, history and people. Most of the potential problems created by this unique environment are solved by riding on an escorted tour but Offroad Vietnam doesn't shield you from engaging with your new environment.

This is a ride that will change your life.

Vietnam. There, I've said it. Depending on your age, this word may trigger memories of a completely unnecessary war that killed millions or, if you're younger, it might just remind you of media you've experienced that told you it was one of the cheapest and most interesting tourist destinations in the world.

Its military history doesn't make it sound like a glam destination although it's punched well above its weight in terms of results. It defeated the Mongols under Kublai Khan, the Chinese, the French, America, China once again, and it freed Cambodia from its despotic ruler, Pol Pot, at a time when the West had no further appetite for war in Southeast Asia – despite Cambodia's leader killing at least two million of his own people in three years.

You wouldn't know any of this as you amble around the fascinating streets of the Old Quarter in Hanoi as most of the population is under 50 and has no direct memory of the terrors their parents and extended families experienced during what Vietnam calls 'The American War'. The population of the country is now over 100,000,000 and the median age is just 32.8 years.

South Koreans fought with the Americans against the Vietnamese but over a million now visit each year as tourists. Americans are understandably a little shy about going back but 320,000 or so are now visiting each year. In fact, there's a large contingent of ex-American soldiers who live there permanently. Australians also contributed troops to assist the American and South Vietnamese against the North. In what sounds miraculous, Vietnam has moved on as a country and appears to harbour no grudges against those who fought against it.

Right Is a tour group of 20 too big? Probably, but we enjoyed every second

 How long?
11 days on the Ha Giang loop.

 When to go
- For Hanoi, October to January is probably the best, but the Tet Festival happens in late January to early February, which pushes up airfares and accommodation prices.
- February to April and June to September are good off-season times but it might rain occasionally and it can get hot.

 Need to know
- To ride legally in Vietnam, you need a licence from your home country that specifies motorcycle riding along with an international driving permit from the 1968 Convention. Many countries (including Australia, UK, USA and Canada) are signatories to a 1949 Convention, which is not accepted in Vietnam. To avoid issues in the unlikely event that the police will ever check your licence, a 1968 Convention IDP is available for all countries from www.e-ita.org/vietnam. The main issue here is to do with medical insurance but you should sort this out with a home insurer who is happy to do it purely on the basis of your home country motorcycle licence. Most insurers work on this basis.
- Prices for the tour vary with the size of the bike you select. It ranges from US$109 per day on a Honda 150 for a group of five or more to US$129 per day for a 250/300cc Honda with the same group size.
- Ride on the right-hand side of the road.

 Ride rating
Intermediate. No high speeds are involved in this trip but the variety of road conditions is considerable and detours, mostly on dirt, are probable in some areas.

 Distances
- The 11-day Ha Giang loop tour covers a distance of around 1600km (994 miles).

 Temperatures
- October to February: 10°C to 32°C (50°F to 90°F)
- March to May: 25°C to 34°C (77°F to 93°F)

 More information
www.offroadvietnam.com
www.vietnam.travel/places-to-go/northern-vietnam

The case for a guided tour

If you're planning to ride in north Vietnam, the case for organising a guided tour is overwhelming. Outside of the capital cities, English is very rarely spoken. It's almost impossible to get local directions or advice on distances or accommodation. Smartphones, Google Translate, Booking.com and the like can be useful in the larger cities but can catch you out if you rely on them in smaller towns and villages. You *can* ride in northern Vietnam on your own but the stress and uncertainty of it may detract from the experience and you'll miss the pleasures local knowledge guides can give you in relation to history, back roads and interacting with the locals.

I've been there on five adventures and actually lived in Hanoi for a year and I still book into a guided tour if I plan to leave the city for any length of time. It's incredibly cheap by Western standards and means you can relax to enjoy the ride without having to worry about where you're going to eat or sleep.

The go-to company in the north is Offroad Vietnam and it operates out of modest premises in the heart of Hanoi's Old Quarter, which also happens to be go-to place for inexpensive hotels and incredible, authentic culture. While I'm writing this, I wish I was there now.

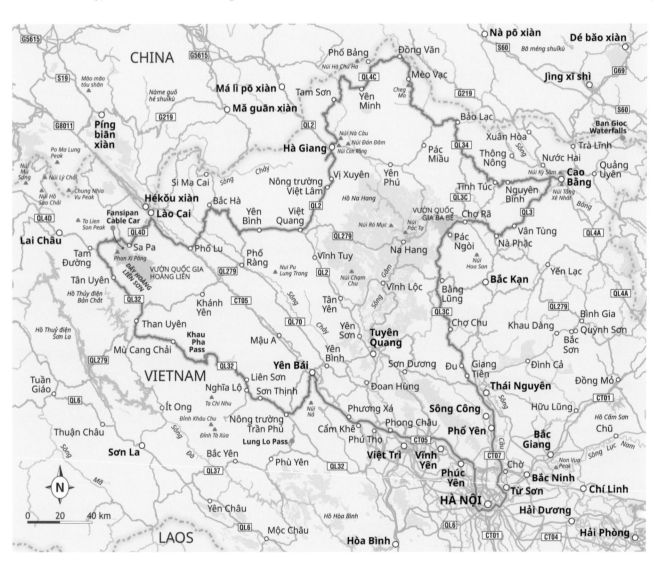

Asia

I've picked Offroad Vietnam's 11-day, Ha Giang motorcycle ride as a sample for this trip that gives you exposure to the best of northern Vietnam's roads and experiences. Doing it will change the person you are forever but it's certainly not for everyone. Medium-level riding skills are probably a minimum and you need to understand that some parts of the north are quite remote. The accommodation on the tour will be the best available, but sometimes that means power outages (you can't use the lifts to get to your room), beds with hard mattresses (or thin mattresses on the floor at homestays) and limited options in the food available, although there's always plenty of it.

Around 80% of registered vehicles in Vietnam are motorcycles and, particularly in the north, roads and trails have been set up with this in mind. If you're not on a bike, you ain't going very far. Registration and licencing costs favour small capacity bikes but so do travel conditions. You'll occasionally have to manhandle your bike onto a bamboo raft to cross a river or ride up the stairs of a hotel to park your bike in its foyer, tasks that would be very difficult on something like a BMW R1300GS. A Honda 150 or 250 (for horsepower freaks) is more than adequate for the task.

Here's how a Vietnam motorcycle adventure might work for you.

Let's do this

Book the Ha Giang loop tour with Offroad Vietnam and get a start date. You'll enjoy it a lot more if you can convince four of your friends to join you as you'll probably have the tour to yourselves. Joining an existing tour is also fine as anyone who does this ride will be worth knowing and you'll make new, lifelong friends.

Book accommodation at one of a number of thin hotels in Ma May street in the Old Quarter to cover before and after the ride. The hotels are thin because property rates are assessed by the width of the frontage. This also explains why, out in the country, you'll see a 10-story building standing by itself in the middle of a field and only being 4.5m wide. Ask to be picked up from the airport and dropped off there after your stay. It's a modest increase in price but it avoids the trap of having to haggle with possibly unscrupulous taxi drivers. Ma May Street is charming with plenty of dining options and is just a short walk to Hoan Kiem lake in the middle of Hanoi.

Offroad Vietnam is in the same area, so once you've settled in wander around to the office, introduce yourself and inspect the bike you've chosen for the trip. The office may appear underwhelming but the professionalism of its business is beyond reproach.

Top Looking down Ma May Street in the Old Quarter of Hanoi
Bottom Bikes in Vietnam carry incredible loads

Above Freedom! *Opposite top* Northern Vietnam is very mountainous and is a great riding environment *Opposite bottom* The engineering behind rice production in mountainous areas is constantly amazing.

Fansipan Cable Car

It's not on the Offroads Vietnam itinerary, but you might be tempted to hire a bike from them afterwards and revisit Sapa. If you do, make sure you take the Fansipan Cable Car trip. It costs about US$40 but it's well worth it.

Not only is this the longest three-line cable car system in the world, it also has a world record for the highest altitude difference. The trip lasts 15 minutes and when you arrive near the top of the mountain, you can either walk the 600 steps to the top or take the funicular, at extra cost.

The cable-car trip crosses valleys and provides extraordinary views before it climbs steeply to its destination.

As you might expect, it can be foggy at the top but if you get a clear day, it feels like looking out the window of an airplane.

Just out of Sapa, you can get to the cable-car station by a short train ride, taxi or by negotiating a price to sit on the back of one of the motorcycle taxis - the cheapest alternative.

Sort your luggage out and leave what you don't need at the hotel, which will also hold a room for you when you return.

The two most extraordinary parts of the ride will be leaving Hanoi in its seemingly feral traffic and returning. Ignore what you currently know about road rules and, as Anh from Offroad says, 'be like a fish swimming in the current'. Eight-abreast in a roundabout is common. There's method in the madness.

On the road again

Day one is Hanoi to Nghia Lo, a 250km journey that'll take around seven hours. It's a relatively big mountain-town that's reached via what the Vietnamese guide will describe as a 'snake road' at the foot of the Hoang Lien Range. It's in the middle of the second-largest rice field in northern Vietnam.

Riding in rural Vietnam does require some fresh learning. Snake roads have plenty of blind corners and you need to assume that what might be coming at you will be two trucks, side by side, in a slow overtaking manoeuvre taking up the entire road. The often narrow roads are also used to move slow-going farm equipment between paddocks, transfer water buffalo to new locations, and dry rice, corn and sometimes clothes. It's very bad manners to ride over any of this. Puppies will leap out from doorways under your wheels and, at school recess, students will flood the streets of rural towns. They'll wave as you pass or attempt high-fives and, if you stop, they'll engage with you to practice the English they're learning.

Natural high

Day two is a more remote road over the **Lung Lo Pass** and then the **Khau Pha Pass**. On this section you'll almost be as high as Vietnam's highest mountain, **Fansipan** (3147m), and you'll see as much of northern Vietnam as you will from any other point in the country. Beautiful.

Day three will take you up a paved mountain road to **Sapa** (population: 38,000), a legendary village from where you can see China. Sapa is a very popular tourist destination but it still has a sense of being very much its own master. You may get the feeling you might like to stay there longer than the tour allows but you can always go back afterwards with a hire-bike from Offroad Vietnam. By then you'll at least know how to find it.

The next day will take you down the mountain to **Lao Cai** (population: 130,671) where you can have a coffee while you watch people moving back and forward across the main bridge that connects Vietnam to China. You'll spend the night in **Bac Ha** (population: 49,000) which is threatening to become the new Sapa. It's a short (100km) day but you're riding along the

Chinese border. Don't be tempted to find a remote part of the road, wade across the river and stand in China. China takes its borders very seriously.

Try the whiskey famously distilled in Bac Ha but do it after you finish riding for the day.

It's a longer day after this to **Ha Giang** (population: 55,559) (200km) and then on to **Dong Van** (population: 81,880) the following day. You need a permit from the police to ride along the Chinese border and this can be provided at the hotel in Dong Van. If you're like me, this border pass will become part of your life-long keepsakes.

Tribe tradition

From the early part of the ride, you'll be encountering hill tribes or, as the Vietnamese prefer to call them, 'ethnic minority people'. They have distinctive culture and dress, and while they're officially Vietnamese, they live very separate lives, which from an outsider's perspective may be judged as disadvantaged. You'll have seen the Hmong and Dao people in Sapa and there are many more Hmong in Dong Van, where you'll be able to wander the streets and see their clay houses built centuries ago and still in use. There are 17 ethnic groups in the area.

Offroad Vietnam does its best to make sure you'll experience a local market on the ride, the fascination of which will never be forgotten. Along with normal market activity is a local, open-air court hearing and dispensing of justice where all (including you) can see and hear. You won't understand the language but you'll be able to tell how severe the punishments are from the look on the defendant's face. Oh, and the market food is exceptional. One such market is in **Bao Lac** (population: 148,000) where you'll be staying after Dong Van, but the Sunday market in **Dong Van** is judged as being one of the most colourful in the entire country. On one of my trips that had a support vehicle, the guides bought a puppy at the markets as a pet. It was wolf-wild and took days to settle down before it could be patted without it biting you. Dog meat is on the menu of many Vietnamese restaurants so at least this one was saved.

The last leg

After Bao Lac, you'll be heading to **Cao Bang** (population: 73,549) and the road is one pass after another. Mesmerising. You'll spend two nights in Cao Bang as the day in between is a ride to the glorious **Ban Gioc Waterfalls**. It's on the same river that separates Vietnam from China and punts meet in the middle to exchange goods and money as, somehow, that's legal

for both countries. Take your bathers as it's possible to swim up to where the 50m-high falls cascade into the river.

Day 10 takes us to the **Ba Be National Park**. The more experienced members of your group can decide to take an adventure track via a stream, but if you're starting to wear out from the constant stimulation, just go with the flow and head for **Pac Ngoi** (population: 400) village in the middle of the park where you'll be sleeping for the night.

Alas, day 11 takes you back to Hanoi but you'll regain the comforts of your chosen hotel and hopefully be able to spend a few days exploring the Old Quarter and soaking up the vibrant culture of the city.

If it sounds like I'm over-selling this ride, it's because I think it's probably the best experience you can have on a bike in Asia. It's unique, affordable and unforgettable. It's not for everyone but if the brief suits your adventurous spirit and open heart, you absolutely aren't going to be disappointed.

Being there

I love Vietnamese food, but while I was living in Hanoi for an extended period I started missing toast. Vietnam doesn't do toast. It took weeks, but I finally located a department store that sold toasters. I was greeted at the door by a young woman who escorted me to the choice of two toasters on display and then went off to advise a salesman of my presence. I picked my toaster and the salesman filled in an order sheet so that the warehouse manager could locate one in the storeroom. He returned saying there were none left. I asked the salesman if I could buy the display model and he arranged for a maintenance staffer to clean and test it.

The salesman then took me to the back of the store where three accountants were located. One filled out a purchase order and passed it on to another who filled out a sales order and, finally, the third one made up a receipt. Suddenly the warehouse manager appeared again saying they'd located a new toaster in the storeroom so the toasters were swapped. I finally paid and attempted to leave but was stopped by a guard at the door to check my receipt and the toaster. Because the receipt had the serial number of the display toaster on it rather than the serial number of the new toaster, the guard assumed I'd swapped a cheaper toaster for the one in the box on the way out.

We returned to the accountant stack and a new purchase order, sales order and receipt were produced before I could finally leave.

Seven of the store's staff were involved in this purchase. In the West, I would have gone to a department store, picked up the toaster and left through a self-checkout, involving no staff at all. Yes, the Vietnamese experience was inefficient, but all the staff in the Hanoi department store had jobs and were earning an income. In the West we have a significant problem with unemployment. I wonder which system is better for social stability?

Now, my next challenge was to buy a bread knife ...

BEST EATS

This is all taken care of by Offroads Vietnam while you're on the road and it does the best job possible with the local providers.

Hanoi and the northern region generally is full of street vendors providing classic Vietnamese dishes at very little expense. Try the following:

PHO BO AND PHO GA - Pho (pronounced 'fur') usually comes with beef (bo) or chicken (ga) and is a rich broth dish that traditionally takes a day to prepare and includes fragrant spices along with noodles, bean sprouts, lime wedges, basil, mint, coriander and other herbs with optional chilli and lemon juice. Delicious.

BANH MI - This is a crusty baguette with a variety of fillings including pork or chicken, pickled daikon and carrot, herbs and often a pâté with optional chilli.

BUN CHA - A specialty of Hanoi, it consists of grilled pork patties and caramelised pork belly slices in a broth made with rice wine vinegar, lime juice, sugar, garlic and chilli. It's usually presented with vermicelli noodles, pickled vegetables, herbs and sprouts.

BAHN XEO - This is a crispy pancake made with rice flower and turmeric and usually filled with pork, shrimp and bean sprouts. It's normally eaten wrapped in a lettuce leaf and dipped in a sauce made from fish, chilli and lime juice.

CHA CA - Hanoi loves *Cha Ca* and while a number of restaurants specialise in it, it's also available from street vendors. It consists of small pieces of fish marinated in turmeric and galangal and grilled at your table and served with dill and peanuts.

CHE - It's not for everyone but many enjoy this coconut milk dessert that has fruit (longans, rambutan, mango and jackfruit), jellies and, occasionally, mung beans and black beans.

BEER HOI - There are beer barns in the big cities serving this beer where you can sit on normal chairs at tables but it's also widely served at less cost on street corners where you'll sit on children's plastic chairs. It's a fresh beer (without preservatives) that only lasts 24 hours in the barrel and is delivered daily by the brewer. It's generally lowish alcohol and very refreshing.

Left Rooms in home-stays are divided by thin curtains but rice wine will help you sleep

Oceania

The Great Ocean Road, Victoria: Australia

Handcarved initially by soldiers returning from WWI, Australia's Great Ocean Road is 243km of riding pleasure.

SNAPSHOT

Despite its popularity working against it in peak seasons, the Great Ocean Road is still one of the world's most interesting roads for riders.

It was hand-built by soldiers returning from WWI who weaved it between rocky outcrops to provide a twisting road with almost constant views of the Southern Ocean. Its closeness to Melbourne means it can be a one-day ride but it deserves more and to learn it could easily take a week.

In this time you could learn to surf, eat lots of fresh seafood and introduce yourself to Australia's First Nations culture – the Eastern Maar, Wadawurrung and Gadubanud Peoples are the Traditional Owners of this region.

Oh, did we mention the corners?

The Great Ocean Road (GOR) is on the southwest coast of Victoria, the lowest of Australia's eastern states, and it runs from the surf town of Torquay for 243km until it technically finishes in the small town of Allansford in Victoria's west. But for most, it's the Twelve Apostles that marks its endpoint.

Its uniqueness comes from both its history and location.

Building it was conceived as a way of providing work for soldiers returning from WWI. Almost half a million Australians had enlisted with 62,000 killed and 150,000 seriously injured. Work was scarce for returning troops in 1918 and a road was needed to link the villages along the southwest coast. It was never going to be a normal road in that it hugged the sea and followed the natural contours of the shale and sandstone costal formations. Even if heavy machinery had been available, it couldn't have been used so the road was built with pick and shovel by over 3000 ex-servicemen and the over-matter taken away by horse-and-cart.

Nobody was thinking about motorcycle tourism then but the result when the road was opened in 1932 was both the largest war memorial in the world and, if corners are your thing, one of the world's great riding experiences.

How long?

It's possible to ride the Great Ocean Road (GOR) and back from Melbourne in a day but at least two days will give you the opportunity to savor its delights. Allow three days if you want to learn to surf or dive for shipwrecks. If you have the time and you like beach culture, it will satisfyingly occupy a week. This will also give you the chance to explore the quiet but challenging roads leaving the GOR and heading into the Otway Ranges.

When to go

- Summers on Victoria's southwest coast tend to be dry and warm but that attracts caravans and buses as well as bikes, so the GOR can get very busy. It's always better mid week and if you're equipped for colder weather riding, the GOR is largely empty over winter. The downside to this is you can't swim but you sure as hell can ride.
- Shoulder seasons (with the exception of school holidays and long weekends) will give you the best opportunity to enjoy the ride.

Need to know

- There are multiple signs on the GOR reminding riders and drivers to stay on the left-hand side of the road. This is important as much of the road is two-lane and there are plenty of visual distractions tempting drivers to drift over the centre line, particularly if they're not used to left-lane driving.
- If you're going to stay on the GOR for a few days book accommodation well in advance, particularly on weekends and school holiday periods. You can usually get motel/hotel accommodation during the week without booking and - with the exception of summer holidays when they're often booked out - campgrounds are plentiful for riders carrying tents.
- The jury is in as far as cafes and diners go. Look for where other motorcycles are parked. They've done the hard yards for you.

- Buses tend to sweep road gravel into the normal line most riders will choose for a corner, so watch for this.
- Kangaroos are mostly active at night and at periods of low light, such as dawn or dusk, so proceed with caution.

Ride rating
The entire road is sealed and there's an 80km/h limit, so if you go with the flow it's a very easy ride. Faster riding will require more attention. Even at 80km/h, the twistier bits of the road can be challenging.

Distances
The distance from Melbourne to the GOR is between 100km (62 miles) and 140km (87 miles) depending on which route you take. Some believe the GOR finishes in either Warrnambool or even Port Fairy but, regardless, the road from Geelong to Port Fairy is 282 Km. The distance from Torquay to Port Campbell is 187km (116 miles), which is where most people finish (though Allansford is the official end of the GOR).

Temperatures
- January: 14°C to 21°C (57°F to 70°F)
- July: 4°C to 13°C (39°F to 55°F)

More information
www.visitapollobay.com
www.iamlorne.com.au

Left The constant corners of the Great Ocean Road encourage enthusiastic riding

Start from Melbourne/Naarm

However you want to get to the start of the Great Ocean Road (B100), you'll probably be departing from Melbourne/Naarm, Victoria's capital. It was ranked as the world's most livable city seven times in a row from 2011 to 2017 and usually comes in thereabouts even if it doesn't get the top gong, so it's not a bad place to get acclimatised before your GOR adventure.

It's also home to a number of motorcycle rental operators if you haven't got your own bike (*see* breakout). There are two ways of getting to Torquay from Melbourne. The more direct route is around 100km via the M1 through the regional city of Geelong, but the more interesting route takes you down the Mornington Peninsula to Sorrento (M11) where you can catch a very scenic 40-minute ferry ride across the heads of Port Phillip Bay to Queenscliff and then on to Torquay. It adds about 1.5–2 hours to the journey. On your way down the M11 to Sorrento, take a left detour at the 85km mark to climb **Arthur's Seat**. It's a steep and twisty ride to a peak that offers extensive views of Port Phillip Bay. The road was used for motorcycle and car hill-climb events from the early 1930s until 2000 and the myriad tight corners and steep rise makes this easy to imagine.

There are hourly ferry departures from Sorrento so time your ride to catch the one you want. You'll arrive in charming **Queenscliff** (population: 1315), a picturesque coastal hamlet famed for its grand 19th-century architecture, which you'll admire as you ride by its ornate streetscapes before heading on to Torquay, a 45km ride along the backroads from where the GOR begins.

If you have the time, **Torquay** (population: 18,534) is a good place to spend a day. This is the home of Australian surfing and, along with the Bells Classic Surf Pro, it's where the brands of Rip Curl and Quicksilver were established. It hosts the Australian National Surfing Museum that pays tribute to the role of Australian surfers in the development of the international surf culture. Over 150 boards are on display including original 100 year-old slab boards. If you're up for it, GOR Surf Tours (www.gorsurftours.com.au) has a one-day program that will take you from scratch to being able to ride a wave at one of Torquay's famed surf beaches. If you can surf already then Jan Juc, Winki Pop and the legendary Bells Beach are less than 5km away. Many of the coastal villages that dot the GOR including Anglesea, Lorne and Apollo Bay also have surf schools catering for beginners. Here's your chance to become a semi-genuine bronzed Aussie surf god!

The road begins

Having already talked up the GOR, you should leave it about 4km out of Torquay for a short loop that takes you past Jan Juc to Bells Beach. Here is the home to the oldest surfing carnival in the world, the Rip Curl Pro that's held every Easter and is as revered by surfers as the Isle of Man is by bikers. Part of its fame internationally comes from the final scenes in *Point Break*,

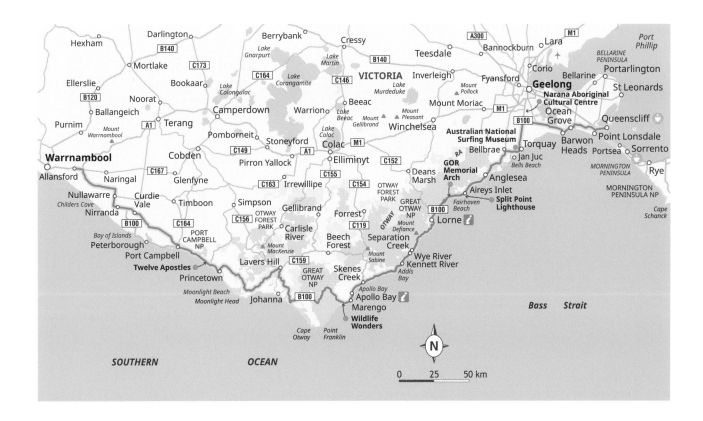

which, though set in Bells, was actually shot at Cannon Beach, Oregon in the US.

There's a car park at the top of the beach with good views but it's a substantial climb down to the actual beach, particularly if you're in your riding gear and it's the middle of summer.

The loop returns you to the GOR 2km later but you haven't missed anything on the early part of the road. It then meanders through coastal scrub until you rejoin the coast proper at the village of Anglesea, just over 20km from where you started in Torquay.

Anglesea (population: 3208) has plenty of restaurants and cafes making it a worthwhile stop for coffee or a bite. From Anglesea, the GOR hugs the coast closely all the way to Apollo Bay offering great corners and spectacular views.

Aireys Inlet (population: 979) is the next town along the route and its lighthouse is well worth a visit. The GOR is also known as the 'Shipwreck Coast' because of the number of vessels that came to grief on this wild coastline. The official estimate is 700 but only about a third of these have been discovered, making

the GOR a magnet for divers looking for their first great find. If you ride and dive, you've struck gold. The GOR boasts four lighthouses but, clearly, that wasn't enough. The most famous disaster was the *Loch Ard*, which hit Mutton Bird Island in 1878, killing 52 of the 56 on board.

Hire bikes from Melbourne and on the GOR

If you're leaving from Melbourne, Garner's Motorcycle Hire (www.garnersmotorcycles.com.au) has been in operation since 1984 and has a very good reputation with reasonably priced rentals ranging from a KTM Adventure 1190R for AUD$150 per day to a humble but competent Kawasaki KLR650 for AUD$75 per day. You might have the best fun on the GOR on a KTM Adventure 390 for just AUD$65 per day.

Down on the Great Ocean Road itself in Apollo Bay you have 73 Moto (www.73moto.com.au) that hires out Royal Enfield Interceptors and Continental GTs along with Triumph Scramblers for AUD$195 per day It also hires out riding gear.

Long and winding road

From Aireys Inlet, the GOR becomes a more technical ride. Its twists and turns were determined by the geography of the coast rather than any concept of safe road-building. The 80km/h speed limit that runs the entire length of the road – apart from the towns which are 60km/h – was set largely to manage high incidents of crashes in a region that attracts up to 2.8 million visitors a year.

Apart from tour buses, which can be a nuisance for riders, midweek the GOR is remarkably free of traffic. Of note between Aireys Inlet and Lorne is the **GOR Memorial Arch**, which acknowledges the hard work of the returned soldiers who provided the labour on this project.

The road itself is mostly well-sealed but you need to be careful of repaired sections. With mountains on one side and cliff drops on the other, there isn't much margin for error. Geography occasionally determines that corners tighten up more than you would otherwise expect and there are enough off-camber corners to encourage a slow-in, fast-out approach. If you glance away from the road itself, it's easy to be distracted by the scenery. Some discipline is required.

It's an argument for a slow ride rather than a fast one, but reason may go out the window in the section between Lorne and Apollo Bay. This is a 44km stretch that swoops and turns to the extent that the ride seems much longer. **Lorne** (population: 1327) is just over 19km from Aireys Inlet and dukes it out with Apollo Bay for being the best coastal town on the GOR. It sits right on the water and was, until 2011, when the old pier was closed for safety reasons, a working fishing port famous for its cray (lobster) catch.

The new pier was opened in 2019 and continues to host the legendary 'Pier to Pub' swimming race in January each year. Around 4000 swimmers leap off the end of the pier and swim 1.2km to the beach making it the largest open-water swim event in the world. Are there sharks? Yes. It's Australia – nobody seems to care.

A further 45km ahead you'll arrive at **Apollo Bay** (population: 1800), a leg that takes you through hundreds of tight corners on a good road surface. Here is an excellent destination to set up camp if the sun is starting to fade. Its fishing fleet is still very active and the local pubs and restaurants rely heavily on the local catch. The Fisherman's Co-op is run by a handful of locals who catch and sell locally. Its boat never really knows what it's going to come back with but it will often include flathead, snapper, King George whiting, flounder, gurnard, leather jacket and red mullet. On top of the menu is the local Southern Rock lobster. On good days, its small shop with plenty of bench seating overlooking the harbour will have a menu of 80% locally caught seafood. The water in the Southern Ocean that faces Apollo Bay is among the cleanest in the world and it's almost worth riding the GOR just to lunch on the incredibly cheap seafood platter available.

You can swim in the ocean all along the GOR but the coastline that sank all those boats has unpredictable tides and currents. Safe options include the patrolled beaches in the major towns. A particularly nice beach where you can swim in between the flags is **Fairhaven**, just west of Aireys Inlet, but you can also swim in patrolled areas in Torquay, Anglesea, Lorne, Wye River and Apollo Bay. Surfers play by their own rules and you'll see them all along the coast wherever the breaks are good. They're the bikers of the sea.

Meet the locals – First Nations experience on the Great Ocean Road

Australia's First Nations' People are part of the oldest, continuous living culture in the world. The GOR is the Traditional Country of the Wadawurrung, Gadubanud and Eastern Maar People of the Kulin Nation. It's a region where, for tens of thousands of years, generations have maintained a deep spiritual and cultural connection to these lands, a timeline stretching continuously as new cultural discoveries are made and dated.

If you continue on B100 past Port Campbell for 140km, you can visit **Budj Bim**, a UNESCO World Heritage-listed site that displays evidence of large, settled Gunditjmarra communities farming and smoking eels for food and trade. Budj Bim is home to one of the oldest aquaculture systems in the world, dating back almost 7,000 years, and ensured a plentiful supply of food year-round for First Peoples.

Previous The view makes it hard to concentrate on the Great Ocean Road *Opposite top* No, not a Twelve Apostle but a sea structure formed by the same process *Opposite left* The GOR is a war memorial *Opposite right* The lighthouse at Aireys Inlet

The wild, wild West

West of Apollo Bay, the GOR heads up to the fringes of the Otway Ranges and away from the coast. Again, the road twists and turns but with the added drama of overhanging trees that don't allow the road enough sunlight to dry properly on overcast days. It's sometimes hard to judge if you're approaching the shadow of a tree or a wet patch in the middle of a corner. To add insult to potential injury, many of the trees are native gums that leak oil onto the road after heavy rain. Proceed with caution.

Close to Apollo Bay (five minutes out, in fact) is **Wildlife Wonders** (www.wildlifewonders.org.au), a 39-acre fenced sanctuary with a focus on endangered native wildlife. It's a modern take on a wildlife park in that it's a social enterprise where money raised is reinvested into the sanctuary in the interests of long-term conservation. Princetown is the lead-in to the road's most famous tourist drawcard: the **Twelve Apostles**. The GOR has been judged the ninth most popular road trip in the world and the Twelve Apostles have a lot to do with it.

The truth is there were never 12 visible at any one time. There were eight, with one toppling over in 2005 to leave seven. The severe erosion caused by the wild Southern Ocean means new stacks are (slowly) being created all the time so the number may vary depending on how long it takes you to visit. Yes, you have to park your bike and take the easy walk to the viewing platforms and, yes, it's worth the effort. It isn't, however, the Grand Canyon.

The Port Campbell National Park is named after the town at its centre, **Port Campbell** (population: 440). It's a cosy, charming coastal town but it's also a remote outpost in a wild part of the eastern seaboard. It's sheltered by high cliffs and Norfolk pines but if you want to get an idea of how powerful the Southern Ocean is, go for a walk out on the jetty when the wind is up. If you're a diver, tours of the canyons on the sea floor are available and, because of its proximity to the Twelve Apostles, there are plenty of helicopter and boat trips available for the cashed-up.

Though the GOR officially finishes at Allansford, a small dairy community just prior to Warrnambool (worth pushing on to if it's whale season), unless you're heading to Port Fairy or the Budj Bim World Heritage site (*see* p.148), in reality Port Campbell marks the endpoint. However, with that said, it's worth taking a short ride farther ahead to admire other spectacular rock stacks such as London Bridge and the Bay of Islands.

There's also an argument about how you should return to Melbourne, if that's indeed the place you're heading. There are roads through the Otways that are full of forest magic and will take you through untypical but lovely Australian bush and small towns.

If you're in a hurry, the most direct route back to Melbourne is through Colac and then on the M1.

What most riders do, though, is turn around and retrace their steps. The vista is different going the other way and it maxes out the pleasure of the GOR journey. You'll understand the road a little better as well, which will enable you to take the last bits off the edges of your bike's tyres. Enjoy.

Being there

It's an ill wind that doesn't blow somebody some good. During the massive disruption to international travel and state-wide lockdowns during the COVID-19 pandemic, the GOR became largely deserted. The pandemic in Australia lasted from the first recorded case in January 2020 to September, 2022 when all restrictions were removed.

There were periods of lockdowns in Victoria where no inner-state travel at all was allowed, but for long periods riders in regional Victoria were allowed to travel while riders in Melbourne weren't.

Many small-town riders, myself included, took full advantage of this and without tourist coaches, national and international visitors, the GOR became our exclusive plaything.

Small businesses suffered but most remained open and often we were the only visitors to the pubs, restaurants and cafes on the road. Not only that, we were actually welcomed!

While the return of coaches and international travel is great news for the local tourist industry, it's once again slowed the down the traffic.

BEST EATS

Totti's, Lorne

Totti's is a busy Italian restaurant attached to the Lorne Hotel. It's trattoria-style dining opposite the beach and its menu is a combination of locally sourced seafood and Italian classics including homemade pasta and woodfired bread to go with a variety of side dishes.

It's busy at night during the summer season but very relaxed if you call in while passing in the afternoon. Modest menu choices result in modest prices but you can splurge with dishes including lobster pasta and King George whiting.
www.merivale.com/venues/tottis-lorne/

Chopstix Noodle Bar, Lorne & Apollo Bay

While this is a chain restaurant, its iterations in both Lorne and Apollo Bay are quite distinctive. The menu is as the title suggests but with a wide range of Thai and Asian-inspired options and plenty for vegetarians. The Lorne Chopstix's signature dish is Thai-styled whole baby snapper and the Tom Yum soup is also recommended with its rich supply of seafood.
www.chopstix.com.au

IPSOS, Lorne

Authentic, Greek taverna restaurant with old-fashioned service and values. It makes the most of its location in Lorne with lots of fresh seafood dishes and tender lamb. Open for lunch and dinner. It's popular so booking is advised.
www.ipsosrestaurant.com.au

Birdhouse, Apollo Bay

This is a gem of a restaurant that makes excellent use of the local seafood along with an eclectic mix of international dishes. It's on the second floor of a building along Apollo Bay's main street with great views of the parkland and ocean. Try the Portuguese seafood broth with blue swimmer crab, prawns, mussels, fish, calamari and chorizo.
www.birdhouseapollobay.com.au

Fishermen's Co-Op, Apollo Bay

The best fresh seafood along the GOR. You can dine on its outdoor tables overlooking Apollo Bay harbour or buy local catch to cook it yourself later. The Southern Rock lobster is excellent and the seafood platter is great value.
www.apollobayfishcoop.com.au

BEST SLEEPS

YHA Apollo Bay Eco, Apollo Bay

Here's a hostel with a difference. Its commitment to sustainability pervades the building but it doesn't mean you compromise on comfort or amenities. Its rooftop deck has great views and it has all the usual hostel features including shared lounges and kitchens. It's located one street away from the GOR and has four-person, multi-share rooms and twin/double rooms available. Like most hostels, it's also kind on your wallet or purse.
www.yha.com.au/hostels/vic/great-ocean-road/apollo-bay

Beachcomber Motel Apollo Bay

This is a traditional, modest motel with prices to match. It's off the main street but only a short walk to all the restaurants and attractions. It's quiet, comfortable and relatively inexpensive. If you stay there, can you ask if they still have my mobile charger?
www.beachcombermotel.com.au

Sea Foam Villas, Port Campbell

Lash out a little with an entire villa to yourself at Port Campbell. The Sea Foam Villas are in the middle of town and many offer bay views. Least expensive is the Queen Suite, which - while lacking views - is clean and comfortable. If you want to see the water from your front verandah, the ground level Bay View villas are your next best option. From there it goes up to the Penthouse Villa.
www.seafoam.squarespace.com

Opposite Every beach along the Great Ocean Road seems better than the one before it

Nullarbor Plain: Western and South Australia

Long, straight roads are usually the death of pleasure for motorcyclists but, strangely, Australia's Nullarbor Plain makes it exciting again.

SNAPSHOT

This is a long, straight road across a desert but it fine tunes your sensibilities to notice the normally insignificant things. This doesn't of course include whales that flock to the Great Australia Bight just off the Eyre Hwy to breed in July and August. They're hardly insignificant.

The ride is a true experience of the remoteness of much of Australia, a giant continent with a population of just 26 million. Crossing the Nullarbor is a rite of passage for Australian motorcyclists and a handy earner for motorcycle tyre retailers.

The vast land that makes up the Nullarbor Plain is the Traditional Land of the Mirning People, who call it Ngargangooridri. When Australia's six states decided to federate in 1901, there was no road or rail link between any of the eastern states and the state on the other side of the country – Western Australia (WA). There wasn't even a telegraph line until 1877. Unless you were an explorer with plenty of time on your hands, the only way to get from one side of the country to the other was by boat.

A rail line was started in 1917 and so flat and open was the Nullarbor Plain that 478km of track was able to be laid in a straight line.

A rough road across the plain was graded in 1941 but it wasn't fully sealed until 1976. It's now known as the Eyre Hwy and runs from Norseman in WA to Ceduna in South Australia (SA), a distance of 1667km. Like its rail line brother, the highway has a very long straight: 146km. Not all of the highway is technically on the Nullarbor Plain. Satellite imaging of the limestone bedrock that underpins the plain gives it as an area of 200,000 sq km, but its stretch is a mere 1100km – certainly enough for a good ride, even if a lot of it is in a straight line.

 How long?
Three days is the safest approach because you can't travel at night and there are things to see and do along the way.

 When to go
May to October is the best time to ride. Not only is the weather cooler (in summer temperatures can reach up to 50°C), but the whales arrive at the Great Australian Bight mostly in July/August.

 Need to know
- Ride on the left-hand side of the road.
- You can usually get fuel at 200km intervals but outback lore is you fill up every time you pass a fuel stop as you can't guarantee the next stop will actually have petrol - even if it says so on the website.
- Take plenty of water as it can get very hot, even in winter. And god forbid your bike breaks down; you might be stuck alone out here for a while.
- You can't take fruit and vegetables either in to or back out from Western Australia.
- Don't ride at night if you can help it - much of Australia's wildlife is nocturnal.

 Ride rating
Easy, but potentially tiring in long spells. If you turn left to check out the Great Australian Bight, you may have some dirt roads to contend with.

 Distances
- Ceduna to Norseman, the accepted start and finish of the Nullarbor Plain, is 1200km (746 miles) but you have to get to Ceduna first and Norseman is 780km (485 miles) from Perth, the capital of Western Australia so your ride will be much longer than this.

 Temperatures
- May: 9°C to 22°C (48°F to 72°F)
- October: 11°C to 24°C (52°F to 75°F)

 More information
www.australia.com
www.westernaustralia.com

Opposite The Nullarbor has a straight section for 146km. There go the tyres and the steering head bearings ...

Doing it the hard way

Edward John Eyre, after whom the highway was named, was the first European to cross the Nullarbor Plain. He had two attempts: his horses died of thirst on the first one in 1840; and two of his indigenous helpers mutinied on the second attempt in 1841, killing his companion and leaving with the remaining expedition supplies. But with the help of a local guide, Eyre finally completed the crossing in June, 1841.

So unimpressed was Eyre that a report on the expedition in 1865 by Henry Kingsly described the region as a 'hideous anomaly, a blot on the face of nature, the sort of place one gets into in bad dreams'.

It obviously wasn't a view shared by the Mirning First Nations People who cared for this country for millennia, sharing a special connection to the land where they lived for many thousands of years. Australia was occupied by the British on the basis of 'Terra nullius' – meaning nobody owned the land before the Brits arrived. This hubris extended to the British testing nuclear devices in Maralinga, just north of the Nullarbor Plain, between 1952 and 1963, largely

ignoring the existence of the Anangu Traditional Owners, marking a horrific chapter in the country's history.

Adventure island

While you're unlikely to have the experience of Edward Eyre, riding across the Nullarbor Plain is still a major adventure that requires a degree of planning. We're riding from east to west and starting from the charming town of Ceduna in South Australia and heading to Norseman in WA. That's the 'Plain plan' done but Norseman is in the middle of nowhere so after that you'll probably turn north to Kalgoorlie and then ride on to Perth, an extra 780km. Oh, and if you're leaving from Adelaide in SA, it's 776km to the starting point of our ride. Australia is a big country.

Ceduna (population: 1959) is known as the gateway to the Nullarbor Plain and a quarter of a million vehicles pass through it each year on their way west. It sits around Murat Bay on the west coast of the Eyre Peninsula. The Far West Language Centre was established in Ceduna in 2005 to help preserve the Wirangu, Kokatha and Mirning First Nations' languages.

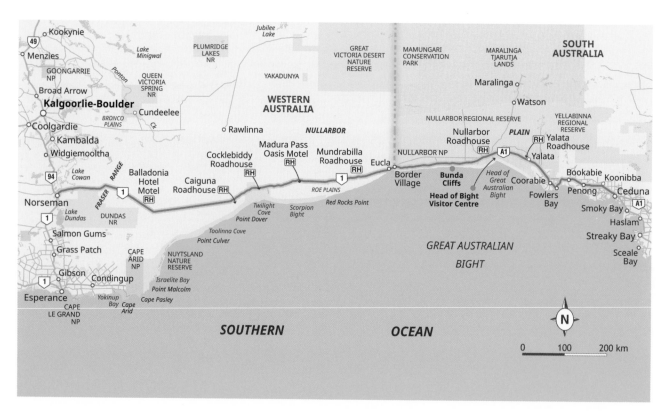

The longest golf course in the world

The Nullarbor Links is an 18-hole, par 72 golf course with 1365km between the first hole and the last. Participating towns and roadhouses along the Eyre Hwy provide a tee and a green linked often by a fairway of natural terrain - dirt and rocks.

Although some holes in the course are at established golf clubs, many boast a synthetic tee area and a synthetic green. This is partly because they don't have to be watered and other environmentally sensitive rules include teeing up (and not riding your bike) on the fairways.

Clubs are available at each hole so you don't have to carry a set on your motorcycle, but bring along a golf ball (or two).

The Eyre Highway Operators Association set the course up to encourage travellers to spend more time (and more money) on the Nullarbor but it also has the road safety benefit of encouraging regular breaks from driving.

Australia used to host the 'Golf Rally' for motorcyclists where an unsuspecting country town would be swamped by riders each year carrying only two clubs for a nine-hole competition. If you're traveling light on the Nullarbor, perhaps strapping two clubs onto the side of your bike mightn't be such a bad idea.

Top The Nullarbor Roadhouse - an oasis in the desert
Bottom One of the holes in the longest golf course in the world.

Above and opposite The Nullarbor Plain suits tourers rather than sports bikes

As you're about to deprive yourself of gourmet food for a few days, take advantage of Ceduna's excellent aquaculture industry and fill up on freshly shucked local oysters and seafood at the Ceduna Oyster Bar (*see* Best Eats).

As you'd expect with a road this long, it's two-lane but mostly in good condition. Within minutes of leaving Ceduna, a sense of isolation will set in so use it to acclimatise yourself for the real isolation you'll be experiencing further down the track.

Some 73km from Ceduna is the small village of **Penong** (population: 289) which has identified itself by establishing a museum for windmills. Yes, perhaps they're an acquired taste but they've provided water for generations of bush farmers in an otherwise dry and occasionally hostile environment. Southern Cross windmills have been made in Australia since 1871 and you'll see the brand name on the vain behind the windmill blades on just about every farm you pass. It's as identifiably Australian as kangaroos.

Fowlers Bay is 69km past Penong and while it's off to the left of the Eyre Hwy, it's a good opportunity for an early look at the cliffs that run almost the entire length of the coast, for the road to Fowlers Bay 15km is sealed and 7km is usually well-maintained dirt. This is where Eyre started

his journey in both 1840 and 1841 to cross the Nullarbor. Its current full-time population of 16 people doesn't sound encouraging but it boasts a caravan park, cabins and is the home of **EP whale-watching cruises** (www.epcruises.com. au) during the southern right whale migration in July, August and September each year. EP Cruises's current record count is 67 sightings in one day, including 27 calves. Its remote location and 28 passenger limit makes it less frenetic than most other whale-watching alternatives.

Back on the highway you'll be heading for the Nullarbor Roadhouse (*see* Best Eats). This will be the first time you really get to feel the isolation of the Nullarbor Plain. Fowler's Bay to the roadhouse is only 175km but the road is mesmerising, and the surroundings so similar that it sometimes feels like you aren't moving forward at all. You need to watch your speed because it will creep up as a result of having nothing on the side of the road with which to compare it. It's as close as you'll get to being a meteorite hurtling through what feels like eternity.

At around half distance you'll see the **Yalata Roadhouse** and caravan park that is run by the Yalata Anangu community. It has probably the best coffee available on the Plain and an art gallery that is a great outlet for the local Indigenous artists.

About 10km from Nullarbor Roadhouse is a sealed road to the left that takes you to the **Head of Bight Visitor Centre**. It overlooks a 15km stretch of coast where southern right whales come each season to mate and give birth. Viewing platforms pretty much guarantee sightings in the peak season between June 1 and October 30 (entrance fee AUD$16) with whale numbers often exceeding 100. The entrance fee reduces to AUD$8 from November 1 to May 31. It's 25km from the visitor centre to Nullarbor Roadhouse.

Sanctuary

Nullarbor Roadhouse has everything the weary traveller needs; fuel, food and motel-style accommodation. But you need to leave 'city thinking' behind you to enjoy it. Be grateful the modest food on offer is hot, the beer is cold and your motel room is private. Forget about comparing prices and comfort with other parts of the world: transport costs are significant here (and rising) and everything is priced accordingly. As they say in the classics, 'suck it up'.

Now it gets more challenging. Fuel is available at roughly 200km intervals across the Nullarbor but the rule of the bush is you fill up every time you see that fuel is present. Some places you might expect to find fuel may be closed or empty because the next delivery hasn't arrived yet. What's the range of your bike's fuel tank? If there's a headwind or you're riding fast, halve it. You can cross the Nullarbor without carrying extra fuel but if you can fit 4 litres in a container somewhere in your luggage, it might make a huge difference to the success of your trip. Having said that, the Eyre Hwy has enough traffic to ensure if anything goes wrong, a good Samaritan won't be too far away.

If you're riding in summer, you'll also need to take plenty of water with you. The drinkable water at roadhouses is held in tanks and their owners are understandably reluctant to give it away. Other water is from bores and the minerals it contains make it a last resort. Bottled water is always available from stores.

While it's not illegal to ride at night, sensible riders don't. Trucks do, though, and you'll see the result of this with the deceased wildlife that litters the highway the next day before the dingoes, eagles and road maintenance crews get to work. Nocturnal wildlife movers include red kangaroos, southern hairy-nosed wombats, dingoes and, believe it or not, camels. Australia is alleged to have the largest feral camel population in the world.

Another good reason not to ride at night is only three roadhouses along the Plain are open 24 hours of the day: Ceduna, Nullarbor Station and Border Village. Other outlets have some self-serve facilities but only for diesel.

While camping isn't allowed in the Nullarbor National Park, most of the roadhouses have campgrounds or caravan parks. There are also plenty of rest areas on the Eyre Hwy where you can bush camp. Many of these have short dirt roads leading to the Bunda Cliffs so you can enjoy the incredible views and do your own whale-watching, but there are no facilities at these sites. Fire restrictions are usually in place between November 1 and April 30 with irregular bans on other days and periods. Check before you light at www.cfs.sa.gov.au, even if the campsite you choose has firepits.

Oh, and check the weather in advance. Locals reckon it can get windy enough on this part of the Nullarbor to blow the milk off your coffee.

The Bunda Cliffs run from Cape Carnot in SA to Cape Pasley in WA, just south of Norseman. The area is called the Great Australian Bight. It should probably be called the Great Australian Bite because it looks like some massive monster bit into the bottom of the country, accounting for the 80m to 120m sheer cliff-line. The Bunda Cliffs run for 1160km and you'll never get tired of looking at them.

From Nullarbor Roadhouse to Border Village, which no surprises is on the border between of SA and WA, is 185km. Depending on what season you're riding in, you'll be able to feel the tread wearing off your bike's tyres, leaving a flat section that ruins handling – not that it matters as there are no corners to speak of along this part of the journey.

Over the borderline

There's a quarantine checkpoint at the state border where you'll have to surrender most of your fresh fruit and vegetables along with odd things like nuts and honey. Western Australia doesn't want SA food diseases and vice versa.

From here the Eyre Hwy moves slightly further away from the coast but there are still plenty of dirt roads leading down to the Bunda Cliffs.

There are very small communities and roadhouses at Mundrabilla, Madura, Cocklebiddy and Caiguna where you can get fuel and supplies. Make sure you fill up at **Caiguna** as you're about to ride on the longest stretch of straight road in Australia – 147km. Fill up at **Balladonia** as well as otherwise the next fuel isn't until Norseman 190km farther down the track.

If you've heard of Balladonia it's because the US Skylab space station crashed there in 1979. Local gossip is that the shire council issued NASA with a littering fine and the then American president, Jimmy Carter, rang to apologise.

Our journey from Ceduna to Norseman has taken you 1200km but since both towns are remote, you probably didn't start or end at either of these places. In all likelihood, you'll be riding from Adelaide in SA to Perth in WA or the other way around, a distance of around 2700km. You'll have experienced the exhilaration and loneliness of one of the world's great rides and it's something you'll never forget.

Being there

Two riders sitting on 190km/h streaking towards the border of WA and SA. I'm on the only Honda CX500 Turbo in Australia and Peter 'Bear' Thoeming is riding Yamaha's new XJ650 Turbo. We're doing a comparison review for the motorcycle magazine *BIKE Australia*.

The Honda coughs twice and then dies. Bear doesn't notice and disappears into the far horizon. There's something wrong with the fuel pump. I rewire it to operate straight from the battery but, of course, the ECU (engine control unit) doesn't just tell the pump '12 volts' and I can't get it going.

I'm struck by the irony of the world's latest motorcycle technology failing on one of the world's oldest plains. The desert spirits watch on silently.

Bear finally returns and we amuse the spirits with our attempts to tow the Honda 20km to Nullarbor Roadhouse from where we make phone contact with the boss of Honda Australia. He immediately understands that if we write about the CX's failure it will kill potential sales but doesn't realise we're 1000km from the nearest Honda technician and a timely rescue is impossible.

That night we drink perhaps too much in the roadhouse bar and canvas the following scenario. Two people in the entire world know that the newly released Honda CX500T has a reliability problem and they're staying in a motel room in one of the most remote spots in the world. Were they to meet with an 'accident', Honda's secret would be safe until the problem could be fixed and the company could go on to make millions. Bear and I agree that if we were Honda, the hit squad would already have been dispatched.

The two-up, three day ride on the Yamaha back to Melbourne was tense. We split the tasks: Bear would watch for approaching black cars with tinted windows and I'd keep my eyes open for helicopters. We finally relaxed after we'd published the story as then everyone knew and there'd be no point in whacking us. Sales of the CX500T tanked.

It took Honda around a month to get the bike back from the Nullarbor Plain.

BEST EATS

Ceduna Oyster Bar, Ceduna
A local institution in Ceduna, this quaint and charming shack has a small indoor dining area and tables and chairs on the roof for overflow - or if you want a great view while you're dining. The bar serves fresh Ceduna oysters, fresh sushi, Asian dishes and local-catch fish and chips. You might as well enjoy yourself here before you confront the Nullarbor proper, where choice becomes greatly reduced.
www.facebook.com/cedunaoyster

Nullarbor Roadhouse
This oasis in the middle of the Nullarbor provides most of the services a traveller would want, including a bar and a restaurant. There's a cafe open all the time but the restaurant operates from 5.30pm to 8pm. Its limited menu includes most of the Australian classics with some nice touches, including bush tomato chutney on the 'Nullar-burger' and fresh, local King George whiting fillets with the fish 'n chips. Make a night of it and use its accommodation as well (*see* Best Sleeps).
www.nullarborroadhouse.com.au

Balladonia Hotel Motel, Balladonia
There's a cafe in the roadhouse and a restaurant in the motel next door so you actually have a choice. The restaurant's menu isn't extensive but it's interesting with a few Malaysian-style options along with a Balladonia Beef & Guinness pie and a classic, Australian 'reef and beef' experience: sirloin steak topped with tiger prawns and a creamy garlic sauce.
www.balladoniahotelmotel.com.au

Below 1160 kilometres of Australia's southern coast look like this

BEST SLEEPS

Yalata Roadhouse and Caravan Park
Yalata is a First Nations community of the Anangu People and their lands cover 4500 sq km and span about 150km of the Eyre Hwy. The roadhouse has 24-hour fuel, food and coffee, and the caravan park has self-contained and semi-contained single, double and family cabins. It likes you to book in advance via email or call ahead. You can, of course, just turn up but accommodation may not be available.

The community and this enterprise have a long and interesting story. Visit the website for more details.
www.yalata.com.au

Nullarbor Roadhouse
Nullarbor Roadhouse has both a motel complex and a caravan park. If you're travelling with a tent, you can pitch it in the caravan park but the motel also has 'budget' rooms if you feel like stepping up for the night. See 'Best Eats' for more information on the Roadhouse's other attractions.
www.nullarborroadhouse.com.au

Fraser Range Station, Norseman
Want a taste of the traditional outback life? Fraser Range station was founded in 1870 and settled by the Dempster brothers in 1872, making it the first Nullarbor Plain station. Accommodation is in a variety of forms including 100-year-old stone rooms, single en-suite rooms and everything in-between, including camping spots for riders with tents. Horses are AUD$15 a night and it's AUD$5 per night for anyone who sleeps with them. There's a set menu meal every night in the kitchen and a bar to help you wash it down. The property is full of native wildlife.
www.fraserrangestation.com.au

Q&A
Cameron Donald

Cameron (Cam) Donald is a road racer best-known for his Isle of Man TT and Classic racing adventures but is also a multi-disciplinary champion in both national and state events in Australia. He rides daily.

How did you get into riding?

Motorcycles were always in the family. I just followed in the footsteps of my grandfather, father and two older brothers, Brad and Darren. What chance did I have of escaping it? Not that I wanted to, of course – I couldn't wait to be old enough for my first bike.

What's in your shed at the moment?

Bikes come and go in the shed on a regular basis but some of them will be there forever. My father's 1954 Velocette 350 MAC is a permanent fixture and so is my '70 Triumph 650 Bonneville. I've got an '04 Harley-Davidson FXDX Superglide which I really enjoy but the star of the show at the moment is a 765 Triumph Street Triple RS, which, in my humble opinion, is the best-handling British bike ever built.

Apart from all the rides we've done together, what's been your favourite road ride?

Two rides stand out. The first was in 2010 when I was in Europe racing and my wife, Kaz, was with me. We were in France and I'd mentioned at a dinner that I'd like to do some touring in Europe. Suzuki immediately organised a 1200 Bandit for me and Kaz and I had the best time roaming around the continent.

I do a lot of riding in Australia with my mates and a highlight has been us taking our naked bikes to Tasmania. I'm not sure if the pleasure comes from the ride itself or the fact that I'm riding with my friends. It's probably a combination of the two.

A racing rival of yours, New Zealand's Bruce Anstey, doesn't have a licence to ride on public roads because he says it just teaches you to ride slow. What's your view on that?

I hear this quite a lot but it certainly hasn't been my experience. I think saddle time helps build your cumulative knowledge of how bikes and tyres work which helps enormously when you turn on the speed.

I remember coaching an otherwise unobtrusive bloke once at a track day and he was a demon in the wet. I asked him afterwards what he did for a living and he told me he was a motorcycle courier. Everything he'd learned from his daily riding helped him on the track.

Your whole family rides. Is this your fault?

I share the blame with Kaz. She had a passion for riding well before she met me and got her learners permit as soon as it was legally possible. Our two daughters were on balance bikes pretty much as soon as they could walk and have progressed to mini-bikes. Riding in the beautiful Australian bush is something we can all do together.

What's your most treasured competition victory?

I know I've had two victories at the Isle of Man TT that are certainly memorable but the result that stands out is coming second to John McGuinness in the 2006 Senior TT. I broke the lap record in that race and knew for certain then that I was in the same league as the big boys.

I still go to the Isle of Man but these days it's to lead tours or do commentary. I'm still involved in competition and still love it but you need to be in a different headspace for TT racing. While it wasn't easy to give it up, having a partner and two kids made the decision a little less painful and it's nice to know I gave up on my own terms.

Opposite (from left) Kaz, Cam, Lola and Joni

Oxley Highway and Thunderbolt's Way, NSW: Australia

Three iconic roads are linked in Australia by First Nations People, bushrangers and wilderness. The Traditional Lands of the Anaiwan and Kamilaroi Peoples, now often referred to as the New England Tablelands, are one of Australia's finest riding areas.

SNAPSHOT

A classic playground for corner-hunters, this triangular ride through NSW covers almost 500km. It takes in a mix of coastal roads and wilderness areas before taking the steep climbs up the Great Dividing Range and finishes with a luge-like ride back down to the coast.

Australia didn't always look the way it looks now. First Nations People cared for this country for more than 65,000 years, with sustainable cultural practices that ensured thriving ecosystems that remained delicately balanced. From 1788 onwards, colonisation introduced Western farming practices along with feral species like cattle and sheep that have had a significant, often hugely detrimental, impact on the country's landscape. The topsoil was once so soft that tracks left in the soil could be retraced some 40 years later.

Australia had other early problems. The prisoners transported from British jails were often victims of their economic circumstances rather than hardened crooks but it's not surprising that those who escaped into the bush had little respect for law and order in the colony.

This ride celebrates an iconic Australian character: the bushranger. We'll start in the New South Wales (NSW) coastal town of Port Macquarie, ride down the coast to Nabiac, home of the Australian Motorcycle Museum, turn right and follow Buckett's Way to Gloucester and then take Thunderbolt's Way up and across the Great Dividing Range to Walcha. From here we'll turn right again and make another crossing of the Great Divide on the Oxley Hwy to end up again in Port Macquarie.

It's a distance of around 490km, which doesn't sound like much but the ride is so involving it feels like it goes forever. That's a good thing: you'll enjoy every centimeter of it.

How long?
You could race it in one day but take two so you can properly value the experience.

When to go
Though this is an all-year round ride, the winter months between June and August are best avoided due to the freezing conditions at night atop of the Great Dividing Range.

Need to know
- Ride on the left-hand side of the road.
- In the warmer months there are increased risks of bushfires, hence you should check weather conditions before you take this ride. Days with total fire bans are becoming increasingly common so keep that in mind if you're camping.
- Both the Oxley Hwy and Thunderbolt's Way are used by logging trucks, usually travelling slowly; watch carefully their entry points from the forests.

Ride rating
Moderate due to climbs, descents, tight corners and changeable road conditions.

Distances
- Port Macquarie to Nabiac: 102km (63 miles)
- Nabiac to Gloucester: 52km (32 miles)
- Gloucester to Walcha: 148km (92 miles)
- Walcha to Port Macquarie: 183km (114 miles)

Temperatures
- March in Walcha: 9°C to 24°C (48°F to 75°F)
- March in Port Macquarie: 18°C to 25°C (64°F to 77°F)
- August in Walcha: -2°C to 13°C (28°F to 55°F)
- August in Port Macquarie: 8°C to 19°C (46°F to 66°F)

More information
www.newenglandhighcountry.com.au

Opposite Thunderbolt's Way, north of Gloucester

Oceania

Above The road sign at Walcha

Any port in a storm

Port Macquarie (population: 50,193) is a bustling coastal town about 390km from NSW's capital, Sydney. We're starting from there because it's a popular holiday destination for east coast locals with lots of nice beaches and a couple of well-regarded motorcycle shops in case you need services or gear.

It wasn't always a holiday town. Birpai People have lived in the area for at least 40,000 to 50,000 years before explorer John Oxley stumbled on the site in 1818. Europeans established a penal settlement there in 1821 for repeat offenders, and a writer who lived there in 1860, Louis Becke, described it as 'the dullest coast town in NSW'. It's moved on a little since then.

There are two options heading south to Nabiac. The first is to take Hwy 1, which is the main route around the coast of Australia. The stretch from Port Macquarie to Nabiac is one of the better sections with lots of forest and a good road surface. If you have time, plan B is to link the coastal roads and ride through places such as Lake Cathie, Camden Haven and Harrington. These are country roads that will be slower but more scenic. Regardless of your decision, you'll end up in Nabiac.

Nabiac (population: 1294) is a small settlement of land of the the Biripi and Worimi Peoples. It now hosts the Australian Motorcycle Museum. It was started by Brian and Margaret Kelleher in Canberra when they discovered that classic bikes in Australia were being bought cheaply by the British and

Americans and being exported. You could argue that the museum is an overreaction, but that's a good thing, because it now has over 800 bikes along with a plethora of memorabilia. Quite a few of the bikes are on loan but many belong to Brian and Margaret. Highlights include legendary motorcycle designer Phil Vincent's own Vincent Black Knight.

You could spend half a day here easily and, if you can't escape the spider web of fascination or you get lost in the collection space (it's possible), there's the clean and inexpensive Nabiac Hotel (www.nabiachotel.com.au/accommodation/), 100m from the museum

To get to the start of Thunderbolt's Way, take Bucketts Way from Nabiac to Gloucester. The full Bucketts Way is the second-oldest tourist ride in NSW but we're only taking part of it. It does take you through the hillside village of **Krambach**, (population: 437) though, which hosts the Commerical Hotel which has a great country kitchen. Bucketts Way has long been a rider's dream but climate change is catching up with it and heavy rain and floods have had an impact on the road surface. It's still scenically beautiful but it ain't the ride it used to be.

Fill up at **Gloucester** and have a drink and a snack at Roadies Café (*see* Best Eats), which is biker-friendly enough to have bikes actually inside the cafe. The whole of Gloucester is bike-friendly which is not surprising given it's the starting point for the very popular Thunderbolt's Way ride.

Captain Thunderbolt

Australia's best-known bushranger is probably Ned Kelly. The country is still torn between people who believe he was just an outlaw police-killer and those who think he was a hero reacting to the oppression of the Irish by a sectarian government. He's been represented in a number of movies and played by, believe it or not, Mick Jagger as well as Heath Ledger.

Regardless, an argument could be made that Captain Thunderbolt should be number one. He spent seven years committing 'robbery under arms' while Ned barely managed three years.

Thunderbolt's real name was Fred Ward who was sentenced to 10 years of jail in 1856 for stealing 75 horses but was given a 'ticket of leave' after just four years. He was a long way from being reformed, though, and spent the rest of his life in the New England Tablelands robbing mail coaches, banks, inns and itinerate travellers. He survived partly because his lover, Mary Anne Bugg, had an Aboriginal mother and Fred was helped in the New England wilderness by her relatives' deep knowledge of the area.

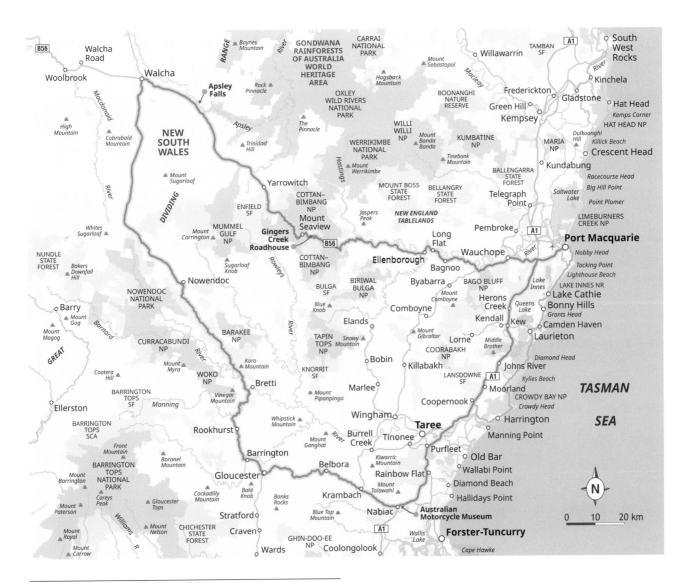

Getting there

Port Macquarie has an airport, which is handy, but it doesn't have any rental bike businesses. If you have your own bike in Australia, no problems. If you don't, Port Macquarie is around 400km from Sydney, which has multiple motorcycle hire businesses with reduced rates if you hire for up to six days. This is perfect for the New England Tablelands route.

Recommendations include:

Aus Motorcycle Rentals who have a range of bikes including Honda CBR500s for AUD$155 per day. www.ausmotorcyclerental.com.au

2 Wheel Adventures offer a wide variety of bikes on offer including a BMW R 1200 GS at AUD$200 per day for rentals lasting for two to six days. www.2wheeladventures.com.au

Eaglerider also has a variety of bikes, but specialises in Harley-Davidsons with either a Road Glide or a Street Glide from AUD$250 per day for bookings three to six days. www.eaglerider.com.au

The New England Ranges are replete with Thunderbolt references, including Thunderbolt's Rock (one of Ward's many hideouts) near Uralla, Thunderbolt's Cave (two of them), Thunderbolt's Hideout and, finally, Thunderbolt's Grave in Uralla.

The Great Divide

As you leave Gloucester, you'll start to climb the Great Dividing Range. It's a collection of mountain ranges, plateaus and hills that runs 3500km across the entire length of the east coast of Australia. It's the fifth longest mountain chain in the world and the longest entirely within a single country. Australian riders bless it because just about every great ride in eastern Australia exists because it either goes up or down the Great Dividing Range.

The section of the Great Divide that Thunderbolt's Way crosses is especially blessed because it crosses World Heritage wilderness areas and part of the Gondwana rainforest area. Only a quarter of Australia's rainforests have survived since 1788.

Within minutes of leaving Gloucester, you're on a two-lane road with origins that are traced back to 1961 when a Gloucester saw miller and road builder finally decided that he couldn't wait for the government to build it so he did it himself. He wanted a route from Nowendoc (up on the plain area of the Great Divide) to Gloucester to transport hardwood but it was eventually adopted by the government and it was then paved.

Like Bucketts Way, the road surface of Thunderbolt's Way can vary in quality partly because it's still being used as a logging road, but it's still an amazing ride. You climb over 1000m as you twist and turn through dense forests. You probably won't see one but you can hear lyrebirds for most of the route. What you might see are dingoes, wombats, the occasional koala and plenty of kangaroos. It also helps explain why Captain Thunderbolt was so hard to catch: imagine what the forest would have been like before the road was built.

There's a bit of plateau after Nowendoc, then a bit more of a climb and then a relatively long stretch of plateau until you pull into Walcha. The tableland area is very open, the road is in better condition because the trucks aren't braking on it and forward visibility is excellent. It can snow in this area and the vegetation reflects the harshness of this.

Walcha (population: 3229) is located on the land of the Dhanggati (Dunghutti) People and evidence from bora grounds where First Nations initiation ceremonies took place, date human use back 6000 years – although it's likely to be far longer than that. Because Walcha is a crossroad for Thunderbolt's Way and the Oxley Hwy, it's become a very motorcycle-friendly town. Sometimes it takes a while but small regional towns on motorcycle routes have finally figured out that motorcycle riders are actually good customers. Unlike car and van tourists, riders can't carry too much with them so they tend to buy what they need when they need it. They don't sleep in their motorhome or eat food they bought in city supermarkets, so hotels and motels do well when they pass through. Furthermore smaller fuel tanks mean they almost always need fuel. Hence signs saying 'Motorcycle-friendly town' are springing up all over Australia.

A standout example in Walcha is the Walcha Royal Cafe (*see* Best Eats), which has lots of different accommodation options to suit solo riders and small groups. It has undercover parking for bikes and lock-up sheds for security.

The Ox

The Oxley Hwy is named after the explorer John Oxley who crossed the Great Dividing Range in this area in 1818. When he stumbled upon the Hastings River, he and his party followed it to discover that it flowed into the sea at a point that Oxley named 'Port Macquarie'.

Oxley had made a number of attempts to head west once he'd crossed the Great Dividing Range only to be continually held back by swamps, leading him to believe Australia had an inland sea and the swamps were on the edge of it. His theory was incorrect and misinformed many other explorers who wasted time and effort trying to find it. Some early expeditions actually took boats.

The Oxley Hwy is longer than the part we're going to be using but this is by far the best bit for riders. It's a 163km section that joins Walcha to Wauchope. Riders from the coast often head up to Walcha, turn around and ride down it again in the same day. The Port Macquarie locals know it like the back of their hand so it's wise not to engage with them when they pass you doing twice your speed. There's no shame in deferring to experience.

Years of this happening has led to increased police interest, though, and most of the route now has an 80 km/h limit. On some parts of the run that's actually fast enough to have a good time and there are some sections of the highway that are so narrow and twisty that there's nowhere for the police to set up. The locals know where they are so follow their advice.

It's not all about speed, though. Around 12km from Walcha is a turn-off to **Aspley Falls.** You can ride to the main viewing area

Above Classic Australian roads with signs everywhere warning of kangaroos. This is just out of Walcha on the way to Wauchope

which alleviates the issue of walking from the main car park past all the signs warning you about snakes on the path. Aspley Falls are just one of a number of waterfalls you can find on the way down to Wauchope.

Walcha is actually in a shallow valley so there's a minor climb out of it before you can enjoy 50km or so across the top of the range. It's open with long straights and sweeping corners. You'll know when you get to the edge of the plateau as the surroundings suddenly wood up again as you start twisting and turning on the way down the side of the range.

After around 65km keep an eye out for the Gingers Creek Roadhouse on the left as it's a very pleasant place to stop for a drink or a light meal. All those other bikes parked there can't be wrong. Ginger's Creek Roadhouse struggled during 2019/20 as a result of the Oxley Hwy being closed for months due to major bushfire damage, but is now firing again on all four cylinders.

The 48km from there to the Mt Seaview turn-off is a mix of corners and great scenery, although the big trees are quite close to the road and you only occasionally get filtered views of the coastal plain you're heading towards. Much of the road was repaired after the 2019 bushfires and the surface now offers large sections of bump-free grip.

Uralla

Around 40km farther on from Walcha is the recently gentrified town of **Uralla** (population: 2358) on the New England Hwy. Here the Traditional Owners are the Anaiwan and Kamilaroi People, who have cared for this country for millennia. Later, Walcha, like many other towns in NSW, saw an influx of people due to the gold rush in 1855. Today, it is home to city tree-changers who are slowly converting it from a sleepy remnant of history to a vibrant art and culture centre.

Just to the south of Uralla is Thunderbolt's Rock, where the bushranger used to keep an eye on passing mail coaches and travellers. Fred Ward (Captain Thunderbolt) brings visitors to Uralla's **McCrossin's Mill**, an award-winning community museum with a fine display of the bushranger's life. Ward was eventually killed by Constable Alexander Walker in 1870 and the pistol allegedly used for this is not only on display at the museum but you can pick it up and handle it. Is it the real thing? Unanswered questions remain about Ward's death. Some claim it was actually his uncle who was killed, so Fred Ward joins that long list of conspiracy-inspired survivors who slipped away from public attention for a quieter life.

Ward's grave is in the Uralla cemetery and the ride from Walcha to Uralla is a continuation of Thunderbolt's Way.

The 27km section from the Mt Seaview turn-off to the Long Flat pub provides a few opportunities for the police to set up camp so keep your eyes open.

Some riders who do this circuit do it anti-clockwise but the benefit of the clockwise run we're doing is you may arrive at the Long Flat Hotel in time for a counter lunch. It's been a biker institution for many years and you get the chance to have a classic pub lunch in the company of most of the riders you've passed or who have passed you. It's hard to decide if you should sit at the front of the pub so you can see the passing parade or sit in the open out the back to admire the view and the calm of the passing river.

Unity in community

Wauchope (pronounced war-hope; population: 6589), the Traditional Land of the Birpai People, awaits 20 minutes further down the road. It's an admirable town in that in the past it could have joined the many country towns in decline in regional Australia but, instead, formed a community co-operative to keep itself alive.

The community owns the department store, the supermarket, the hardware store, the farm supply outlet, the liquor store and even a rent-a-car outlet. The money spent in Wauchope stays in town and the co-operative in its wider spread employs over 300 people, many of who are young and who would probably

Above Aspley Falls

have left town were it not for the job opportunities the co-op has provided.

If you spend some money there, you'll know its supporting the town.

The run from Wauchope back to Port Macquarie gradually re-enters civilisation which slows the pace a little and gets you thinking about a swim in the Pacific Ocean once you finally climb off your bike. As the hippies of the '60s were fond of saying, 'What a trip'.

Being there

Winter on the New England Tablelands can be, in turn, miserable and magnificent, and you can be easily fooled. If the sky is blue and there's no wind in Uralla in the middle of winter, it can get to a balmy 18°C.

It's Friday afternoon and we're sitting in the Top Pub in front of a fire.

'Why don't we ride down the Oxley to Port for the weekend? If we leave soon we can be there by nightfall'.

What an excellent idea. The 'leaving soon' bit turned out to be a joke, though, as various of us had to check tyre pressures, fuel up, pack, unpack to find the bike keys, pack again and then wait for everyone else.

It was relatively hot when we left Uralla but it was freezing by the time we'd travelled the 40km to Walcha and pretty much all of us were seriously underdressed. Walcha is blessed with two very good op (thrift) shops but both closed at 2.30pm, which was hours before we'd arrived. There was still someone working inside the St Vincent de Paul shop, however, who took pity on the five of us huddled outside the front door and let us in to raid the warm clothes section.

I have a theory about the generous people who donate to op shops: they tend to be shorter and more on the plump side. Or compared to me, anyway, as I'm long and (relatively) thin and it's rare I can find anything that actually fits me. On this occasion fitting came second to warmth, which is why in the bottom of my bedroom cupboard, there's a Walcha Golf Club jacket, a Walcha school uniform jumper and a pair of hand-knitted women's bed socks.

The bill came to AUD$12 and the ride was saved. St Vincent de Paul has since been my patron saint.

BEST EATS

Bills Fishhouse and Bar, Port Macquarie
It's not the cheapest restaurant in Port Macquarie to enjoy the local seafood catch but it's a long way from being the most expensive and it has a nice, casual ambience about it which is reflected in the name. The mostly seafood menu is often presented in unusual and novel ways. Mains are all around AUD$40.
www.billsfishhouse.com.au

Roadies Café, Gloucester
You won't have any trouble finding this cafe in the main street of Gloucester because there'll be bikes parked outside (and inside!) It's a favourite haunt for riders heading up Thunderbolt's Way with a straightforward but extensive menu with no mains being over AUD$20. It's licensed, too.
www.facebook.com/roadiescafe2422

Terracotta Trattoria Italian Restaurant, Wauchope
This restaurant does pizzas, of course, but plenty of other Italian dishes too including traditional favourites as well as the more exotic.
38 Cameron St, Wauchope; 02-65851824

BEST SLEEPS

Walcha Royal Cafe, Walcha
This motorcycle-friendly cafe and accommodation has plenty of options including a cottage for five to seven people for AUD$260 a night or, at the other end, king single rooms for AUD$90. It has a locked yard for overnight motorcycle parking with undercover options as well.

The former hotel bar has been converted to a '60s style cafe with an interesting and varied menu.
www.walcharoyalcafe.com.au

Gloucester Country Lodge, Gloucester
A modest motel in a bush setting with modest pricing, the Gloucester Country Lodge has a large pool and outdoor barbecue facilities that you'll appreciate in summer. Parking is free and secure. Most rooms have a rear sliding door so you can sit outside and admire the mountains.

Single rooms from AUD$120 and Queen doubles from AUD$135.
www.gloucestercountrylodge.com.au

Ozzie Possie Backpackers, Port Macquarie
This is a very cute youth hostel with twin en-suites from AUD$89 and queen en-suites from AUD$99. It also has the usual shared dorms and rooms for small groups. It's well located in Port Macquarie and you can park your bike in the grounds.
www.yha.com.au/hostels/nsw/mid-north-coast/ozzie-pozzie-backpackers

Above 'Is that Aoraki/Mount Cook?' Sometimes it's hard to tell as the beautiful scenery constantly replicates itself

South Island: Aotearoa/ New Zealand

Aotearoa/New Zealand's physical beauty and deep mystery is well captured in Peter Jackson's Lord of the Rings. *The South Island looks spectacular on the big screen but there's nothing like the real thing.*

SNAPSHOT

The South Island of Aotearoa/New Zealand is one of the most contained, beautiful rides in the world. Narrow roads and bridges mean there's not much heavy industry to clog up the roads with trucks. The enchantment of the scenery never seems to stop and New Zealanders are among the nicest people you'll ever meet.

Do you know what a Tuatara is? Probably not. It's a beak-headed reptile that has been extinct for somewhere between 60 and 100 million years everywhere else in the world except Aotearoa/New Zealand. It survived here because it is one of the last large, habitable places in the world to be populated and settled.

The country is located in the extreme southwestern part of Polynesia and is 1600km (1000 miles) southeast of its nearest neighbour, Australia. It's slightly smaller than Colorado in the US and slightly larger than the United Kingdom. It's also one of the world's great motorcycle destinations.

Maori arrived in the 1300s from other parts of Polynesia, but not in great numbers – probably due to the arduous nature of the canoe journey required to get there. When Abel Tasman saw it for the first time in 1642 and James Cook followed up in 1769, it's estimated the Maori population was around 100,000. This declined to around 42,000 by 1896 as a result of European diseases (to which the Maori had no resistance) along with both inter-tribal warfare and clashes with the largely British colonisers.

New Zealand (Aotearoa in the Maori language) was annexed by Great Britain in 1840. The Treaty of Waitangi was signed in 1840 between the British Crown and around 540 Maori chiefs. Differences of interpretation eventually emerged in the languages of the agreement. Regardless, the treaty facilitated European settlement as it ensured the Europeans could buy land from the Maori.

The relatively short period of human occupation in NZ (around 700 years) enabled a unique physical environment. Two-thirds of it is covered by mixed, evergreen forests and nine-tenths of its indigenous plants only exist on this island.

 How long?
Give yourself 10 days to two weeks to fully enjoy it, although it's possible to ride it in three days.

 When to go
December to March provides the best weather for riding. Most motorcycle-related activities take place during this period.

 Need to know
- Ride on the left-hand side of the road.
- Hire car crashes are common on the South Island as many tourists aren't used to the open spaces, narrow roads and the need to park safely if they want to take photos.

 Ride rating
Easy. Roads are clearly defined, well sealed and not chopped up by heavy vehicle movement. The only issue is both the roads and bridges can be narrow.

 Distances
- The big loop is around 1700km (1056 miles) but allow for a bit extra for deviations

 Temperatures
- December: 10°C to 21°C (50°F to 70°F)
- March: 10°C to 17°C (50°F to 63°F)

 More information
www.discovernewzealand.com

The ride to Paradise

There's actually a location in NZ called Paradise and we'll get to it eventually but, first, we have to decide on which of the two parts of the country we're going to ride: the North Island or the South. All of NZ is worthy of your interest but the South Island is a rider's dream due to its great roads, sparse population and phenomenal scenery.

We're starting from **Christchurch** (population: 399,700), which is the largest city on the South Island and home to an international airport, making it relatively easy to get to. It's also home to many bike hire companies, so there's no problem getting a bike and hitting one of the world's great road networks.

Christchurch itself is worth a few days of inspection. It was severely damaged by an earthquake (not uncommon in NZ) in 2011, which killed 185 people and there are still parts of what used to be the central business district that have an unsettling silence. A promenade along Brockworth St with all its attractions revives the spirits and a gondola ride up to Mt Cavendish will introduce you to the spectacular scenery you'll be exposed to once you ride out of the city limits.

It's also always worth checking what's going on at **Ruapuna Park** (Euromarque Motorsport Park) while you're in Christchurch as there are frequent motorcycle race events there.

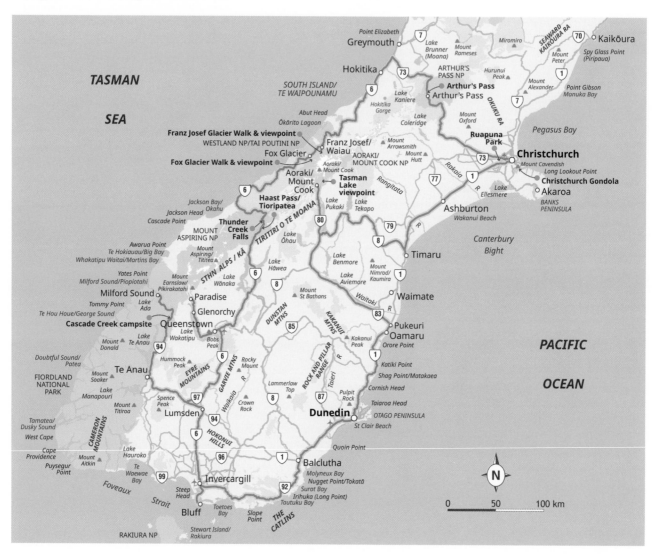

Oceania

Our ride loop is around 1700km and the start requires you to ride 380km across the Island to the Franz Josef Glacier. The best part of this is crossing Arthur's Pass with its viaducts, gorged rivers, bridges and waterfalls. The lack of heavy industries on the South Island means most of the two-lane roads are in very good condition and well suited to spirited riding. The pass takes you up to 900m and by the time you get to Franz Joseph Glacier you'll be a little disorientated from the hundreds of corners and will appreciate a rest.

Put your walking shoes on and take the one hour (return) trail to the **Franz Joseph Glacier** viewpoint. New Zealand, because of its location, has a reduced impact of climate change but its glaciers are receding. Franz Joseph has lost over 2km in the past 10 years but it's still well worth the walk. After your exercise, climb into the natural hot pools in the town and think about the 350km you'll be doing the next day to get to Queenstown.

Closer to the South Pole

Depending on how much time you have, breaking up the ride to Queenstown isn't a bad idea in that it will give you more time to take in the spectacle of the Fox Glacier and the Haast Pass. There's a one hour walk on a viewpoint trail at the **Fox Glacier**, which is enchanting but, if you can afford it, a half-hour helicopter flight over Fox Glacier and Aoraki/ Mt Cook is something you won't forget in a hurry. It costs less than NZ$400 in a six-seat chopper and, weather permitting, you actually land on the upper reaches of the glacier for a short walk on its surface. Magic.

Haast Pass is just as energising as Arthur's Pass with myriad corners and a good road surface along with great views. Thunder Creek Falls is on this road and is just a five minute walk from the highway.

Something to keep in mind on the passes is that NZ attracts tourists from many countries that drive on the right-hand side of the road. Recent figures indicate that foreign tourists were responsible or partly responsible for up to 80% of crashes on the South Island. Many are unaccustomed to the open driving conditions and are prone to stop in inappropriate spots to take photographs. Ride with this in mind.

Town of queens

Queenstown (population: 15,800) is a highlight of the South Island loop. On the surface it shouldn't be, as it looks like a typical tourist trap but its concentration on physical activities means it's usually full of young, fit adventurers and their energy electrifies the surroundings.

Above Florence Hill Lookout on the Southern Scenic Route

Punching above weight

New Zealand is by any definition a remote country. Keep it in mind if you need to emigrate before the nuclear holocaust. Despite it's relatively tiny population of 5.5 million (New York alone has 8.5 million), NZ has produced a well-above average list of stellar international performers.

Ernest Rutherford (1871-1937) practically invented atomic and nuclear physics. Kate Sheppard (1848-1934) was instrumental in NZ being the first country in the world in which women could vote (1893). Edmund Hillary (1919-2008) along with Tenzing Norgay was the first up Mt Everest in 1953. Peter Jackson (*Lord of the Rings* director) and Russell Crowe (*Gladiator*) are New Zealanders, so was the late Denny Hulme and 2023 rookie Liam Lawson (F1 drivers) and musicians Neil and Tim Finn from Split Enz and Crowded House.

You already know about Burt Munro, but what about Hugh Anderson (four times motorcycle world champion) and Graeme Crosby (legendary racer)?

Then, of course, there's the All Blacks. This tiny nation has absolutely dominated world rugby to the point where there's an expectation they'll always win, no matter who they're playing. Remember, they draw from a population of 5.5 million, while Great Britain, where the game was invented, has 68 million.

Top Road design is determined by the location of the surrounding mountains *Bottom left* Beach racing at the Burt Munro Classic *Bottom right* Returning to Invercargill after the Hill Climb event at the Burt Munro event

Jet boating, canyon swings, bungy jumping, skydiving, luge – you imagine it and it's probably there along with more sedate pastimes like lake cruises and bushwalking. Taking the gondola up to Bob's Peak will let you get some perspective on your surroundings, but if you're going to spend some time there, get on your bike and ride alongside Lake Wakatipu to Glenorchy (46km). This isn't a famous road and nobody talks about it much because, despite its stunning nature, its glory is masked by all the other stunning roads you've already been on to get there. If it was in any other part of the world, you'd be paying an admission fee to ride it.

Paradise (the village, not the state of mind; population: 6443) is a little farther past Glenorchy and is beautiful but some of the road to it is unsealed. It was used as a location for both the *Lord of the Rings* and *Hobbit* films.

Back in Queenstown, book yourself into the -5 Degrees Ice Bar for an hour. They'll give you a warm coat at the door so you don't freeze to death and you can drink cocktails from ice glasses while sitting on ice furniture. Afterwards, join the queue in Shotover St waiting to order a Fernburger. It's a Queenstown institution and is as good as burgers get.

Okay, enough mucking around in tourist town. Fire up your bike and head to the exquisite **Milford Sound**. It's 288km from Queenstown via Te Anau and its natural beauty is unmatched by any other location in Aotearoa. The ride on the Te Anau/Milford Sound section is wild and twisty with an excellent, grippy surface and plenty vision in its open spaces. Perfect.

You're going to Milford Sound both for the ride and for the views, and the best way to enjoy the latter is on a boat cruise. Leave Queenstown early as buses packed with tourists are also going to be visiting on the same day. You'll enjoy an early morning (or late afternoon) cruise as it won't be as crowded. Waterfalls, myriad wildlife and a bar – what more could you wish for?

There's only one accommodation option: Milford Sound Lodge. It has choices from dorms to upper-end suites. If you're travelling with a tent, nearby Cascade Creek campsite is cheap but it can't be booked in advance and can fill up in the summer season. There's a handful of other campsites on the road from Te Anue and you could consider staying in Te Anue itself, which has more accommodation options and is within easy riding distance to Milford Sound.

You need to backtrack on the same road to Milford Sound (94) but it's no burden as you'll enjoy the ride just as much going the other way. You're heading to Lumsden where you'll link up with Hwy 6 to take you down to Invercargill. One thing you'll have noticed by now is how narrow the frequent bridges are on the South Island – some are one lane only. It's one of the reasons the roads are so lightly trafficked: the narrow bridges and twisty roads aren't suited to transporting goods by truck. It limits the potential commercial growth of the Island but makes it all the better for riding.

Start your engines

Invercargill (population: 57,100) is the unlikeliest town to be a focus for motorcyclists but it is and it's largely down to one man: Burt Munro (1899–1978). Burt's story was told in the movie *World's Fastest Indian* and it brought international attention to someone who had always been a national hero.

The movie uses a bit of dramatic license (as all movies do) but the framework is an absolutely true story. An impoverished Bert developed his 1920, 600cc Indian Scout with a standard top speed of 90km/h into a fire-breathing 950cc monster that set a world record for bikes under 1000cc at the Bonneville Salt Flats in 1967 topping 296km/h (184mph). Burt was 68 at the time and his bike was 47 years old. He died in 1978 and is buried in his hometown cemetery.

His bikes and memorabilia are on display in **E Hayes' hardware store** in Invercargill and the town comes alive each February for the Burt Monro Challenge, a festival of motorcycle sport that includes a hill climb, beach races, sprints, speedway and street racing. If the planets align for you, your New Zealand trip should coincide with this event. It's an absolute hoot.

Also in Invercargill is the **Classic Motorcycle Mecca Museum** with 300 bikes on display, including four examples of the legendary Britten – a superbike designed and built in NZ by John Britten, which, among other things, set four world speed records and won the Daytona Battle of the Twins in 1994. John only built 10 of these bikes so having four in the one place is indeed special.

It's slightly out of the way but 25km south of Invercargill is **Bluff** (population: 1840), home of the world famous Bluff oysters. These come from the pristine Foveaux Strait and are widely considered to be the best oysters in the world.

Once you've exhausted Invercargill, stay on the coast on 92 until it links up with Hwy 1 at Balclutha and proceed to Dunedin. This takes you through the Catlins region, which is the leafy, undulating land between the sea and the start of the inland ranges. It's called the 'Southern Scenic Route', which has a little irony in it – show me a part of the South Island that isn't scenic. If waterfalls are your thing, there are plenty

of them, all well signposted, as you start heading north. Keep your eyes open for fur seals, sea lions, elephant seals, dolphins and yellow-eyed penguins.

Dunedin (population: 114,347) is the second largest town on the South Island and has architecture that reflects the influence of the many Scots who settled the area. It's also home to the main campus of NZ's oldest university: Otago. This makes it very much a student town with all the attendant cheap bars and restaurants. St Clair beach is a go-to haunt for excellent seafood.

Oh, and if you're after a little exercise, Baldwin St in Dunedin holds the current *Guinness Book of Record* for being the steepest street in the world.

Onwards and upwards

Staying on Hwy 1 from Dunedin, we're sticking to the coast until we get to just above Oamaru at Pukeuri Junction, where we turn left onto 83 and follow the Waitaki River up to where 83 meets Hwy 8. Here we turn right, heading to Lake Pukaki. Another left onto Hwy 80 takes us alongside the lake to Aoraki/Mount Cook Village, a total distance of 317km.

Aotearoa has a number of blue lakes but **Lake Pukaki** is by far the bluest. As you twist and wind along 80 you'll get very clear views of Aotearoa's highest mountain, **Aoraki/Mt Cook**. It's a very popular destination for locals and visitors, so if your intention is to stay there you need to book well in advance. It's full of great walks that can be matched to your level of fitness.

The beautiful Mueller Hut walk is seven hours return (you can stay the night there but, if it's summer, you need to book) but the Tasman Lake viewpoint is less than a kilometre return.

You'll need to follow Hwy 80 in the opposite direction to get back onto Hwy 8 and head north again past Lake Tekapo on your way back to Christchurch. Highway 8 rejoins Hwy 1 at Timaru. The trip back to Christchurch is scenic but you'll be so overwhelmed by the physical beauty of the roads you've travelled so far that 'scenic' will no longer be enough. You'll have to be dragged kicking and screaming to your seat on your flight home.

If you're like thousands of other riders, New Zealand/Aotearoa will become your stock answer to the perennial question: 'Where would you live if you had to leave your home country?'

Being there

The New Zealand accent takes some getting used to if you're not actually from there. Nominally, the language is English but with enough influences from outside it sometimes makes it hard to follow. The main intonation feature is the high, rising terminal that makes most statements end up sounding like questions. Australians do it as well.

Then there's the slang - different words for things you already know.

'Fish and chips' sounds like 'fush 'nd chups' and 'six' sounds either like 'sux' or 'sex'.

All is lost in the South in places like Dunedin where the accent is heavily contaminated by Scottish ancestry. It can sound like a completely foreign language.

I flew into New Zealand when it was possible in COVID-19 times and was put through the third degree at the arrival counter and the immigration desk. Understandably, they wanted to know where I'd really come from, what was I doing there and when would I be leaving. After 30 minutes of this I was finally standing in front of what I thought was the last line of questioning.

'What do you want me to do now?'
The tourist visa clerk fixed me with his steely glare and said, 'Sing Auld Lang Syne for me'. In the split second I had to think about this, I decided he wanted me to make a cultural gesture to prove that I really was from where it said on my passport. So as I began to sing he looked suitably astounded. 'What are you doing'
"Didn't you ask me to sing 'Auld Lang Syne'?"
'No, I said, "See that line behind me?"'

He let me in, regardless, but he's probably still telling his friends about it at dinner parties.

BEST EATS

Buccleugh's on High, Greymouth
This is a restaurant at the Recreation Hotel on High St, Greymouth, and it's an opportunity to sample one of the secret pleasures of locals: whitebait fritters. Whitebait is immature native freshwater fish, usually about an inch long and prevalent from August to November. The fritters are made from a combination of whitebait and eggs fried in butter and coated with salt and white pepper. Tradition has it that it's served as a sandwich. Buccleugh's other local options include venison and blue cod.
www.rechotel.co.nz/restaurant

Bunrunners Cafe, Christchurch
The Scottish influence in NZ extends to the Southland Cheese Roll. It's simple and cheap: a slice of white bread spread with a cheese mixture, rolled up, grilled and then coated with butter. Be still my beating heart! You'll also find a variety of other Scottish-inspired items on its menu.
www.bunrunners.co.nz

Captain's Steak and Seafood Restaurant and Bar, Queenstown
You've spent all that money to get to Queenstown so don't sweat spending a bit more on an upmarket local dining experience. Captain's is in the middle of Queenstown Mall and has an extensive menu featuring all the things for which NZ is famous: mussels, oysters, crayfish and, of course, lamb. Enjoy.
www.captains.co.nz

BEST SLEEPS

Jailhouse Accommodation, Christchurch
Yep, it's an actual old jail but very tastefully converted into inexpensive accommodation. It's a 20 minute walk to the arts centre, museum and botanical gardens. It has dorms but also well-priced private rooms. It's also got parking for motorcycles and all the other features you expect from a hostel. There are plenty of other hostel options in Christchurch, too.
www.jail.co.nz

Tasman Holiday Park, Te Anau
There's an argument for staying in Te Anau if you plan to visit Milford Sound. It's a 120km ride, you beat the buses from Queenstown and it's much cheaper with a lot more accommodation options than Milford Sound itself.

Tasman Holiday Park is adjacent to Lake Te Anau, and is a five minute walk to restaurants and shops, and offers a range of accommodation options along with secure bike parking. It's also got a hot tub and sauna to soothe away the aches after a hard ride. Go for the deluxe queen studio but there are also tent spaces if you're camping.
www.tasmanholidayparks.com/nz/te-anau/accommodation

Tower Lodge Motel, Invercargill
Okay, this place is a motel but it's a very good one and it's in the heart of Invercargill. Its rooms have kitchenettes and satellite TVs in case MotoGP is on. It's also modestly priced and has free motorcycle parking. It's one of a hundred accommodation options but the price and location make it a winner.
www.towerlodgemotel.co.nz

Above Bluff oysters - arguably the best in the world *Opposite* Fox Glacier walk

More Rides

Blue Ridge Parkway: USA

The Blue Ridge Parkway in Virginia and North Carolina is one of America's favourite rides. 16,000,000 visitors each year can't be wrong.

The Blue Ridge Parkway runs between the Shenandoah National Park in Virginia to the Great Smoky Mountains in North Carolina. It's officially 469 miles long.

Constructing the Parkway was one of President Roosevelt's 'new deal' projects to provide work after the Great Depression that started in 1929. Work commenced in 1935 and was interrupted by WWII to finally be completed in 1987. The route includes six viaducts and 168 bridges.

It's not actually a national park but the road and land either side of it is under the control of the National Park Service and it's regularly the most visited site on the national park register.

The speed limit on the road reflects building difficulties in its early years where corners were determined by what was physically possible rather than any thinking about contemporary corner design. Some corners don't play by the rules and you need to keep this in mind during your ride.

Start your engines

Starting from Waynesboro near Afton in Virginia is probably the correct approach but riding it the other way has some advantages. One of them is bike hire at Asheville (www.ashevillemotorcyclerentals.com) where a Royal Enfield Interceptor is US$149 a day and a Harley-Davidson Softail Lowrider is US$169 per day. Insurance is US$25 per day.

Camping on the Blue Ridge Parkway is a great option. The route has eight designated camping areas open from May to October and, with the exception of two relatively expensive lodges, precious little accommodation exist on the Parkway itself. Plenty exist off the Parkway's many exits, of course, and a business ecosystem built around Parkway travelers is alive and well. You'll have to leave the Parkway regardless to get fuel as 469 miles is a big ask for most motorcycle fuel tanks.

Planning your ride is assisted by milestones along the entire route from the Shenandoah Valley to its end in North Carolina. The planning app you now have on your mobile will tell you what's going on mile after mile and where you should turn off for attractions that catch your eye.

The road itself is, apart from the traffic, everything a rider would want: sweeping corners, climbs and descents, plenty of roadside stop places and genuinely startling views.

Before you get to Waynesboro (if you're starting from that end), stop at **Staunton** and have a walk down the main drag to admire the Woodrow

 How long?
How long is a piece of string? To fully explore the Blue Ridge Parkway would take weeks but you'll get plenty of riding pleasure from three days.

 When to go
While the route is open all year (snow notwithstanding), May to September are the best months but also the busiest. April and October will be less hectic.

 Need to know
- Ride on the right-hand side of the road.
- There's no fuel available on the Blue Ridge Parkway but plenty close by on the many Parkway exits.
- There's a speed limit of 45 mph (72km/h), which may sound frustrating but helps you enjoy the scenery.
- For a country where capitalism is a religion as well as an economic system, it's pleasing to know riding the Blue Ridge Parkway is free.

 Ride rating
Easy. The roads are well maintained to accommodate the massive number of visitors, and tooling along at 45mph isn't going to tax your riding ability.

 Distances
- 469 miles (755km)

 Temperatures
- June: 63°F to 83°F (17°C to 28°C)
- February: 30°F to 50°F (-1°C to 10°C)

 More information
For information and useful planning app you can use offline visit www.blueridgeparkway.org

Opposite top Mabry Mill *Opposite bottom* A tight curve along the Blue Ridge Parkway

Wilson Presidential Library and collect some maps from the Staunton Visitor Centre.

The **Peaks of Otter** at milepost 86 are worth a stop, and although many walks start from there, you can always just sit in one of the lawn chairs near the lake and admire the views.

Mabry Mill at milepost 176 is a glimpse of former times but is also a good opportunity to introduce yourself to Appalachian music, which has had a big influence on American music generally. Follow this up at milepost 213 where you can visit the **Blue Ridge Music Center** and enjoy the free concerts that seem to run continuously in the outdoor amphitheatre. This is where Loretta Lynn, Dolly Parton, Chet Atkins and Dwight Yoakam came from.

At milepost 304, check out the **Linn Cove Viaduct**, and at 305 admire **Grandfather Mountain**. It's a state park with an entrance fee but it enables you to walk on the Mile High Swinging Bridge. Don't say you weren't warned.

Like most tourist destinations, the Blue Ridge Parkway is popular because it delivers what it promises. Enjoy the ride.

Cherohala Skyway & Tail of the Dragon: USA

Two extraordinary rides, side by side near the Great Smoky Mountains National Park, will focus on your riding skills and expand your mind at exactly the same time. Not for the faint-hearted.

If you're unused to America, something that will surprise you is how much empty space there is in it. New York, Los Angeles and the like seem massive in the movies but head out to places like the Great Smoky Mountains National Park and be prepared for a surprising amount of wilderness.

The Cherokee People have lived here from around 8000BCE, well before one of their trails became the Cherohala Skyway we know today. It was finished in 1996 after decades of planning and at a huge cost. It was designed to be a tourist drawcard but it's become a route dominated by visiting motorcyclists. We own it.

How long?
These rides could be completed in a day but you'll want to do them more than once. You can make a loop that takes in both but you'll sleep well that night.

When to go
May to October. It may rain in the afternoons but only for a few hours and will then pass.

Need to know
- Ride on the right-hand side of the road.
- The Cherohala Skyway connects Robbinsville with Tellico Plains with no facilities to speak of in its 41-mile (66km) length. It's desolate so be prepared. Tail of the Dragon is more civilised but its 11 miles consists almost entirely of corners. When you ride it, it seems longer than its stated length.

Ride rating
Moderate. You can relax on both these roads but if you ride them with enthusiasm, they can challenge you.

Distances
- Cherohala Skyway: 41 miles (70km)
- Tail of the Dragon: 11 miles (18km).

Temperatures
- June: 61°F to 84°F (16°C to 29°C)
- February: 32°F to 55°F (0°C to 13°C)

More information
www.cherohala.com
www.tailofthedragon.com

Left A dragon sculpture across from Deals Gap Motorcycle Resort *Opposite* October is peak autumn leaf colour season along the Cherohala Skyway

It climbs 5400ft for 18 miles in North Carolina and then drops 23 miles into heavily forested Tennessee. You leave Robbinsville and head towards Tellico Plains on a snake road with a great surface as it's so little used by four-wheelers (except the occasional sports car). There's nothing to speak of along the route: no fuel, no restaurants and no civilisation. Though 41 miles doesn't sound long, be sure you're prepared for the isolation. The reward is that the views are spectacular.

If you head northwest from Robbinsville, you'll find the Tail of the Dragon. This part of eastern USA boast plenty of dragon roads: the claw, the spine, the head and most other parts, but the tail is the area that has captured international attention.

The road is between the Great Smoky Mountains National Park and the Cherokee National Forest with the benefit for riders of having almost no intersecting roads. Bliss. There are 318 corners in 11 miles with highlights including the Hump, the chicanes, and esses just before Cattail Straight. Ride it during the week rather than on weekends.

The loop

Making a loop of the two roads involves riding the Tail of the Dragon first and continuing through Tallassee (watch out for the bridge) before turning left on the 411 and then left again at Vonore towards Tellico Plains. This is the area where 'Bigfoot' sightings are common so keep your eyes open.

The Cherohala Skyway starts as the 165 and then becomes the 143 as it approaches Robinsville where you can re-engage with civilisation. The area is very motorcycle-friendly with the Deal's Gap Motorcycle Resort being one of two businesses on the Tail of the Dragon and motorcycle-specific hotels being a feature of Robbinsville.

The scenery is excellent but you may not notice as the road takes hold of your concentration. If your ambition is riding rather than touring, here's your soul destination.

London to Anglesey: Wales

Wales is full of history and great roads. Although you stay on the A5 for the entire ride, you'll be tempted to deviate on many occasions. The adventurous will always succumb …

We're starting from London partly because it's a great city but also because it's a convenient place to hire a motorcycle if you don't have your own with you. Raceways (www.raceways.net) have a good reputation with large capacity bikes like Triumph's Bonneville, available from £100 a day (minimum-hire two days plus insurance etc).

Taking the A5 out of London will not fill you with wonder and awe but it will give you time to reflect on the history of the road before it starts being fun to ride when you get closer to Wales.

In part, it follows a section of the Roman Iter XI route but it wasn't until 1815 that Thomas Telford was tasked with joining existing turnpike roads and linking them with new roads where necessary to make a direct route from London to the newly unified Ireland. Yes, there's a body of water in the way called the Irish Sea but Holyhead on the island of Anglesey was as close as you could get by land and mail was then carried by boat.

This made it the first major state-funded road building project in England since the Romans left in AD 410 and is part of the answer to the question, 'What did the Romans ever do for us?' The road was mostly a communications route between London and Dublin and was designed for stagecoaches and mail coaches rather than motorcycles.

Some 100 miles into your journey you will have already noticed the absence of hills and mountains with very little change in the road gradient. Wales changes all of that.

Tales of Wales

You cross into Wales near Chirk Castle and the riding improves on the A5. The A55 is now the preferred route for four-wheeler travel to Holyhead as it doesn't pass through the twists, turns and climbs of Snowdonia. This leaves the best route just for us. As we all know, the fewer cars the better.

As tempting as it is to cross the Menai suspension bridge to the island of Anglesey, turn right on the A55 just before Bangor and ride along the coast for 16 miles to the walled city of **Conwy** (population: 15, 715) that dates back to 1283. The city and the castle are mesmerising.

On the way back to Anglesey and once over the Menai Bridge (you have another bridge option but take this), you can either stay on the A55 to Holyhead or reconnect with the older A5, which is a far more pleasant ride.

How long?
You could sprint this in a day but you'd miss the main reason for going in the first place - the beauty and spectacle of Wales. Allow a minimum of three days.

When to go
Winter in this part of Wales can be miserable: long, cold, wet and windy - take your pick. Even summer can be cool but early July to late August will provide the best weather.

Need to know
- Ride on the left-hand side of the road.
- Great Britain has its own currency and it's usually called British pound sterling (BPS). The slang term for a pound is a 'quid'. New polymer notes have entered circulation since 2016 and paper notes are no longer accepted by businesses.

Ride rating
Easy. The roads are generally in good condition and as the A5 was originally built for stage coaches, the gradient rarely exceeds 5% until you ride through Wales.

Distances
- 260 miles (418km)

Temperatures
- July: 15°C (59°F) average
- February 4°C (39°F) average

More information
www.visitwales.com/info
www.wales-tourist-information.co.uk

Opposite top left Chirk Castle *Opposite top right* South Stack Lighthouse *Opposite bottom* Snowdonia National Park

Visit the lighthouse at **Ynys Lawd South Stack** and **Trac Môn** (Anglesey racing circuit), which is called the Welsh Phillip Island due to its coastal views.

Oh, and lastly, get a Wales resident to pronounce **Llanfairpwllg wyngyllgogerychwyrndrobwllllantysiliogogogoch** for you. It's a little village (population: 3028) on Anglesey with the longest name in all of Europe.

Q&A
Brian Rix and
Shirley Hardy-Rix

Brian Rix and Shirley Hardy-Rix have published three books on their epic rides: 'Two for the Road', 'Circle to Circle' and 'The Long Road to Vladivostok'. You can buy them directly, signed, from aussiesoverland@hardyrix.com.au and they're also available from Amazon.com

You can also hear Brian and Shirley on the adventureriderradio.com podcast.

What was your motorcycle background, Shirley?

I grew up in Manly, a suburb of Sydney in Australia and it was a beach culture rather than a bike culture. I had a few pillion rides but I didn't even ride a bicycle. Brian's bike when we met was a Yamaha XV1000 and I hated it. His next bike was a BMW K100LT with a Corbin seat and a top-box for me to lean on and that was a lot more comfortable.

What about you, Brian? When did you start riding?

I was a farm boy from Merbein in country Victoria and I had a Yamaha 100 trail bike before I entered my teenage years. My mates and I rode our bikes on the common beside the Murray River. It wasn't legal, of course, but the coppers turned a blind eye to it as it kept us out of trouble. I've had bikes ever since.

What prompted the first of your big three rides?

It was probably Horizons Unlimited's fault. It inspired us with its message of 'don't wait!' so Brian took long-service leave and we shipped his BMW R 1150 GS to England and rode it home to Australia. This was in 2003/04 when it was still relatively easy to ride through Iran and Pakistan but it was very much pre-internet in those parts of the world. You can read all about it in the book we jointly wrote, *Two for the Road*.

This was followed by 'Circle to Circle'?

Yes. That was a big one. We rode from the bottom of South America (Antarctic Circle) to the top of North America (Arctic Circle). We had the time as Brian had just retired and the ride took 16 months. We had a new bike, too. Brian had upgraded to a BMW R 1200 GS.

For most people, 80,000km would have been enough but you backed up for another epic ride. It seems like the more difficult the route, the more you liked it.

Well, we had an itch to scratch in that we hadn't ridden in Scandinavia or the Russian regions. We made it to Nordcapp, the northern-most point of Europe and then followed the legendary Silk Road to Vladivostok. This was in 2015 on the same bike we'd used for the 'Circle to Circle' ride. The three trips covered 175,633km and a total of 67 countries – 68 if you count Australia.

Many crashes?

We had a few but they were mostly low-speed crashes in difficult riding conditions. There was a slip on an icy bridge in Nepal and a fall on a steep climb on sand and rocks in Kazakhstan. Even with Brian's skill and experience, you can't really expect to escape 175,000km unscathed. I was never seriously hurt. Ironically, the most serious injury I suffered in relation to these trips was at the launch of *The Long Way to Vladivostok* at BMW Southbank in Melbourne. Someone had dropped a grape on the floor and I slid on it and broke my shoulder!

What status does a pillion passenger have on rides like this?

I've discussed this with Susan Johnson, the co-founder of Horizons Unlimited (www.horizonsunlimited.com) who spent years on the back of her partner Grant's bike. You aren't 'just' a pillion. A trip together is more complete than a ride on your own. Susan says a ride shared is a ride doubled and I'm sure Brian agrees with this. The books we wrote were a result of us being able to share our observations each night and fill in the blanks for each other.

Hey, Brian, how many kilometres has your R 1200 GS got on it now?

Big Red has just clocked up 350,000km and the ride isn't over yet.

Opposite Brian Rix and Shirley Hardy-Rix somewhere in the 'Stans

Tasmania East Coast loop: Australia

Tasmania is more like Aotearoa/New Zealand than mainland Australia and its natural beauty is a major seducer of motorcycle riders.

You have a couple of options if you want to go to Tasmania (or Lutruwita in palawa kani, the language of the Traditional Owners, and sometimes just 'Tassie' to locals). If you're already in Australia on the mainland with a bike you can book yourself on the Spirit of Tasmania ferry (www.spiritoftasmania.com.au) that operates out of Geelong in Victoria. Spirit offers overnight and day trips but it pays to plan well in advance as it's generally heavily booked. On-board options include seats or cabins with plenty of entertainment.

You can also fly into Launceston or the international airport at Hobart and hire a bike for your ride adventure. Southern Cross Motorbike Tours (www.southerncrossmotorbiketours.com.au) for example, will pick you up from the airport (or the terminal in Devonport if you've arrived by ferry) and take you to its operations centre to collect your gear. Our route covers a near-600km loop that takes you across the rugged northeast section of Tassie and then down the east coast to Bicheno before returning to Launceston/Devonport. If you're on your own bike, though, and you have time, almost all of the rest of Tasmania is equally worth riding and it's not a huge island. To circumnavigate it by road is just 1500km.

 How long?
You could do this ride in a day but since Tasmania is a little hard to get to, allow yourself a week to explore the rest of the island.

 When to go
September to March; it's cold in winter but summer is beautiful.

Need to know
- Ride on the left-hand side of the road.
- There is an abundance of wildlife in Tasmania that regularly wanders across the roads. This includes wombats, wallabies, pademelons and Tasmanian devils. There's more road-kill here than in any other of Australia's states.
- Keep an eye out for logging trucks on rural and winding roads. They can be hidden around bends and will be travelling slower than you.
- Mobile phone reception is very patchy in wilderness areas.
- Garages in country towns often close early in the evening.
- The east coast of Tasmania doesn't get as much rain as the west coast but it can still rain so be prepared.

 Ride rating
Easy. The roads are generally in good condition as Tasmania's location works against it having lots of heavy industry.

 Distances
- 577km (360 miles).

 Temperatures
- October: 7°C to 18°C (45°F to 64°F)
- February: 12°C to 25°C (54°F to 77°F)

 More information
www.discovertasmania.com.au

Out of Launceston

Following the Tasman Hwy east from Launceston will take you over a couple of passes but mostly you'll be riding through valleys with mountains on either side. You'll turn southeast just after Derby and head towards **St Helens** on the east coast – a game fishing town known for the quality of its oysters.

There are two pubs on this route well worth a stop. The **Welbourough Hotel** has great stories to tell about the Chinese miners who worked there in the past and **The Pub in the Paddock** at Pyengana is a state icon. There used to be a sign on the door as you left saying, 'Don't come back' but they never really meant it.

Heading south, you stick to the coast still on the Tasman Hwy and enjoy the sweeping road and vistas of the Tasman Sea.

It's worth taking a small detour at the turnoff to St Marys just before Falmouth. This takes you over St Marys Pass on a steep, winding road with tight corners that hugs the cliff-like hillside. At St Marys, take the A4 signposted to Chain of Lagoons to investigate **Elephant Pass**. This is a little less challenging with more sweepers and can be a very fast run back to the Tasman Hwy although there's a very motorcycle-friendly pancake house on Elephant Pass to tempt you if you're hungry. Look for the elephant on a motorcycle sign.

Keep heading south but have a break at the beautiful little town of **Bicheno** (population: 1049), which is as good a place as any for fresh crayfish.

Turn right after that onto Lake Leake Rd, which will take you across more mountains and valleys back to Campbell Town where you'll turn right up the Midland Hwy back to Launceston.

On the way, stop at **Longford** where the Australian TT motorcycle races were held from 1953 to 1966. Parts of the road circuit are still able to be ridden and there's a pub in town dedicated to the area's racing history. World champions Geoff Duke and John Surtees raced there (Surtees in a car after he'd switched to four wheels) along with Zimbabwean star Jim Redman.

Tasmania is infectious. Make sure you allow enough time there to fully explore it.

Top The iconic oranges and greys of the Bicheno foreshore *Middle* Farmland and vineyards along the route *Bottom* The fishing town of St Helens *Opposite* Open road on the Tasman Highway

Garden Route: South Africa

There's much to see and do at the bottom of Africa and riding the Garden Route will deliver it all.

More Rides

You'll be starting from Cape Town where, if you haven't ridden down the entire length of South Africa on your own mount, you'll probably be hiring. There are a few options for bike hire but Cape Bike Travel (www.capebiketravel.com) is a good example of what's available with a Triumph Tiger 900 Rally Pro available if you think you might be engaging in a little off-road adventure for ZAR2300 a day (US$125) or a Triumph Bonneville T120 for normal road touring for ZAR2000 (US$105).

Cape Bike has plenty of alternative hire options but keep in mind the maximum daily travel distance of 350km.

Why is what you're about to do called the 'Garden Route'? It's because of the distinctive type of vegetation (fynbos) found only on the southern tip of South Africa. It's shrubland and heathland with incredible biodiversity. The area in which it exists is only 0.5% of Africa but it houses 20% of the continent's plant species. If you were indifferent to plant life before you arrived, you won't be afterwards.

The ocean is calling

It's almost 400km to Mossel Bay, the start of the Garden Route, but the trip there is worth it in itself. Head to **Hermanus** (population: 79,636) to begin with where you can find out what 'rugged' means when people say 'rugged coast'. In season (June to December), it's a world-famous whale-watching spot. It's only a 90-minute ride from Cape Town, and an extra 30 minutes if you go on to Gansbaai where you can try out cage shark diving.

While you're in the area, stay on the coast and call in at **Cape Aghulas**, the most southern point of the African continent. It's where the Indian Ocean stops and the Atlantic Ocean begins. Cape Aghulas is 90 minutes from Gansbaai and three hours from there to Mossel Bay.

While Mossel Bay is where the Garden Route officially commences, **George**, 30 minutes farther on, has a botanical garden that'll tell you most of what you might want to know about fynbos.

From George you can stay on the coast route to Knysna or take the Seven Passes Road that twists and turns through the Outeniqua Mountains with lots of corners and plenty of high bridges.

Knysna (population: 75, 918) is a beautiful town that sits above a lagoon harbouring myriad sailing boats. It's also full of restaurants and, if you're there in late June, you'll enjoy its annual oyster festival.

Not much farther east (30 minutes) is **Plettenberg Bay** (population: 30,000), known internationally by surfers who come just for the beaches

How long?
Six days will give you time to explore as well as ride but you could easily spend 14 days on this route.

When to go
The spring, summer and autumn months between September to May are great but the generally temperate climate makes it an all-year destination.

Need to know
- Ride on the left-hand side of the road.
- Though wildlife is generally confined to the reserves in this part of South Africa, native animals still occasionally make it onto the roads. Ride with care.

Ride rating
Easy. The roads to the Garden Route and the route itself are in very good condition and well-maintained.

Distances
- Garden Route from Mossel Bay to Storms River: 200km (124 miles)
- Cape Town to Mossel: 390km (242 miles)

Temperatures
- September: 13°C to 21°C (54°F to 70°F)
- January: 17°C to 29°C (63°F to 84°F)
- May: 13°C to 22°C (54°F to 72°F)

More information
www.garden-route-info.co.za
www.capebiketravel.com

Opposite left A beautiful day in Knysna
Opposite top right On the way to Cape Agulhas, the southern most point of Africa
Opposite bottom right Bloukrans Bridge

and the waves. The whale season here seems to be a year-round event but if you don't see whales, you'll certainly see dolphins and seals.

Not getting enough adrenaline from riding? Plettenberg boasts the Bloukrans Bridge which is the highest in Africa and hosts one of the highest bungy jumps in the world. Go on – you know you want to …

Some 45 minutes on is the end of the Garden Route at **Storms River**, where the river enters the Indian Ocean.

Homeward bound

If you've enjoyed the N4 highway this far, you may want to use it again to return to Cape Town. But you do have the option of turning right when you get back to George and following the N12 to Oudtshoorn over the spectacular Outeniqua Pass.

You reach the summit of the pass just 14km from George, which will give you some idea of the gradient of the 800m climb.

From Oudtshoorn back to Cape Town is 420km on Route 62, which *CNN Travel* decided was the best road trip in the world. Make sure you visit **Ronnie's Sex Shop** (it was just 'Ronnie's Shop' until the locals altered the saloon sign outside). Motorcycle riders are particularly welcome for a cooling drink. You might also like to spend some time at Robertson, the wine centre of South Africa.

Motorcycling is big in South Africa as the landscape lends itself to both off- and on-road riding. Here's your chance to discover what the locals have known for many, many years.

INDEX

ABOUT THE AUTHOR

Grant Roff is an Australian who has been writing professionally about motorcycles since 1978. He has been a contributor to international publications and most of Australia's print media motorcycle titles. He's also been the editor of two of the country's most successful motorcycle magazines: *Motorcycle Trader and Two Wheels.*

Grant has an arts degree and a master's degree in communications and has lectured in writing in Australia, India, Singapore and Vietnam. Along with his motorcycle travel writing, he is a current contributor to INFO MOTO, a prominent motorcycle website and social media platform.

He's ridden every kilometre of the 20 great rides features in this book and says he's not done yet. Watch out, South America ...

ACKNOWLEDGEMENTS

Thanks to my frequent and admirable travelling companion, Julia Kearton, for her patience, support and advice. She literally and metaphorically rides her own bike but has the generosity to include me in her life. Thanks also to my brother, Stuart, and my nephew, Zac, for their company on the America adventure. Every potential disaster was met with common sense and humour. Similarly, Jon Leevers was enormous help in Europe, where his curiosity revealed many otherwise hidden stories.

For advice, suggested routes and encouragement, thanks to Bill McKinnon, Lee Atkinson, the Lemmings MC, Chris Roberts, Eddie Garner, Guy Allen, Nic Booker and the University of New England Motorcycle Club.

Special thanks to Chris Harris, Triumph Australia, Triumph UK, Harley-Davidson Australia and H-D in the US for the timely provision of the most appropriate motorcycles.

Photo Credits

All images © Grant Roff, with the exception of the following:

Front cover, pages iv-v, 6, 17 (top), 53 (bottom), 83, 106, 110 (bottom), 113, 122-123, 138 (top), 152, 156, 174 (top), 182, 189 (middle), 191 (top right) Alamy; xi, xviii-1, 3, 7, 9, 10, 12, 14 (top and bottom left), 17 (middle and bottom), 24, 42, 43, 44, 46, 50, 56, 59, 60, 66, 68 (bottom right), 72, 74, 76-77, 79, 84, 87, 93, 98-99, 108-109, 142-143, 155, 157, 159, 163, 168, 176, 178-179, 181, 183, 185, 188, 189 (top and bottom), 191 (left and bottom right) Shutterstock; xvi Lavi and Ollie; 26 Michelle Lamphere; 80 Elspeth Beard; 132 Heather Ellis; 150 Visit Victoria; 160 Cameron Donald; 186 Brian Rix and Shirley Hardy-Rix; 41 Stuart Roff; 69, 127 Julia Kearton; 91, 97 Jon Leevers; 124, 129, 131 Lee Atkinson; 139 Lee Nichols; vi, 170 Jeff Crow; 173 Chris McLennan; 174, 177 Great South.

Published in 2024 by Hardie Grant Explore,
an imprint of Hardie Grant Publishing

Hardie Grant Explore
(Melbourne)
Wurundjeri Country
Building 1, 658 Church Street
Richmond, Victoria 3121

Hardie Grant Explore
(Sydney)
Gadigal Country
Level 7, 45 Jones Street
Ultimo, NSW 2007

www.hardiegrant.com/au/explore

The maps in this publication incorporate data from the following sources:
OpenStreetMap www.openstreetmap.org/copyright OpenStreetMap is
open data, licensed under the Open Data Commons Open Database
License (ODbL) by the OpenStreetMap Foundation (OSMF). https://
opendatacommons.org/licenses/odbl/1-0/. Any rights in individual
contents of the database are licensed under the Database Contents
License: https://opendatacommons.org/licenses/dbcl/1-0/ Data extracts
via Geofabrik GmbH https://www.geofabrik.de

Land Information New Zealand (LINZ) Data Service licensed for
re-use under CC BY 4.0. © All data and other material produced by
Land Information New Zealand (LINZ) constitutes Crown copyright
administered by LINZ.Natural Earth.

Free vector and raster map data @ naturalearthdata.com. The maps in
this publication incorporate data

© Commonwealth of Australia (Geoscience Australia), 2006. Geoscience
Australia has not evaluated the data as altered and incorporated within
this publication, and therefore gives no warranty regarding accuracy,
completeness, currency or suitability for any particular purpose.

*Incorporates or developed using [Roads May 2023, Hydrology Nov 2012, Airports Aug
2015] © Geoscape Australia for Copyright and Disclaimer Notice see geoscape.com.au/
legal/data-copyright-and-disclaimer*

Maps contain parks and reserves data which is owned by and copyright
of the relevant state and territory government authorities. © Australian
Capital Territory. www.ACTmapi.act.gov.au Creative Commons
Attribution 4.0 International (CC BY 4.0) © State of New South Wales
(Department of Planning, Industry and Environment) Creative Commons
Attribution 4.0 International (CC BY 4.0) © State of New South Wales
(Department of Primary Industries) Creative Commons Attribution
4.0 International (CC BY 4.0) © State of Victoria (Department of
Environment, Land, Water and Planning) Creative Commons Attribution
4.0 international (CC BY 4.0) © State of South Australia (Department
for Environment and Water) Creative Commons Attribution 4.0 Australia
(CC BY 4.0) © State of Western Australia (Department of Biodiversity,
Conservation and Attractions) Creative Commons Attribution 3.0
Australia (CC BY 3.0 AU) © Northern Territory Government of
Australia (Department of Environment, Parks and Water Security)
Creative Commons Attribution 4.0 International (CC BY 4.0) © The
State of Queensland (Department of Environment and Science) Creative
Commons Attribution 4.0 International (CC BY 4.0) © Commonwealth
of Australia (Great Barrier Reef Marine Park Authority) Creative
Commons Attribution 4.0 International (CC BY 4.0) © State of Tasmania
(Department of Primary Industries, Parks, Water and Environment)
Creative Commons Attribution 3.0 Australia (CC BY 3.0 AU)

A catalogue record for this
book is available from the
National Library of Australia

Hardie Grant acknowledges the Traditional Owners of the Country on
which we work, the Wurundjeri People of the Kulin Nation and the
Gadigal People of the Eora Nation, and recognises their continuing
connection to the land, waters and culture. We pay our respects to their
Elders past and present.

For all relevant publications, Hardie Grant Explore commissions a First
Nations consultant to review relevant content and provide feedback
to ensure suitable language and information is included in the final
book. Hardie Grant Explore also includes traditional place names and
acknowledges Traditional Owners, where possible, in both the text and
mapping for their publications.

Traditional place names are included in *palawa kani*, the language
of Tasmanian Aboriginal People, with thanks to the Tasmanian
Aboriginal Centre.

Ultimate Motorcycle Tours
ISBN 9781741177367

10 9 8 7 6 5 4 3 2 1

Publisher Melissa Kayser
Project editor Megan Cuthbert
Editor Trent Holden
Proofreader Collin Vogt
Editorial assistance
  Jenny Varghese
First Nations consultant
  Jamil Tye, Yorta Yorta

Cartographer Emily Maffei,
  Claire Johnston
Design Andy Warren
Typesetting Susanne Geppert
Index Max McMaster
Production coordinator
  Simone Wall

Colour reproduction by Megan Ellis and Splitting Image Colour Studio

Printed and bound in China by LEO Paper Products LTD.

MIX
Paper | Supporting
responsible forestry
FSC® C020056

The paper this book is printed on is certified
against the Forest Stewardship Council®
Standards and other sources. FSC® promotes
environmentally responsible, socially
beneficial and economically viable
management of the world's forests.